International Journal on Advances in Internet Technology

2017 vol. 10 nr. 3&4

Printed from e-media with permission by:

Curran Associates, Inc.
57 Morehouse Lane
Red Hook, NY 12571

Some format issues inherent in the e-media version may also appear in this print version.

Printed by Curran Associates, Inc. (2018)

International Academy, Research, and Industry Association (IARIA)
412 Derby Way
Wilmington, DE 19810

Phone: (408) 893-6407
Fax: (408) 527-6351

petre@iaria.org

Additional copies of this publication are available from:

Curran Associates, Inc.
57 Morehouse Lane
Red Hook, NY 12571 USA
Phone: 845-758-0400
Fax: 845-758-2633
Email: curran@proceedings.com
Web: www.proceedings.com

The *International Journal on Advances in Internet Technology* is published by IARIA.
ISSN: 1942-2652
journals site: http://www.iariajournals.org
contact: petre@iaria.org

International Journal on Advances in Internet Technology
Volume 10, Number 3 & 4, 2017

International Journal on Advances in Internet Technology
Volume 10, Numbers 3 & 4, 2017

CONTENTS

Internet Access Service Quality Perceived by the User

Janusz H. Klink
Telecommunications and Teleinformatics Department
Wroclaw University of Science and Technology
Wroclaw, Poland
e-mail: janusz.klink@pwr.edu.pl

Abstract— **This paper presents the selected issues of Internet Access Service quality. A special attention was paid to the user's point of view. According to the European documents, users have right to be informed of IT services offered by their providers. The providers are involved in service quality measurement, but they often put emphasis on the objective parameters, which are relatively easy to measure and to compare with other competitors' offers. The issue is: how service quality is perceived by users and, finally, how to correlate these two different points of view. The author discusses the selected objective measures of the Internet Access Service and presents different factors that influence the Internet quality perceived by users. The author shows how the users assess Internet Access through the lens of services they use. An example of building the Quality of Experience model for the WWW service will be presented.**

Keywords-Internet access; quality assessment; QoS; QoE; WWW quality model.

I. Introduction

The Internet is supposed to be used as a vital medium for conducting business, as well as aiding work, play and communication between users in the next years. I will also be the center of the future economy, which will be based on network-based knowledge. Therefore, it has a wide appeal with service providers and consumers, research and regulation authorities, etc. [1][2][3].

In March 2010, the European Commission has launched a strategy titled "Europe 2020", which sets the objectives for smart, sustainable and inclusive growth of the European Union by 2020. The Digital Agenda forms one of the seven pillars of the strategy and defines the key enabling role that the use of Information and Communication Technologies (ICT) will have to play in Europe in future years. It is supposed to support a better quality of life, e.g., through better health care, safer and more efficient transport, a cleaner environment, new media opportunities and easier access to public services and cultural content. It is assumed that by 2020 all Europeans will have access to Internet speeds of above 30 Mbps and at least 50% of the households will subscribe to Internet connections above 100 Mbps.

According to the European Commission, the digital sector grows seven times faster than other parts of industry. Thus, in September 2016, new Commission strategy documents on Connectivity for a European Gigabit Society were adopted [4]. They set a vision of Europe where "availability and take-up of very high capacity networks enable the widespread use of products, services and applications in the Single Digital Market". A vision of "Broadband Europe" assumes the building of the Gigabit Society by 2025 and relies on three main strategic objectives:

- Gigabit connectivity for all main of socio-economic drivers,
- uninterrupted 5G coverage for all urban areas and major terrestrial transport paths,
- access to connectivity offering at least 100 Mbps for all European households.

Consumer research has revealed that price is still the most important attribute taken into account when choosing an Internet access service for 20% of users [5]. The second decision-making factor is the data cap, i.e., the monthly limit on the amount of data a user can use with an Internet connection. Moreover, what happens when a user hits their limit is a very important issue. Internet Service Providers then (ISPs) engage in different actions such as slowing down data speeds, charging extra fees, or preventing further usage.

The next important factors, which may influence user attitude to an ISP offer, are service differentiation and traffic management such as prioritization, blocking or throttling. These practices aim to preserve the appropriate conditions for providing high-quality services. Nonetheless, in recent years these activities have raised questions about network neutrality, which assumes that all content and applications should receive equal treatment. Moreover, neutrality also means that providers neither impose nor discriminate in favor of using a particular type of technology [6][7].

Consumer awareness of network neutrality and traffic management is rather low. On one hand most people have very little knowledge about these terms and, on the other hand, they do not see the influence of these issues on their Internet usage. As is shown in [8], consumers care very little for all the technicalities connected with data transport and the role of ISPs. Users are not interested in net neutrality or traffic management practices and instead are tied to their experience of traffic management effects.

The WIK-Consult study, which concentrates on contract-based consulting services for public and private institutions, asked a series of questions about the way consumers would respond to specific changes in the traffic management policies operated by their ISP, e.g., the introduction of throttling on video traffic, or of data caps. A significant majority of respondents said that they would even change the provider in response to some significant changes in the traffic management policies of their ISP [5].

The issues mentioned above show a much higher interest of users in their ISP traffic engineering operations when these activities touch the concrete services and influence the users' experience. Nowadays, users not only trust the service level agreements of their providers, but also want to be able to check them.

This paper, as an extended version of [1], is organized as follows. In Section II the author presents a general overview of IAS structure. Next, in Section III, the main parameters that may influence quality are discussed and the objective quality measurements of IAS, according to the present standards, are presented. Section IV describes the subjective service quality issues, i.e., perceived by users. The author underlines the difference between objective quality measures and the subjective users' perception of different services used by them. He validates the need to build quality models for the most popular services and mentions WWW browsing as one of them. In Section V, the Quality of Experience (QoE) model for the WWW service is discussed. The author presents the laboratory test-bed, measurement results and method of the model derivation. The paper ends with a conclusion and the plans for future work.

II. INTERNET ACCESS SERVICE

One of the major factors influencing the decision of users when choosing an ISP is the Internet Access connection throughput offered by the provider. However, there are many misunderstandings regarding this term. Physically, it is a combination of different connections and services that are needed to establish a functioning Internet access. Each of them can be treated as a separate service. Most users, however, treat Internet access as an access to the end-to-end services available on the Internet. A purely physical access to the Internet has no practical meaning to them. Thus, Internet access is generally understood as a platform that provides access to Internet services.

It should be noted that some e2e services, that require two-way communication, engage Internet accesses of each end-user taking part in the meeting (Fig. 1).

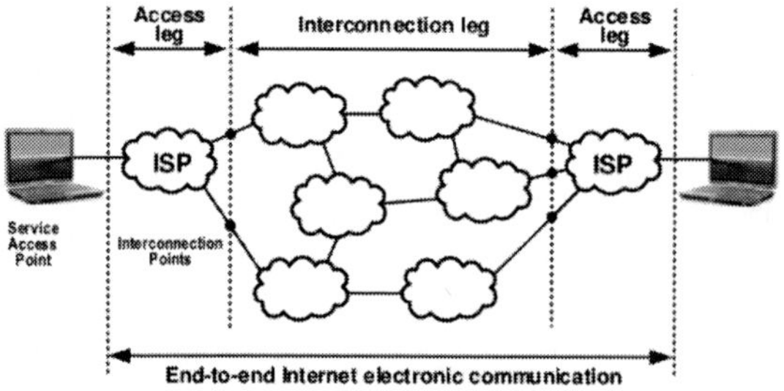

Figure 1. Illustration of the contributing elements of the e2e communication [28].

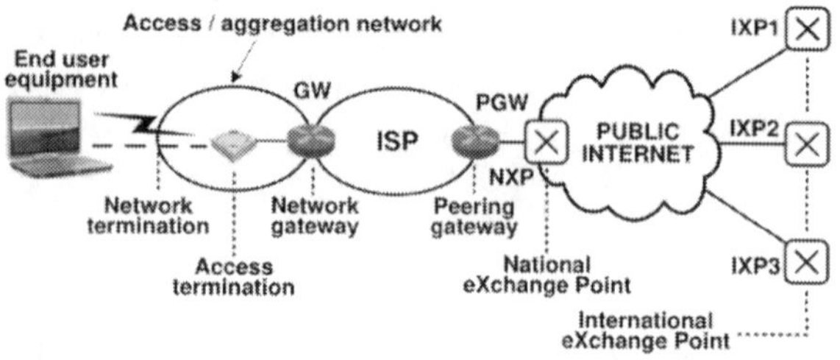

Figure 2. General overview of elements and network sections of IAS.

From the technical point of view, however, the primary meaning of the term Internet access should be understood as a physical and logical access to the core of the network, including all functionalities needed to enable the user to establish a connection to further entities in the Internet and to run advanced services [9].

Providers often advertise the maximum values of the throughput, which is rarely accessible, due to variable traffic load and the still increasing demand for data transmission bandwidth in recent years. Many users often expect such throughputs for most of the day, irrespective of the time and network conditions. According to the CISCO forecast, presented in Visual Networking Index [10], global IP traffic will increase nearly threefold over the next 5 years and by 2020 will reach 2.3 ZB per year. Moreover, traffic load varies significantly during the day. Busy-hour (the busiest 60-minute period in a day) Internet traffic is growing more rapidly than average Internet traffic. It increased by 51 percent in 2015, compared with a 29-percent growth in average traffic. It means that service providers will face even higher network load fluctuations and more serious traffic engineering problems than up to now.

Users can be connected to the various ISPs via the access networks, using wired or wireless connections. Communication over the Internet requires data interchange over different National and International eXchange Points (NXPs and IXPs). Fig. 2 presents a generic overview of the elements, network sections and interfaces of the IAS according to [11].

A very important issue is the proper definition of the Internet Access Service (IAS). The answer to this question is not only crucial for the users, who are usually not familiar with the technical details, but also for the providers as well, because it determines the user-to-network and network-to-network interfaces and also the responsibilities of the providers.

Finally, it says how IAS quality should be measured and how the results can be interpreted and compared between different providers and their end-users. It is especially important in the light of European regulation [12] on the rights of users to be informed about the quality of their services.

III. IAS MEASUREMENTS

Identifying the parameters that may affect the quality of service, locating the points at which the measurements should be performed and specifying the measurement scenarios is a sequence that should be done before the measurements. Simply speaking, one should specify "what, where and how" should be measured to provide ISPs and users with a thorough knowledge of the quality of service.

The measurements fall into two groups: so called "In-net" and "Over-The-Top" (OTT). The first case covers the ISP's area - the area on which it acts. European Consumer Center (ECC) Report [11] specifies a list of technical quality parameters proposed to be measured during a technical evaluation of IAS.

Many National Regulatory Authorities (NRAs) or other national institutions agree that the list is too long. They also consider it to be too complicated and incomprehensible to the average user. Thus, they propose the selection of a subset of parameters. After consulting an abundance of documents [9][11][13] and different points of view, the ECC has proposed a list of minimum technical parameters that take their influence on the most popular Internet applications into account. Table I, based on [11], illustrates popular services and the relevance of the network performance parameters to the performance or quality of those services. The relevance ranges from "–" (irrelevant) to "+++" (very relevant). The following quality metrics have been selected: data transmission rate, delay, delay variation, packet loss ratio, and packet error ratio.

The data transmission rate is probably the most relevant parameter, nearly mentioned in every ISP's offer. It is defined as the data transmission rate that is achieved separately for downloading and uploading specified test files between a remote website and a user's terminal equipment [9]. The next parameter is delay, defined as half the time (in ms) that is needed for an ICMP packet to reach a valid IP address. This parameter also has a significant influence on many applications available over the Internet and is already being used by many NRAs, operators and web-based speed meters. There are also some applications that are very sensitive to delay variation and this parameter is therefore selected for measurements. The exact definition of delay variation can be found in [13][14].

IP packets can sometimes be dropped, e.g., due to a small buffer size of the network nodes or poor (radio) connection, even if the transmission rate, delay, and delay variation remain good enough. Such packet loss can significantly affect all data-based applications.

TABLE I. RELEVANCE OF NETWORK IMPAIRMENT PARAMETERS TO VARIOUS APPLICATIONS

Service	*Data transmission speed*		*Delay*	*Delay variation*	*Packet loss*	*Packet error*
	Down	*Up*				
Browse (text)	++	–	++	–	+++	+++
Browse (media)	+++	–	++	+	+++	+++
Download file	+++	–	+	–	+++	+++
Transactions	–	–	++	–	+++	+++
Streaming media	+++	–	+	–	+	+
VoIP	+	+	+++	+++	+	+
Gaming	+	+	+++	++	+++	+++

Moreover, UDP-based applications, such as Voice over IP may also not work properly in such conditions. Packet loss ratio can be defined as the ratio of the total lost IP packet occurrences to the total number of packets in the population under examination [14]. The parameter that may have an influence on the quality of service is the packet error rate and was therefore also included in the basic set of measured parameters shown in Table 1. The IP packet error ratio is sometimes called the packet error ratio and is defined as the ratio of the total faulty IP packet occurrences to the total number of successful IP packet deliveries plus the faulty IP packet occurrences within a population of interest.

Internet access is no longer provided by a single network or service provider, as was the case with traditional voice communication in Public Switched Telephone Networks (PSTNs). Nowadays, a user gains an indirect access to the public Internet, as shown in Fig 2. Therefore, the overall quality of services (or, in general, Internet access) is a combination of the performance of all the elements involved in the connection.

Different approaches to QoS measurements are discussed in literature. One of the classifications points out the methods as follows:

- carried out by the carefully selected users running the measurement tests from designated locations (or users' homes) and using special purpose equipment [11][15][16],
- large-scale user-driven tests, performed by software agents installed on PCs, tablets, smartphones, etc. [15].

On the other hand, the measurements can be performed by network or service providers, regulators or designated third-party institutions. Different solutions are used in different countries. Many providers do it individually but their results may be regarded by users as non-objective. Thus, external institutions are needed here. Such institutions are very often national regulators or the external companies hired by the regulators. The first solution is used, e.g., in Portugal [15], while the second approach, based on "QoS Memorandum" [17], is used in Poland.

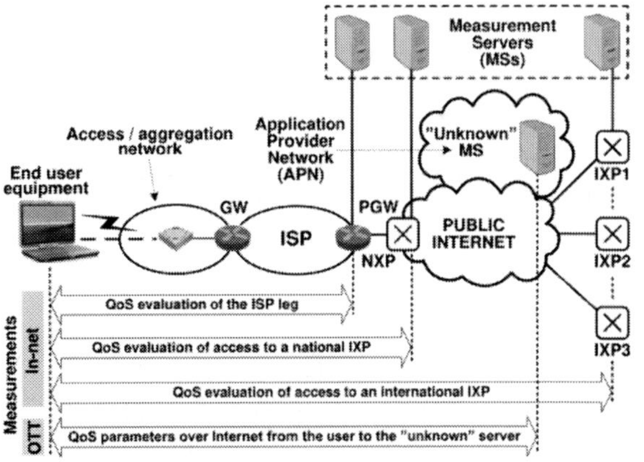

Figure 3. Internet Access Service quality assessment.

On the European level, the minimum set of QoS parameters and measurement methods for retail Internet Access Service has been described in [11]. According to this, the measuring points to be used during the IAS quality assessment may be specified (Fig. 3).

Three evaluation methods (scenarios) are relevant to the measurements connected with IAS quality assessment. The methods encompass an examination of the access network, the ISP network and the network connections to NXP or IXP.

Their names are listed below:

- QoS evaluation within the ISP leg,
- QoS evaluation between the Network Termination Point (NTP) and NXP(s),
- QoS evaluation between the NTP and IXP(s).

Depending on the scenario, the measurement server should be located in the right place (cf. Fig. 3).

In order to test only the access network, the test server should be located as close as possible to the gateway (GW) between the access network and the ISP network. In the case of evaluating the entire ISP leg quality, the test server should be placed near the public Internet interface (PGW in Fig. 3). According to the definition, the ISP leg consists of the access network part and the ISP network part of the connection of the customer to the ISP [11]. Based on [9], a measurement set-up for the ISP leg quality evaluation is presented in Fig. 4.

It should be possible to perform the tests both by the ISP and the user (assuming that the ISP provides a software client or a web based application for this purpose).

The test server shall be connected to the edge of the ISP network (Fig. 5) [11].

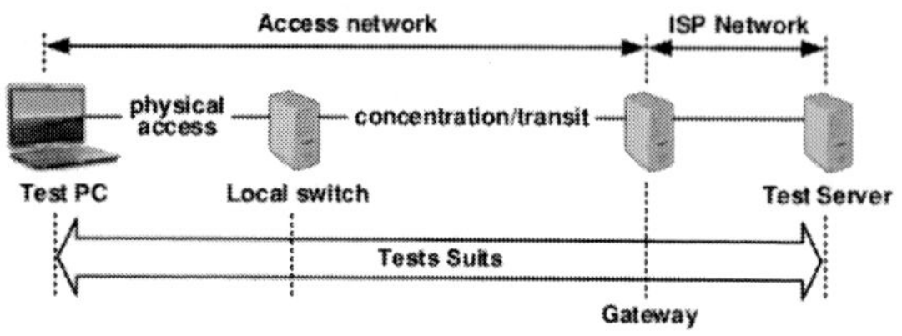

Figure 4. Measurement set-up for the ISP leg quality evaluation.

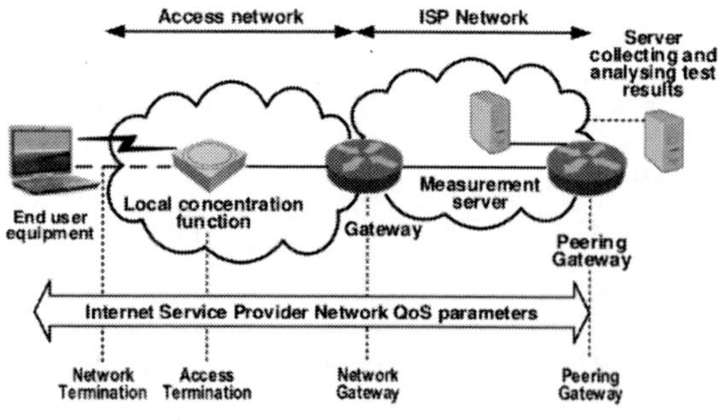

Figure 5. QoS evaluation of the ISP leg.

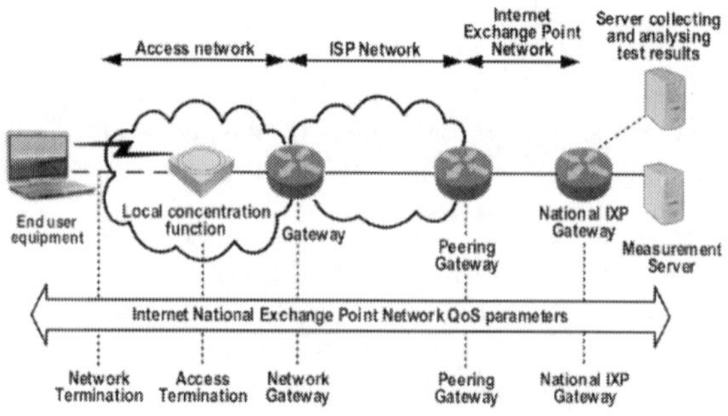

Figure 6. QoS evaluation of access to a national IXP.

Locating the test server in the National eXchange Point (NXP) allows the network performance parameters of different ISPs to be compared (Fig. 6).

The comparability of the IASs of different ISPs can be reached in the best way, if all ISPs are connected on a similar way to the central measuring point.

In the case of bigger countries it can be difficult to fulfill this condition. There may be few IXPs present and due to that, the ISPs are not connected on a similar way to the central measuring point. However, the impact of these circumstances may not be considered significant enough to make the values incomparable, because the bottleneck of the ISP's network usually do not lie within the backbone of the ISP's network but within the Access leg and/or Interconnection points [11].

The quality results achieved in this scenario seem to be far closer to the quality of Internet connection, as perceived by users, than the results in the "ISP leg" scenario.

It is recommended to perform this kind of measurements by the measuring organization, which can be NRA, other relevant national institution or an independent organization. The measuring tools are not strictly specified by any standardization document. These can be dedicated hardware solution, software client or web based applications.

It can be seen that the Internet Access Service quality assessment is therefore a very demanding issue, especially as users care about their own quality experience, which is commonly understood as unrestricted, high-quality and having a reliable access to the applications they use and the content they seek out online. This is the reason for performing the second type of measurements presented in Fig. 3. They were called "OTT measurements", because they allow the performance parameters of specific applications run by the users to be tested and thus they, in general, better reflect the quality of service as perceived by the user.

Nonetheless, these are measurements of the objective parameters and, in the next step, should be transformed into the quality measures as perceived by users. Mapping the measured QoS factors to the QoE ones is often quite a complicated process. The next paragraph presents an example of WWW service quality assessment as perceived by users.

IV. Service Quality Perceived By Users

In this paragraph, the author presents an example of the service quality assessment procedure based on the WWW service. The WWW is one of the most popular services, if not the most important of all, used by Internet users. Many of them assess the Internet quality through the lens of web browsing and information searching on the Internet. The main parameter that influences the service quality, as perceived by the user, is web page opening (loading) time. In other words, the end-to-end (e2e) delay between the user's request and the time when the page is open on the user's display is the most important. The WWW service quality evaluation procedure will be treated as one of the factors that influence the user's perception of the IAS. The WWW service evaluation in the real network may be performed as shown in Fig. 7.

The objective QoS parameter that is measured here is delay between the times when user sends a request to open required web page and the time when the information appears on the display of his PC.

Beside objective measuring of the web page opening times, the subjective user's perception of the service should be determined. In another words, service quality perceived by the end-users, i.e., the relation between QoS and QoE, should be found. It means that the QoE model for the service should be determined. By presenting the WWW quality assessment, the author would like to underline that measuring and presenting only the objective network performance parameters to the customers, discussed in previous sections of the paper, may not be sufficient for determining the IAS quality as perceived by the users. There is a need to check the service quality experienced by them. Building such a model requires a big amount of tests to be conducted. The best way to determine the QoS-QoE relation is to perform the tests in a controlled environment.

One of the important things is to prepare a proper measurement scenario, taking into account main factors influencing web-QoE. Many of these factors are known, but in literature they are sometimes grouped into different categories and not all of them are taken into account in every research.

According to [18], the influence factors (IFs) may be grouped according to the following categories:

- user influence factors (UIFs),
- system influence factors (SIFs),
- context influence factors (CIFs).

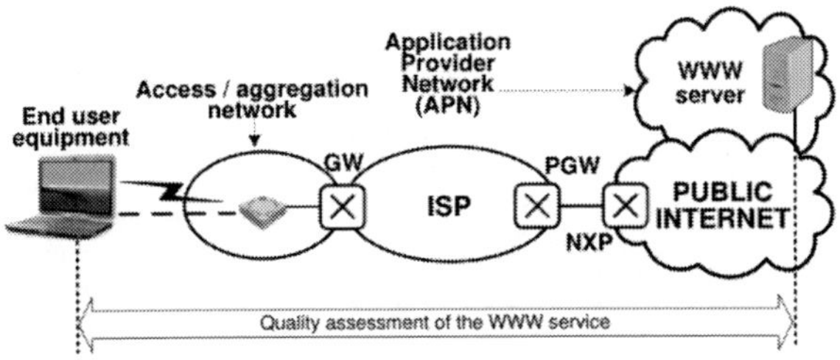

Figure 7. WWW service quality assessment.

A very similar, but a little bit different, categorization is presented in [19], where four categories are listed, as follows:

- user,
- technology,
- content,
- environment.

Referring to the previous classification, it can be noted that the most significant UIFs seem to be user's perception, interest, expectations, experience of application and/or network performance, etc. In today's ICT environment, the users' expectations, satisfaction and (perceived) quality of experience (QoE), are being recognized as crucial determinants for the success of the technology, even more important than technological performance and excellence [20].

The set of SIFs consists of:

- server-related influence factors,
- content-related influence factors,
- delivery network influence factors,
- client influence factors.

To better understand the relations between SIFs, a typical Web-QoE delivery chain was shown in Fig. 8 [18].

According to the classification listed above, the most important SIFs are response time (determined by CPU, operating system, memory, software, etc.) and capacity of the links connecting the server to the Internet. However, the perceived response times may be lowered by the cashing elements in the delivery network.

The next sub-set of SIFs constitute content-related influence factors. They are very crucial for web-QoE, especially because the Web content is typically constituted by a mix of different element types. It consists of text, pictures, audio and video files. Additionally, the structure of the HTML pages (and the scripts) determines the actual loading behavior of the page according to the utilized objects (number, type, size, order, etc.) [21].

Another group of SIFs are client influence factors. These are: web-page loading procedure, processing power, browser implementation, operating system, TCP/IP stack, configuration etc.

The last, but not least, factor which may have a critical influence on the user behavior and his QoE is the context in which a web page is accessed. The range of CIFs spans:

- location: cafeteria, office, home,
- interactivity: high/low level interactivity,
- task type: business, entertainment,
- task urgency: urgent vs. casual (without time constraints).

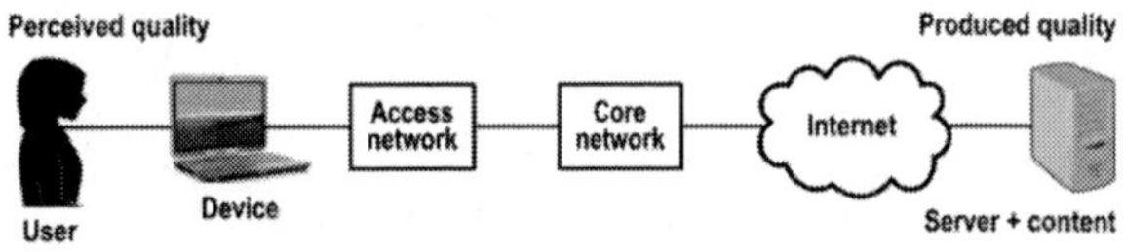

Figure 8. Delivery chain for a typical web-page.

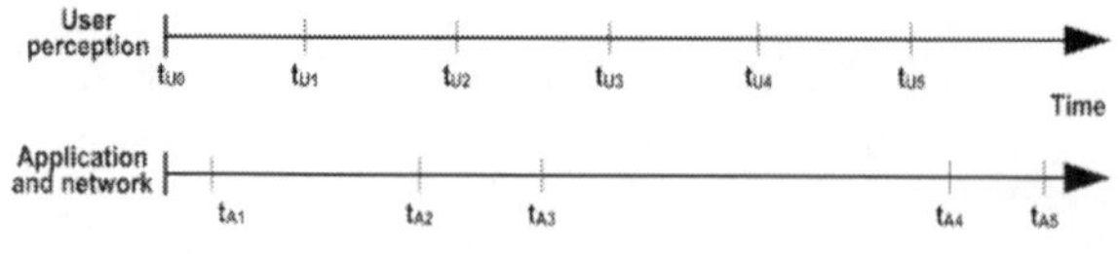

Figure 9. User's perspective of the perceptual events in a web page view cycle.

As it was mentioned before, the time (delay) is one of the main factors that influence user perception of the service. When user requests a web page, the download of content from web server is initiated and progressively fetched and rendered by the browser. During this time the user encounters several events that indicate the progress of the page loading process. However, the objectively measureable times are a little bit different from the characteristic moments of web browsing process that are perceived by the user and decide on user's appraisal of the service (see Fig. 9). For more details regarding the impact of these different points of view on the web-QoE assessment please see [22] and [18].

According to [18], the meaning of the times presented in Fig. 9 is as follows:

- t_{U0} the moment in time when the user requests a new web page (typically by clicking or pressing enter "Enter"),
- t_{U1} the moment in time when a change in the status bar happens,
- t_{U2} the moment in time when the previously viewed web page vanishes (the content of the requested page has not yet started to render),
- t_{U3} the moment in time when the first element of the requested page appears on the screen,
- t_{U4} the moment in time when, from the user's point of view, the page is sufficiently rendered such that he can access the required information,
- t_{U5} the moment of time when the visible portion of the web page (as determined by screen or browser windows size) is fully rendered,
- t_{A1} the moment in time when the initial HTTP request is sent by the browser,
- t_{A2} the moment in time when the first HTML element is received,
- t_{A3} the moment in time when the HTML page is processed by the browser (observed at application level),
- t_{A4} the moment of time when all objects of the page are downloaded from the server at the browser's device,
- t_{A5} the moment of time when the page is completely rendered and displayed on the screen.

It should be noted that the distance between the perceptual events in Fig. 9 is shown as being equal, but in real-world browser implementations they may be different.

The influence factors listed above show that the Web-QoE description is not a simple task. It requires a big effort and usually is time-consuming and expensive. The question arises: how to measure the users' satisfaction of IP-based services as WWW?

One of the methods of expressing the users' satisfaction is an Application Performance Index (APDEX) [23]. It is an industry open standard that allows to measure the satisfaction with the response times of web applications and/or services and their conversion into one commonly understood factor (AI).

The magnitude of this factor can be described as a value on a scale between 0 and 1. It can be calculated using (1) as follows:

$$AI = (S_R + (T_R / 2)) / N_R \qquad (1)$$

where: AI – an evaluation score according to the Apdex method; S_R – satisfied requests (number of users' requests when the service response times were satisfied for them); T_R – tolerating requests (number of users' requests when the service response times were tolerated by them); N_R – the total number of users' requests.

The final result (AI) depends heavily on the threshold time T. It is the value of the delay which, in the user's opinion, represents a negligible reduction of service quality (Fig. 10). Thus, it can be assumed that the web page load time of no longer than T guarantees high user satisfaction of WWW service. On the other hand, it was observed that $4T$ is the upper limit of delay tolerated by the user. In practice, this problem involves fixing the maximum value of T that will guarantee, in the user's opinion, a very good quality of service. In other words, T should be the maximum time which does not distract the user's attention from the service during waiting for an application response. For delays which are longer than T and do not exceed $F = 4T$, users notice a deterioration in the service quality, but they tolerate it.

APDEX can also be treated as a simplified Service Level Agreement (SLA) solution that gives application owners better insight into how satisfied users are, in contrast to traditional metrics like average response time, which can be skewed by a few very long responses.

Finding the QoS/QoE relation is often a starting point to the cost-effective service provision and quality management process. This often leads to finding of more sophisticated relationships between objectively measured parameters and subjective quality as perceived by the users. Such kind of investigation, including preparation of the a special laboratory test-bed and measurement scenario, and performing of the tests, was presented in the next section.

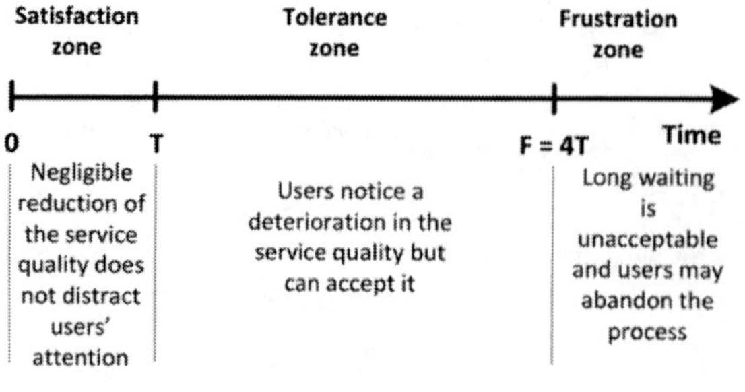

Figure 10. Threshold values for the Apdex Method.

V. The Laboratory Test-Bed

The laboratory test-bed used by the author is presented in Fig. 11. It consists of a WWW client with a dedicated measuring tool, a test server that hosts a set of special prepared WWW pages and the Network Emulator (NE).

All the machines and software run under the MS Windows operating system. As a user client, the Mozilla Firefox browser was used while the measuring tool was the Wireshark protocol analyzer. The NE was capable of emulating the impairment parameters such as network delay, jitter and packet loss. This stage of the measurements only studied the impact of the delay on the service quality as perceived by the users. The delays were randomly generated by the NE on the interval from 0 to 20 s, while the users tried to open the web pages on the test server. Next, the packets were captured by the Wireshark and analyzed. The users did not know the strict values of the delays, but they did see the effects of the delay and tried to assess whether the web page opening time was acceptable or not. It was clear that these delays had a decisive influence on the WWW service quality as experienced by the users. It was expected that increase in end-to-end delay would lead to deterioration of users' satisfaction of the service. Quality of Experience was expressed by the user's evaluation grades according to the Mean Opinion Score (MOS) scale [24].

During the experiment the subjects (testers) were asked to independently rate each sample and provide their opinions using a "rating scale". The purpose of the scale was to translate a subject's quality assessment into a numerical value that can be averaged across subjects and other experimental factors. The Absolute Category Rating (ACR) 5-point scale (most common) was used, as follows:

- Excellent 5,
- Good 4,
- Fair 3,
- Poor 2,
- Bad 1.

The ACR scale is a discrete scale, meaning that the subject's response is limited to one of the five values listed above. However, the averaging process used to combine results from different subjects means that MOS values are not confined to integer values [25]. The first observations confirmed the expectations, that users' grades should be inversely proportional to the e2e delays. It was also noticed that the subjective opinion of users depended highly on the page properties, i.e., their content, layout, construction (static, dynamic), etc. For subjective measurements the WWW reference page was needed. Static web pages were launched on the test server and the contents of these pages were different, but they were of the same style. In this experiment as a content a photo gallery was used.

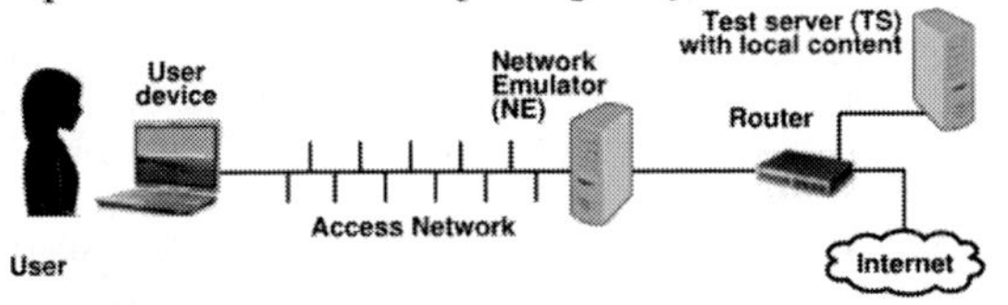

Figure 11. The laboratory test-bed for the WWW QoE assessment.

The main goal was to build as simple web page as possible, but with interesting content.

As a result, the obtained QoE model was similar to the presented in [22], where the test page was prepared according to the ETSI reference page requirements [26]. The relatively small differences require further study. Therefore, the next investigations will be devoted to carry out more detail QoE analysis, taking into account different contents of the web, i.a. based on the ETSI recommendations. It should also give the answer the question of the impact of the content on the experiment results.

It should be also noted that the structure and preparation of the test groups can have the influence. The testers evaluating the quality of the WWW service, as described in [22], were divided into two categories: the first consisted of professionals, the second included non-professionals, i.e. people with little computer experience. Evaluation results presented by the two categories had similar trends, though the marks they awarded were inversely proportionate to the page opening delays. In long-period observations, however, a significant difference between these groups was observed: professionals tended to be more radical in their evaluations than non-professionals, who were relatively moderate.

The current scenario assumed that every user, when evaluating web opening times (equivalents of end-to-end delays during normal web browser use), should give his grade after seeing several photos so that he would be better able to make a judgment. The test was performed on a user's PC (WWW client with a measurement tool). Additionally, Wireshark software installed on the client's PC (as a second tool) was used to capture IP packet streams and to register the end-to-end delay time. This was defined as the difference between the point in time at which the web page was requested and the point in time at which all data needed for the display of the web page were received. The end-to-end delay was varied throughout the course of the experiment using the NE. It was noticed that the web page opening times that were registered at the user site played a crucial role in the subjective evaluation of WWW service quality (QoE). There were groups of "professional" users (each group of 10) taking part in the experiment (70 users in total). They gave their subjective grades for WWW service quality in a range from 1 to 5 on the MOS scale. More than 1500 test measurements were conducted. In the next step the statistical analysis has been performed.

VI. The QoE Model

The measurements show that the grades of users are inversely proportionate to the web page opening times. To speak in more detail, the people who took part in the evaluation test were quite critical with regards to the service under analysis: a rapid decrease in the quality can be observed for the web page opening times (T) covered in the first few seconds. It shows that users are very critical in their opinions and do not accept long delays. The longer the web opening times, the lower grades users give. For the delays exceeding 10 s, the grades of users tend to be significantly lower at a level of 2, which means that such long times are unacceptable for WWW users.

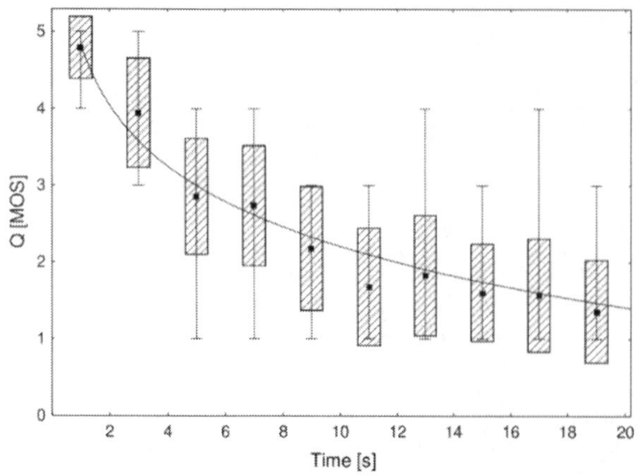

Figure 12. Subjective evaluation of WWW page opening times in MOS scale.

The analysis of the results leads to the conclusion that users had a considerable problem with evaluating web page opening times with very high fluctuations. The measurement results obtained by the author are consistent with those presented in literature [22]. It can be noticed that users are willing to award very high grades for the service (MOS = 5) when opening times are under 2 s, while the lower grades (MOS less than 2) are given when opening times are 8 s and more. In individual cases the evaluation grades may differ significantly from the majority of the scores and thorough statistical analysis should therefore should be carried out. As can be seen in Fig. 12, the mean values for the specific page opening times were not only determined, but min and max values and standard deviation as well.

The correlation between the opening times and the user grades achieved here is at a level of 80 %. The standard deviation is indicated by the boxes in Fig. 12, while whiskers represent the distances between the minimal and maximal values of the captured page opening times. This shows a high level of user uncertainty during the evaluation process.

As it is known from the former experiments [22][27], during long waiting times many users begin to consider whether waiting for the page to open makes sense, and many of them resign. To find a precise relation between the captured values of web opening times and the quality experienced by users, a regression model was used.

This model derived by the author can be described by the following formula:

$$\begin{cases} Q = 5 & \text{for } T < 1\text{s}, \\ Q = 4.84 - 2.63 \log_{10} T & \text{for } T \in [1\text{s}; 1\text{min}], \end{cases} \quad (2)$$

where: T is the web page opening time.

The logarithmic line (Fig. 12) represents the Q value (in MOS scale) as a function of web opening times. The statistical analysis proved that the model fits the data very well, with the coefficient of determination (R2) above 0.9. It means that the obtained outcomes are replicated by the model in at least 90 % of the time. This model is valid for the page opening times T not exceeding 1 minute, which is even more than the longest times emulated in the experiments (20 s). Subjective evaluation however showed that web-page opening times longer than 10 s are not acceptable by the users, thus they may not be taken into account in further practical applications.

A confirmation of the user's QoE distribution, obtained in the paper, can be found in the analysis results presented by the above-mentioned ITU-T recommendation [22], where attention had also been drawn to the logarithmic nature of the relation between QoS and QoE in such a case. A possibility of determining the prospective MOS value by managing the opening times is very valuable and more convenient for the provider than performing the subjective evaluations, which are time consuming and more expensive.

VII. Conclusion and Future Work

Internet Access Service is a key factor that influences a user's perception of all the services provided on the Web. Thus, service providers have to do all their best to offer a good quality IAS. Moreover, they should monitor the network transmission parameters and be up to date with their values. Usage of the appropriate measurement methods is therefore very important. The methods can use different scenarios. In order to make the results credible and comparable with others, these scenarios should be clear and measurement interfaces and procedures have to be clearly defined.

The paper shows the different measurement solutions that can be used. In the second part of the paper the author stressed the importance of subjective quality assessment methods, which are based on the experience of users and give more information about their perception. They assess the Internet Access quality through the quality of the services that they use. One of the most popular is the WWW service. Therefore, the author presented the example of a web browsing quality evaluation scenario, specified the key quality parameter and showed the results of measurements. At the end, the QoE model was proposed and discussed. The main conclusion is that the quality measurements should not only take into account the objective parameters, but subjective parameters as well. Obviously, the set of the parameters depends on the service.

Future work will be devoted to WWW QoE model enhancement by specifying a wider set of parameters to be measured and to also build reference web pages that will be more representative for current Internet content.

Acknowledgment

The paper presents partial results of the statutory research carried out at Wroclaw University of Science and Technology, Poland. The author would like to express special thanks to Pawel Bardowski and Zbigniew Sałamacha for their contribution to the test-bed set-up and help during the editorial process.

References

[1] J. H. Klink, "Selected Issues of Internet Access Service Quality Assessment," ComputationWorld 2017. The Ninth International Conferences on Advanced Service Computing. Service Computation 2017 IARIA, February 19 - 23, 2017, pp. 31-36.

[2] European Commission. *EUROPE 2020 - A strategy for smart, sustainable and inclusive growth.* [Online]. Available from: https://ec.europa.eu/digital-single-market/en/europe-2020-strategy, [retrieved: 12, 2016].

[3] European Commission. *A Digital Agenda for Europe.* [Online]. Available from: http://eur-lex.europa.eu/legal-content/EN/TXT/PDF/?uri=CELEX:52010DC0245&from=EN, [retrieved: 12, 2016].

[4] European Commission. *Connectivity for a Competitive Digital Single Market - Towards a European Gigabit Society.* [Online]. Available from: http://ec.europa.eu/newsroom/dae/document.cfm?doc_id=17182, [retrieved: 12, 2016].

[5] BEREC. *How do consumers value Net Neutrality in an evolving Internet marketplace?* [Online]. Available from: http://www.berec.europa.eu/eng/netneutrality/, [retrieved: 12, 2016].

[6] Official Journal of the European Union. *Regulation (EU) 2015/2120 of the European Parliament and of the Council of 25 November 2015.* [Online]. Available from: http://eur-lex.europa.eu/legal-content/EN/TXT/PDF/?uri=CELEX:32015R2120&from=en, [retrieved: 12, 2016].

[7] BEREC. *Guidelines on Transparency.* [Online]. Available from: https://ec.europa.eu/digital-single-market/en/news/berec-guidelines-transparency-scope-net-neutrality-best-practices-and-recommended-approaches, [retrieved: 12, 2016].

[8] BEREC. *The value of Network Neutrality to European Consumers.* [Online]. Available from: http://www.berec.europa.eu/eng/netneutrality/, [retrieved: 12, 2016].

[9] ETSI. *EG 202 057-4. Speech Processing, Transmission and Quality Aspects (STQ); User related QoS parameter definitions and measurements; Part 4: Internet access.* [Online]. Available from: http://www.etsi.org/deliver/etsi_eg/202000_202099/20205704/01.02.01_60/eg_20205704v010201p.pdf, [retrieved: 12, 2016].

[10] CISCO. *White paper: Cisco VNI Forecast and Methodology, 2015-2020, June 2016.* [Online]. Available from: http://www.cisco.com/c/en/us/solutions/collateral/service-provider/visual-networking-index-vni/complete-white-paper-c11-481360.html, [retrieved: 12, 2016].

[11] ECC Report 195. *Minimum Set of Quality of Service Parameters and Measurement Methods for Retail Internet Access Services, April2013.* [Online]. Available from: http://www.erodocdb.dk/Docs/doc98/official/pdf/ECCREP195.PDF, [retrieved: 12, 2016].

[12] Official Journal of the European Union. *DIRECTIVE 2009/136/EC of the European Parliament and of the Council, 337/11, 25 Nov. 2009.* [Online]. Available from: http://eur-lex.europa.eu/legal-content/EN/TXT/?uri=celex:32009L0136, [retrieved: 12, 2016].

[13] ITU-T. *Rec. Y.1541: Network performance objectives for IP-based services.* [Online]. Available from: https://www.itu.int/rec/T-REC-Y.1541/en, [retrieved: 12, 2016].

[14] ITU-T. *Rec. Y.1540: Internet protocol data communication service - IP packet transfer and availability performance parameters.* [Online]. Available from: https://www.itu.int/rec/T-REC-Y.1540/en, [retrieved: 12, 2016].

[15] R. Nunes, R. Pereira, Rui Valadas, and S. Parranc, "Agent-Based Platform for Continuous Measurement of Internet Access Quality of Service," 16th International Telecommunications Network Strategy and Planning Symposium (Networks), Funchal, 2014, pp. 1-6, doi: 10.1109/NETWKS.2014.6959251.

[16] SamKnows. *The global platform for internet measurement.* [Online]. https://www.samknows.com, [retrieved: 12, 2016].

[17] UKE. *Memorandum QoS report* (in Polish). [Online]. Available from: https://www.uke.gov.pl/raport-koncowy-memorandum-jakosci-13373, [retrieved: 12, 2016].

[18] ITU-T. *Rec. G.1031: Multimedia Quality of Service and performance – Generic and user-related aspects. QoE factors in web-browsing.* [Online]. Available from: https://www.itu.int/rec/T-REC-G.1031/en, [retrieved: 08, 2017].

[19] M. Alreshoodi and J. Woods, "Survey on QoE/QoS Correlation Models for Multimedia Services," International Journal of Distributed and Parallel Systems (IJDPS), 2013, vol. 4, No. 3, pp. 53-72, doi: 10.5121/ijdps.2013.4305.

[20] D. Geerts, K. De Moor, I. Ketyko, A. Jacobs, J. Van den Bergh, W. Joseph, L. Martens, and L. De Marez, "Linking an Integrated Framework with Appropriate Methods for Measuring QoE," Quality of Multimedia Experience (QoMEX), 2010 Second International Workshop on. IEEE, 2010. pp. 158-163.

[21] D. Strohmeier, S. Jumisko-Pyykkö, and A. Raake, "Toward task-dependent evaluation of web-QoE: Free exploration vs. who ate what?," Globecom Workshops (GC Wkshps), 2012 IEEE, pp. 1309-1313.

[22] ITU-T. *Rec. G.1030: Estimating end-to-end performance in IP networks for data applications.* [Online]. Available from: https://www.itu.int/rec/T-REC-G.1030/en, [retrieved: 12, 2016].

[23] APDEX. [Online]. Available from: https://www.apdex.org, [retrieved: 08, 2017].

[24] ITU-T. *Rec. P.800.1: Mean opinion score (MOS) terminology.* [Online]. Available from: https://www.itu.int/rec/T-REC-P.800.1/en, [retrieved: 08, 2017].

[25] ITU-T. *Rec. P.800.2: Methods for objective and subjective assessment of speech and video quality. Mean opinion score interpretation and reporting.* [Online]. Available from: http://www.itu.int/itu-t/recommendations/rec.aspx?rec=12973, [retrieved: 08, 2017].

[26] ETSI. *Kepler reference web page.* [Online]. Available: http://docbox.etsi.org/STQ/Open/Kepler/, [retrieved: 08, 2017].

[27] P. Bardowski, J. Klink, and T. Uhl, "New metrics for WWW service quality assessment," Przegląd Telekomunikacyjny (in Polish), No. 8-9, 2013, pp. 644-649.

[28] BEREC. *Guidelines for quality of service in the scope of net neutrality* [Online]. Available from: http://berec.europa.eu/eng/document_register/subject_matter/berec/regulatory best practices/guidelines, [retrieved: 08, 2017].

Internet of Things Patterns for Devices: Powering, Operating, and Sensing

Lukas Reinfurt[1], Uwe Breitenbücher,
Michael Falkenthal, Frank Leymann
Institute of Architecture of Application Systems
University of Stuttgart
Stuttgart, Germany
email: {firstname.lastname}@iaas.uni-stuttgart.de

Andreas Riegg
[1]Daimler AG
Stuttgart, Germany
email: {firstname.lastname}@daimler.com

Abstract—**A central part of the Internet of Things are devices. By collecting data about themselves and their environment using sensors, they provide the raw resources for later analytics stages. Based on the results of these analytics they can also act back on their environment through actuators. Depending on their use case, these devices come in all shapes and sizes, are placed in various environments, and often have to operate under constraints such as limited access to energy or requirements for mobility. All these factors have an impact on how they are supplied with energy, how they operate, and how they sense. In this paper, we describe the resulting types of energy supplies, operating modes, and sensing techniques as Internet of Things Patterns based on existing terminology and known implementations. We show that these patterns are interconnected with others and that they form the beginning of an Internet of Things Pattern Language, which allows readers to find and navigate through abstract solutions for often reoccurring problems.**

Keywords—Internet of Things; Patterns; Devices; Constraints; Energy Supply; Operation Mode; Sensing.

I. INTRODUCTION

The development of the Internet of Things (IoT) is gaining momentum. Companies and research institutes create new technologies, standards, platforms, applications, and devices in rapid succession. As a result, it becomes increasingly hard to keep track of these developments.

We started creating IoT Patterns to help individuals working in this area. This work is an extension of our paper "Internet of Things Patterns for Devices" we presented at the ninth International Conferences on Pervasive Patterns and Applications (PATTERNS) 2017 [1]. We also have published other patterns in several categories in [2][3]. By methodically collecting common problems and their solutions and abstracting them into patterns, we are building up an IoT Pattern Language. These patterns help others understand the core issues and solutions in the IoT space and provide them with the means to apply these solutions to their own problems.

Devices are an important part of the IoT, as they are the point where sensors and actuators bridge the gap between the real world and its digital representation. To fulfill the vision of the IoT, a world where nearly everything works together to react and automatically adjusts to its environment, devices have to be ubiquitous. They come in all shapes and sizes and are located not only in controlled indoor environments but also outside and in harsh conditions. For example, some of them are required to be mobile, are located off the power grid, or are placed under water.

Such requirements lead to constraints in cost, size, weight, or available power and hence influence the choice of power source. Different power sources also require different operation modes. For example, Bormann et al. describe different energy sources and operation modes in their terminology for constrained-node networks [4]. These choices and other factors then also have an impact on how devices are able to operate and use their sensors.

Based on the terminology by Bormann et al. [4] and additional sources describing the application of IoT devices in real world scenarios, we created eight patterns for IoT devices with different energy sources, operation modes, and sensing techniques. Devices can be ALWAYS-ON DEVICES, PERIOD ENERGY-LIMITED DEVICES, LIFETIME ENERGY-LIMITED DEVICES, or ENERGY-HARVESTING DEVICES, depending on the energy source they use. The energy source also influences a device's operation mode, thus it can be an ALWAYS-ON DEVICE or a NORMALLY-SLEEPING DEVICE. Three of these patterns have been described in detail in [1], namely PERIOD ENERGY-LIMITED DEVICE, ENERGY-HARVESTING DEVICE, and NORMALLY-SLEEPING DEVICE. This paper expands on [1] by adding detailed descriptions of the other three patterns, which where only shortly summarized in [1]. Moreover, we present two new patterns for SCHEDULE-BASED SENSING and EVENT-BASED SENSING.

The rest of this paper is structured as follows: Section II provides a short overview of previous work related to patterns in general and to our IoT Patterns. Section III briefly summarizes our understanding of patterns, our pattern format, and our previously published IoT Patterns. Section IV introduces the eight IoT Patterns for devices in three categories: The four energy supply type patterns ALWAYS-ON DEVICE, PERIOD ENERGY-LIMITED DEVICE, LIFETIME ENERGY-LIMITED DEVICE, and ENERGY-HARVESTING DEVICE, the two operation mode patterns ALWAYS-ON DEVICE and NORMALLY-SLEEPING DEVICE, and the two sensing patterns SCHEDULE-BASED SENSING, and EVENT-BASED SENSING. We also show how they are connected among themselves and to the already presented IoT Patterns. Section V describes these eight patterns in detail following the pattern format described in Section III. Finally, Section VI provides a summary and an outlook on our planned future work.

II. RELATED WORK

The pattern concept was first introduced by Alexander et al. in the architecture domain [5]. Since then, the concept has been applied in other domains. Examples from IT include the Messaging Patterns by Hohpe et al. [6] or the Cloud Computing Patterns by Fehling et al. [7]. There has also been work on the pattern writing process itself [8][9][10][11]. Others are working on making abstract patterns more usable by linking them to technology specific patterns [12] or to solutions implementations [13][14] and, thus, building solutions languages [15].

We presented our first five IoT Patterns, DEVICE GATEWAY, DEVICE SHADOW, RULES ENGINE, DEVICE WAKEUP TRIGGER, and REMOTE LOCK AND WIPE [2]. We later added more patterns in [3]. These patterns are not concerned with IoT devices themselves but do already mention the terminology by Bormann et. al [4]. They present a terminology for constrained nodes, constrained networks, and constrained-node networks. They describe some aspects of why and how different energy sources and operation modes occur, but not in the form of patterns. The pattern format used in this paper adds more to this description in form of the forces, the result section, and the benefits and drawbacks, as well as the interconnection with other patterns.

Eloranta et. al published a pattern language for designing distributed control systems [16]. These patterns focus on larger machinery and are not concerned with small constrained devices and the implications of these constraints. Other patterns in the IoT space exist, which are not concerned with the devices themselves. Qanbari et. al present four patterns for edge application provisioning, deployment, orchestration, and monitoring, which use existing technologies like Docker or Git that are not suited for constrained devices [17]. Another publication collected other existing patterns, many just blog posts without much substance, and categorized them into a pattern language [18]. Many of these patterns are just one or two sentences long and they all are lacking the interconnections between them.

III. IOT PATTERNS OVERVIEW

The IoT Patterns presented in this paper and our previous work follow the ideas of Alexander [5] and others [8][9][10][11]. As described in more detail in [2][3], we identified these patterns by collecting material from product pages, manuals, documentation, standards, whitepapers, and research papers. Once reoccurring descriptions became evident, we grouped them and extracted the core principles into the more abstract pattern format. The format is also described in more detail in [2][3], but, in short, is made up of the following elements: The **Name**, **Icon**, and **Aliases** help to identify the pattern. The icons are also intended as a visual summary of the core solution and should be usable in architecture diagrams to represent the patterns. A brief summary section gives an overview. The short **Problem** and **Solution** sections contain the core issue and steps to resolve it. The **Context** and **Forces** describe where the problem occurs and why it is hard to solve, while the **Solution Details** section gives more details on the solution. Other relevant patterns are listed as **Related Patterns**. Existing products, which implement the pattern and are used as sources for the pattern writing process, are summarized under **Known Uses**.

Table I provides an overview of our earlier patterns, including a short summary of the problems (P) they are solving and a brief description of how they solve it (S). These and future patterns are available online in shortened versions at http://www.internetofthingspatterns.com.

TABLE I. OVERVIEW OF OUR PREVIOUS IOT PATTERNS

DEVICE GATEWAY [2] 	**P.:** You want to connect many different devices to an already existing network, but some of them might not support the networks communication technology or protocol. **S.:** Connect devices to an intermediary DEVICE GATEWAY that translates the communication technology supported by the device to the communication technology of the network and vice-versa.
DEVICE SHADOW [2] 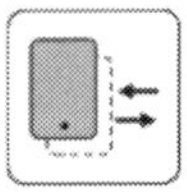	**P.:** Some devices are only intermittently online to save energy or because of network outages. Other components want to interact with them but do not know when they will be reachable. **S.:** Store a persistent virtual representation of each device on some backend server. Include the latest received state from the device, as well as commands not yet sent to the device. Do all communication from and to the device through this virtual representation. Synchronize the virtual representation with the actual device state when the device is online.
RULES ENGINE [2] 	**P.:** Throughout its operation, a system receives a wide range of messages from devices and other components. You want to react in different ways to these messages. **S.:** Pass all messages received from devices to a RULES ENGINE. Allow users to define rules that evaluate the content of incoming messages or metadata about the message against a set of comparators. Also, allow external data sources to be included in these comparisons. Let users associate a set of actions with these rules. Apply each rule on each message and trigger the associated actions if a rule matches.
DEVICE WAKEUP TRIGGER [2] 	**P.:** Some devices might go into a sleep mode to conserve energy and only wake up from time to time to reconnect to the network. During sleep they are not reachable on their regular communication channels. In some instances, other components might have to contact sleeping devices immediately. **S.:** Implement a mechanism that allows the server to send a trigger message to the device via a low energy communication channel. Have the device listening for these triggering messages and immediately establish communication with the server when it receives such a message.

Remote Lock and Wipe [2] 	**P.:** Some devices might be lost or stolen. You want to prevent attackers from misusing the functionality of the device, or from gaining access to the data on the device or to the network through the device. **S.:** Make the device a managed device that can receive and execute management operations from the backend server. Allow authorized users to use the backend server to trigger functionality on the device that can delete files, folders, applications or memory areas, revoke or remove permissions, keys, and certificates, or enable additional security features. Execute triggered functions as soon as the device receives them and provide an acknowledgment to the backend.
Delta Update [3] 	**P.:** You want to reduce the size of messages containing sensor data without losing any information. **S.:** Store the last message send. Calculate the delta from the current data to this message. Also calculate a hash of the current data. Send only the delta and the hash to the receiver. Let the receiver merge the delta with its current state and check if it matches the received hash.
Remote Device Management [3] 	**P.:** You want to manage a large number of devices remotely. **S.:** Set up a management server on the backend. Install management clients on the device which you want to manage. Send management commands from the server to the client and let the client execute these commands locally on the device.
Visible Light Communication [3] 	**P.:** You need to use wireless communication in a crowded area, but you cannot use the crowded radio spectrum. **S.:** Use visible light for short distance wireless communication. Modulate messages into the light by turning the light on and off. Do it fast to not impede normal light usage and to be invisible to the human eye.

IV. IoT Patterns for Devices

In this paper, we add eight IoT Patterns for devices. This section presents an overview of all of them in Table II, Table III, and Table IV. Related patterns are organized into three groups. The first group, *Energy Supply Types*, is summarized in Table II and describes patterns based on different forms of energy sources a device might use. Which one of these is applicable depends on the use case and its environment. If, for example, a device is required for a wearable use case, then a Mains-Powered Device is not an option. However, the environment of the use case might also not provide sufficient ambient energy for an Energy-Harvesting Device.

The second group, *Operation Modes*, is summarized in Table III and lists different patterns based on a device's mode of operation. These often depend on the amount of energy available to the device. For example, if a device is an Energy-Harvesting Device, it will in many cases not have enough energy to be an Always-On Device and has to be a Normally-Sleeping Device.

TABLE II. OVERVIEW OF THE NEW IOT PATTERNS CONCERNED WITH DEVICE ENERGY SOURCES

Energy Supply Types	
Mains-Powered Device (Section V.A) 	**P.:** You need to power a stationary device, which requires a lot of energy. **S.:** Connect the device to mains power. Transform higher voltages to a low voltage, which you can use. Convert alternating current to direct current and filter it to get smooth voltage.
Period Energy-Limited Device (Section V.B) 	**P.:** You need to power a device, which requires a fair amount of power. The device is mobile or located in a remote place. Moreover, mains power is not available. **S.:** Use a replaceable or rechargeable source of energy to power the device. Implement a notification mechanism that informs you when the power source is nearly empty. Replace or recharge the power source when needed.
Lifetime Energy-Limited Device (Section V.C) 	**P.:** You need to power a device, which requires a small amount of power. The device is mobile or located in a remote place. You want to minimize maintenance. **S.:** Build an energy source into the device, which will last for the entire expected lifetime of the device.
Energy-Harvesting Device (Section V.D) 	**P.:** You need to power a device with very little power needs. The device is mobile or located in a remote place. Its environment is stable and predictable. **S.:** Integrate an energy-harvesting component, such as a solar cell, into the device. Use it to turn the energy available in the device's surroundings into power for the device. Use components and technologies optimized for low-power usage to make the most of the harvested energy.

The third group, *Sensing*, shown in Table IV, contains patterns which describe different sensing techniques. These are influenced by the energy supply type and operation mode used, as well as by other forces, for example the preexisting knowledge about the domain. For example, Event-Based Sensing is a good option for Normally-Sleeping Devices, but requires the events that should be observed to be known and understood beforehand.

Period Energy-Limited Device, Energy-Harvesting Device, and Normally-Sleeping Device have been presented in detail before in [1], while the other energy supply and operation mode patterns where only briefly summarized. This work adds detailed descriptions of these patterns as well as the new sensing patterns.

TABLE III. OVERVIEW OF THE NEW IOT PATTERNS CONCERNED WITH DEVICE OPERATION MODES

Operation Modes	
ALWAYS-ON DEVICE (Section V.E) 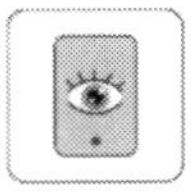	**P.:** You have a device with an unlimited energy supply and need to have it available and responsive at all times. **S.:** Leave the device turned on and connected at all times.
NORMALLY-SLEEPING DEVICE (Section V.F) 	**P.:** You have a device with a limited energy supply. You want to minimize the power used by the device. **S.:** Program the device to disable its main components when they are not needed. Leave a small circuit powered which reactivates the components after a predefined amount of time has passed or when an event occurs.

TABLE IV. OVERVIEW OF THE NEW IOT PATTERNS CONCERNED WITH SENSING

Sensing	
SCHEDULE-BASED SENSING (Section V.G) 	**P.:** You do not know what kinds of events you are looking for in your measurements or you need a general overview of the trend of the phenomenon that you are measuring. **S.:** Define a schedule for sensor reading which fits with your use case's requirements. Program the device to power up its sensors and read their values according to this schedule. Power down the sensors after reading.
EVENT-BASED SENSING (Section V.H) 	**P.:** You have a use case where you are interested in irregularly occurring events that are represented in sensor values. Reading the sensor in regular intervals is wasteful because those events occur rarely and the other values are of no interest to you. Besides, it is possible that you miss such an event if it falls between two sensor readings. **S.:** Define the events that are of interest to you in the form of sensor values. Use low-power sensors and power them continuously. Program low energy comparator circuits to read those sensors and watch for the events. Only propagate measurements to the device if a sensor value triggers such a comparator circuit.

These patterns do not exist in a vacuum. They are connected among themselves and to the patterns we previously presented [2][3]. Fig. 1 shows an overview of all the connections between the IoT Patterns. A black box in a row means that the pattern represented by this row relates to the pattern represented by the column in which the box is placed (the gray boxes show, where a pattern is compared with itself).

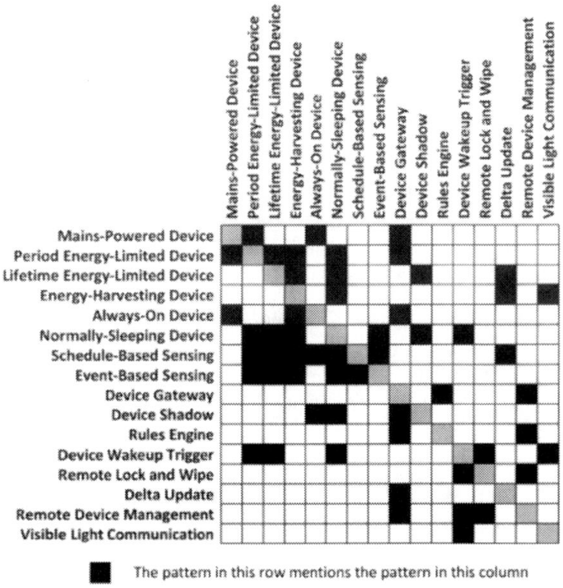

Figure 1. Connections between IoT Patterns.

For example, in row four, a black box in column six shows that the ENERGY-HARVESTING DEVICE pattern mentions the NORMALLY-SLEEPING DEVICE pattern. The nature of the connection is not further elaborated in this figure but could be interesting for future research.

As the applicability of the IoT Patterns for devices presented in this paper is heavily influenced by the particular use case, it seems reasonable to choose them as entry points into the IoT Pattern Language when designing an IoT system. Their selection then greatly influences the design of the remaining system by suggesting or forcing certain additional patterns. For example, if a use case requires a PERIOD ENERGY-LIMITED DEVICE, then also being a NORMALLY-SLEEPING DEVICE will greatly enhance its energy efficiency. Adding a DEVICE SHADOW will make the overall system more robust and using a DEVICE WAKEUP TRIGGER will allow you to communicate with a NORMALLY-SLEEPING DEVICE in an instant if necessary.

In turn, if new devices should be added to an existing IoT system, the design decisions elaborated in the architecture of the existing system will dictate which kinds of devices can be added without modifications, or what modifications have to be made to support a specific kind of device.

V. DETAILED IOT PATTERNS FOR DEVICES

In this section, we describe the IoT device patterns presented in this paper in more detail. We start with the *Energy Supply Types* category, followed by the *Operation Modes*, and then the *Sensing* category.

A. *MAINS-POWERED DEVICE*

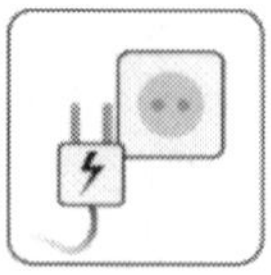

Some devices require a lot of power or are stationary. Power them by connecting them to mains power.

Aliases: Mains-operated

Context: You have a device that needs to be powered. It may be an ALWAYS-ON DEVICE that has to run continuously to fulfill its intended function. It may also be a device that does a lot of local processing which requires large amounts of energy.

Problem: You need to power a stationary device, which requires a lot of energy over its lifetime.

Forces:

- **Energy Requirements:** The device needs a large amount of energy over its lifetime. Making it a LIFETIME ENERGY-LIMITED DEVICE is not an option because the device needs more energy over its lifetime than current batteries can provide in a reasonable form factor without being replaced or recharged. Making it an ENERGY-HARVESTING DEVICE is not an option because ambient energy does not deliver the required power.
- **Environmental Constraints:** The environment of the device may have some constraints, such as not having a suitable source of ambient energy, thus making it not possible to use an ENERGY-HARVESTING DEVICE.
- **Maintenance:** Making it a PERIOD ENERGY-LIMITED DEVICE is not an option because replacing or recharging a battery in frequent intervals is too much effort.
- **Mobility:** The device does not have to be mobile.
- **Infrastructure:** Mains power is available in many places, but voltages and outlet designs vary depending on location.

Solution: Connect the device to mains power. Transform higher voltages to a lower voltage that you can use. Convert alternating current to direct current and filter it to get smooth voltage.

Solution Details: A MAINS-POWERED DEVICE requires a bit more than adding a cable to a power outlet. As many devices operate on lower voltages than provided by the power grid, a transformer, which converts high voltages to lower voltages, is required. Moreover, often alternating current (AC) has to be converted to direct current (DC) using a rectifier.

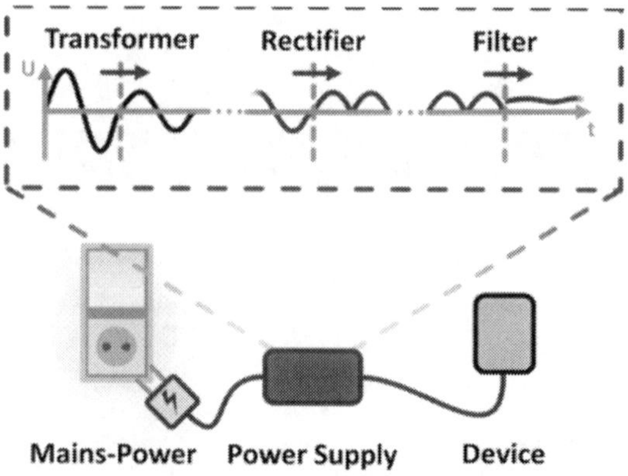

Figure 2. Sketch of the MAINS-POWERED DEVICE pattern.

It should also be filtered to provide a smooth voltage that does not damage components. Fig. 2 shows this process with an external power supply. Besides, a regulator might be necessary to receive a constant voltage level.

All these components have to be added to the device, either externally or internally. Both options have different benefits and drawbacks. An external power supply increases portability as the weight and size of the device can be kept small. The device can be used with different adapters to connect it to different power sources and if an adapter fails, it can be easily replaced. Besides, heat and electrical noise production is reduced and kept away from the device itself. In addition, production and inventory is simplified. The drawbacks of an external power supply are that it still uses some power if the device is not connected or powered, and possible confusion and compatibility problems when looking for an appropriate power supply for a device. An internal power supply reverses these benefits and drawbacks. These aspects should be taken into account when designing a MAINS-POWERED DEVICE.

Benefits:

- **Energy Requirements:** The device has large amounts of energy at its disposal allowing it to perform energy intensive tasks.
- **Maintenance:** There are no batteries that have to be recharged or replaced.

Drawbacks:

- **Dependence:** The device is dependent on the power grid. If there is a power outage, it will stop functioning. Additionally making the device a LIFETIME ENERGY-LIMITED DEVICE or PERIOD ENERGY-LIMITED DEVICE provides it with some backup power in such cases.
- **Mobility:** As the device is bound to the power grid, its mobility is severely limited.
- **Infrastructure:** If power lines are not already available it might be expensive and a lot of effort to build the required infrastructure.

Related Patterns:

- **Lifetime Energy-Limited Device:** A built-in battery can be used as backup power in case of a power outage.
- **Period Energy-Limited Device:** A rechargeable or replaceable power source can be used to provide backup power in case of a power outage. The Mains-Powered Device can recharge it once the power is up again.
- **Normally-Off:** A Mains-Powered Device might also be a Normally-Off Device to reduce its energy consumption.
- **Always-On:** A Mains-Powered Device can be an Always-On Device if it is required.

Known Uses: Common examples for Mains-Powered Devices are those that offer functionality that requires larger amounts of energy or that is used very frequently. Examples are *Philips Hue* lights [19], the *Xiaomi Mi Air Purifier 2* [20], the *Airboxlab Foobot* [21], or the many other home appliances that are increasingly connected to the internet. Device-Gateways are also often Mains-Powered Devices, like the *WeR@Home Hub*, which is powered with a power supply, but is also a Period Energy-Limited Device as it has a replaceable battery as backup to make it resilient against power outages [22]. Similarly, the *Afero Hub* is a Mains-Powered Device but is also equipped with a port where a backup battery can be connected [23].

B. *Period Energy-Limited Device*

Devices that are mobile or located in remote places cannot rely on fixed infrastructure. When they require a fair amount of power, use a replaceable or rechargeable energy source and renew it regularly.

Aliases: Rechargeable

Context: You have a device, which needs a fair amount of energy to work but does not necessarily require mains power, such as a device that takes regular sensor readings, communicates, and powers actuators. Besides, your use case dictates a specific location for this device, which restricts available energy sources. For example, the device has to be mobile, wearable, or in a remote location.

Problem: You need to power a device that requires a fair amount of power. The device is mobile or located in a remote place. Moreover, mains-power is not available.

Forces:

- **Energy Needs:** The device needs a fair amount of energy to work. A Lifetime Energy-Limited Device is not an option if it needs more in its lifetime than current batteries offer in a reasonable form factor. An Energy-Harvesting Device is not an option if the device needs more power for a cycle than the harvesting generates between cycles.
- **Environmental Constraints:** Your use case enforces a specific location for the device. For example, the device has to be mobile or wearable, or the device location is in an area where mains power is not available. Thus, being a Mains-Powered Device is not an option. Besides, an Energy-Harvesting Device is not an option if no suitable form of ambient energy source is available at the device's location.
- **Costs:** Replacing or recharging the power source is an option but has a cost associated with it, especially if the device is located in a remote or inaccessible location. For your use case, it makes economically and physically sense to do this in the time frame that allows the device to sustain its functionality.
- **Uptime:** You want to minimize the periods where the device is not operating because of power source renewal.

Solution: Use a replaceable or rechargeable source of energy to power the device. Implement a notification mechanism that informs you when the power source is nearly empty. Replace or recharge the power source when needed.

Solution Details: Using a replaceable or rechargeable power source is a common occurrence in today's devices. Increasingly energy efficient electronic components now allow manufacturers to build devices that run on one charge for weeks to months, if not years. For the rest of this text, we equate a Period Energy-Limited Device with using batteries, as they are common in the domain of IoT. But, for example, fuel for a generator is another valid form of a power source for a Period Energy-Limited Device.

Fig. 3 shows the lifecycle of a Period Energy-Limited Device. It can be roughly divided into three phases: Most of the time, the device operates normally and, thus, *discharges* the power source, as shown at the bottom. Once a certain threshold is reached, the device starts to *notify*, as shown at the top left. Then, the depleted power source is *renewed*, as shown at the top right, before the cycle begins again.

Batteries come in different forms and sizes and are renewable in two ways. The first way to renew power for a Period Energy-Limited Device is to replace depleted batteries with full ones. The replacement battery is either a new non-rechargeable battery or a recharged battery. In this case, it makes no difference to the device if the battery is rechargeable or not. If you recharge the battery, it happens outside of the device through a separate charger. Integrating this replacement mechanism into a device is straightforward. It requires a connector to which you attach the battery. An optional compartment housing this connector offers protection for the battery and the device internals from the outside.

The second way to renew the battery is to allow it to be recharged inside the device. This requires integrating a charging circuit into the device. When the battery is empty, you connect another energy source to the device to recharge the battery, for example, a power bank. Alternatively, you bring the device near to mains power and plug in a power supply.

The complexity of the charging circuit varies depending on the type of battery and the desired recharge time. A slow charge circuit is simple because it cannot damage the battery and thus requires no end-of-charge detection. A fast charge circuit has to detect end-of-charge through voltage or temperature to prevent overcharging the battery. In this case, the battery has to be rechargeable but not replaceable. If it is rechargeable and not replaceable, replacing the battery when it malfunctions becomes difficult, but it allows for a tighter integration and closed housing.

Depending on the intended use case of the device, you have to take care to shield it from its environment. Dust or waterproof battery compartments offer protection from outside elements. For integrated rechargeable batteries, nothing but the charging contact has to be accessible from the outside. This further prevents environmental factors of deteriorating the device.

Since the power renewal of the PERIOD ENERGY-LIMITED DEVICE requires another entity to act, the device needs a notification mechanism to trigger power source renewal, as shown at the top left in Fig. 3. If the device sends out messages, adding the battery status to these messages is one way to inform others about the device's battery status. Besides, a repeating light or sound indicating low energy is another option. To minimize downtime, you have to choose the notification threshold to allow time for power source renewal before it runs out.

Benefits:

- **Independence:** The device is independent of the grid and of its environment. It has power regardless of power outages or bad weather as long as you replace its energy source in time.
- **Lifetime:** The power source does not limit the lifetime of the device if it is replaceable.
- **Cost:** The costs for the device itself and for its installation are low. A battery connector and compartment or a charging circuit do not add high costs and wires are not required.

Drawbacks:

- **Lifetime:** The power source limits the lifetime of a device if it is a rechargeable but not replaceable battery because aging batteries deteriorate with time and batteries have a maximum charge cycle count. This is not a problem if the maximum number of charge cycles allows the device to run until its intended end of life. Otherwise, making the battery replaceable solves this problem.

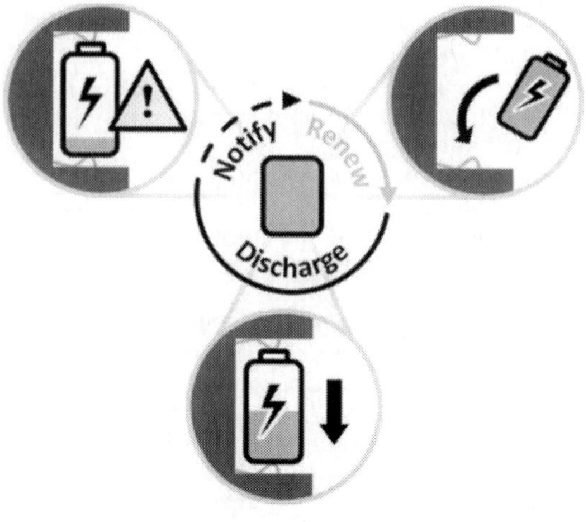

Figure 3. Sketch of the PERIOD ENERGY-LIMITED DEVICE pattern.

- **Costs:** You need to replace or recharge the power source in regular intervals, which increase maintenance costs. Also being an ENERGY-HARVESTING DEVICE or a NORMALLY-SLEEPING DEVICE increases the interval length.
- **Durability:** The device has to support replacing or recharging the power source, which requires access to the power source or the recharging contacts. If the device exposes these points to the environment, they may deteriorate in harsh conditions. One option is to build these points dust or waterproof but doing this does not offer full protection and increases costs. Wireless charging is another option that allows sealing the device.
- **Uptime:** The device is not operational when you replace its power source instead of recharging it. Making the power source rechargeable besides being replaceable is one way to guarantee uptime. Another option is to have two power sources in the device, where it uses one as a backup while you replace the other one.

Related Patterns:

- **ENERGY-HARVESTING DEVICE:** One way to increase the time needed between power source replacements or recharging is energy-harvesting. An example is adding a small solar cell, which trickle charges the battery.
- **NORMALLY-SLEEPING DEVICE:** A NORMALLY-SLEEPING DEVICE saves energy when the device is not needed. This can increase the interval length between power source replacement or recharging for PERIOD ENERGY-LIMITED DEVICES.
- **MAINS-POWERED DEVICE:** A MAINS-POWERED DEVICE can also be a PERIOD ENERGY-LIMITED DEVICE if it uses a battery as a backup in case of power outage.

Known Uses: One example of a PERIOD ENERGY-LIMITED DEVICE is the *Flic Wireless Smart Button*. It claims to last one year or more on its replaceable battery [24]. A similar device, *Logitech's POP Home Switch*, claims up to 5 years battery life from its replaceable battery [25]. *Sen.se's ThermoPeanut* is a wireless temperature sensor with a replaceable battery that lasts up to 6 months, depending on the frequency of sensor reading [26]. Another example is the *Nest Learning Thermostat*, which comes with a rechargeable lithium-ion battery [27]. The *Roost Smart Battery* is a replacement battery, which adds WiFi connectivity to smoke detectors. It notifies users via an app when the alarm is triggered or the battery runs low [28]. Besides, some MAINS-POWERED DEVICES are also PERIOD ENERGY-LIMITED DEVICES as they use batteries as a backup to increase their resilience against power outages. Examples include the DEVICE GATEWAYS from *SmartThings*, *Essence*, or *Afero*. They either include a backup battery or offer connection options for external batteries [22][23][29].

C. LIFETIME ENERGY-LIMITED DEVICE

Devices that are mobile or located in remote places cannot rely on fixed infrastructure. When they require a small amount of power and need a robust construction, use a built-in power source.

Aliases: Non-replaceable Battery

Context: You have a device that needs to be powered. The device needs only a small amount of energy to function.

Problem: You need to power a device, which requires a small amount of power. The device is mobile or located in a remote place. You want to minimize maintenance.

Forces:

- **Mobility:** The device has to be mobile, thus, being a MAINS-POWERED DEVICE is not an option.
- **Location:** The device may be placed in a remote location far of the grid, where common infrastructure such as powerlines are not available. Thus, being a MAINS-POWERED DEVICE is not an option. The location may also provide no suitable form of ambient energy for an ENERGY-HARVESTING DEVICE.
- **Maintenance:** A PERIOD ENERGY-LIMITED DEVICE is not an option because replacing or recharging a battery in frequent intervals is too much effort.
- **Energy Requirements:** Being an ENERGY-HARVESTING DEVICE on its own is not an option, because it does not deliver the required power.
- **Lifetime:** You know the maximum lifetime of the device.
- **Ruggedness:** The device is intended to be used in environments where a rugged device enclosure is needed.

Solution: Build an energy source into the device, which will last for the entire expected lifetime of the device.

Solution Details: For many applications, being MAINS-POWERED DEVICE or a PERIOD ENERGY-LIMITED DEVICE would be too complicated or simply not possible. For example, a sensor network might be located deep down at the bottom of the ocean, which would make these tasks very difficult. In such cases, using a built-in battery that has enough capacity to last for the expected lifetime of the device would be a better solution. Even in cases where mains power would be available or replacing a battery would be possible, using a built-in battery can make the design, manufacturing, and usage of a device much simpler.

Fig. 4 shows the different phases of a LIFETIME ENERGY-LIMITED DEVICE. During production, a charged battery is wired or soldered into the device. Then, during the normal operation of the device, the battery is slowly discharged. At some point, the battery level reaches a critical point where it may make sense to notify a responsible person about the imminent end of life of the device. Once the battery is fully discharged, the device has reached its end of life.

Benefits:

- **Simplicity:** A LIFETIME ENERGY-LIMITED DEVICE is simple and cheap to build. Only a battery has to be soldered into the device. There is no need for charging circuits, charging ports, access to the battery through the enclosure, or energy-harvesting components.
- **Maintenance:** There is no maintenance required for the built-in battery, since it cannot be replaced or recharged.
- **Costs:** There are no additional costs apart from the onetime costs of building the battery into the device.
- **Independence:** The device is independent of existing infrastructure.
- **Location:** The device is not bound to a particular location, as it does not depend on its environment.
- **Mobility:** The device can be freely moved, as it is not bound to the power grid or other environmental factors.
- **Ruggedness:** The device enclosure can be build more rugged since access to the battery is not required and all power related parts are internal.

Drawbacks:

- **Lifetime:** The overall lifetime of the device is limited by the energy supply. Once the energy supply is depleted the device becomes useless and the whole device has to be replaced which require some effort, especially if the device is located at a remote place.

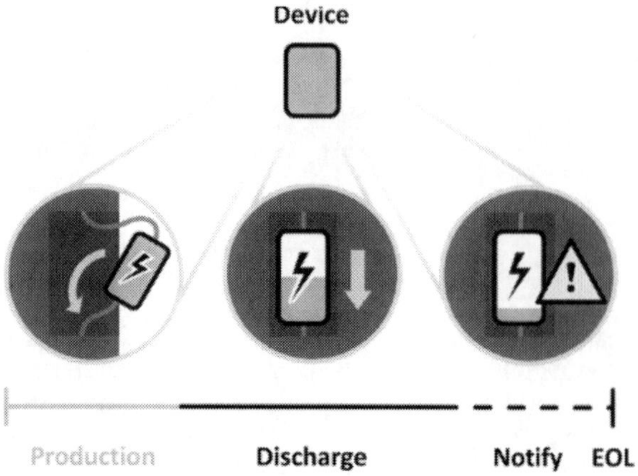

Figure 4. Sketch of the LIFETIME ENERGY-LIMITED DEVICE pattern.

The overall lifetime of the energy supply can be increased by also being an ENERGY-HARVESTING DEVICE to trickle charge the battery. However, this then also negates some of the benefits of a pure LIFETIME ENERGY-LIMITED DEVICE.

- **Energy Requirements:** The total available energy is limited and dictates the use cases where a LIFETIME ENERGY-LIMITED DEVICE makes sense. In general, using a built-in power source only makes sense for devices with very low energy requirements. Besides, to make the most out of its limited energy supply, the device should also be a NORMALLY-SLEEPING DEVICE that turns off most of the time.

Related Patterns:

- **ENERGY-HARVESTING DEVICE:** Energy-harvesting can be used to extend the lifetime of LIFETIME ENERGY-LIMITED DEVICES.
- **NORMALLY-OFF DEVICE:** LIFETIME ENERGY-LIMITED DEVICES may also be NORMALLY-OFF DEVICES to extend the lifetime of their energy source.
- **MAINS-POWERED DEVICE:** A MAINS-POWERED DEVICE can have an additional non-replaceable and non-rechargeable backup battery in case of a power outage.

Known Uses: *Amazon's Dash Button* has a built-in battery that is claimed to last 1000 button presses. It cannot be replaced or recharged once empty [30]. The *Tile Mate* is a small Bluetooth tag, which can be used to keep track of your belongings. The battery is guaranteed to last for a year after which a replacement Tile (which may include updated technology) can be automatically ordered for a reduced price [31]. The *Chipolo Plus* tag is sold in a similar fashion [32].

D. Energy-Harvesting Device

Devices that are mobile or located in remote places cannot rely on mains power infrastructure. When they require a small amount of power and the environment allows it, use energy-harvesting to gather its required power.

Aliases: Ambient Energy, Event Energy-Limited, Event-Based Harvesting

Context: You have a device that needs to be powered. The device needs only a small amount of energy to function. Besides, your use case dictates a specific location for this device, which restricts available energy sources. For example, the device has to be mobile, wearable, or in a remote location.

Problem: You need to power a device with very little power needs. The device is mobile or located in a remote place. Its environment is stable and predictable.

Forces:

- **Location:** The device has to be mobile or is located at a remote place. Thus, it cannot be a MAINS-POWERED DEVICE.
- **Effort:** Replacing or recharging a battery in frequent intervals is too much effort or not possible at all. Thus, using a PERIOD ENERGY-LIMITED DEVICE is not an option.
- **Energy Requirements:** The device needs very little energy to function.
- **Lifetime Energy Requirements:** The device needs more energy over its lifetime than current batteries can provide in a reasonable form factor without being replaced or recharged. Thus, using a LIFETIME ENERGY-LIMITED DEVICE is not an option.

Solution: Integrate an energy-harvesting component, such as a solar cell, into the device. Use it to turn the energy available in the device's surroundings into power for the device. Use components and technologies optimized for low-power usage to make the most of the harvested energy.

Solution Details: An ENERGY-HARVESTING DEVICE transforms ambient energy into electrical energy, as depicted in Fig. 5. Ambient energy can be in form of radiant energy (solar, infrared, radio frequency), thermal energy, mechanical energy, or biomechanical energy. Each of these energy forms comes with its own benefits and drawbacks that have to be taken into account for each use case separately.

Figure 5. Sketch of the Energy-Harvesting Device Pattern.

Radiant energy in form of sunlight or other light sources is a common source of energy for ENERGY-HARVESTING DEVICES. Miniature solar modules are able to harvest enough energy, even from indoor lights, to perpetually transmit a measurement a few times per hour. However, especially when using sunlight, it has to be taken into account that it is only available for a limited time each day. Another form of radiant energy, radio frequency, is produced by the many wireless communication technologies we use today and can be harvested. Because it is purposely generated and heavily regulated, it is more predictable than other forms of ambient energy. However, to be usable, a sufficient level of energy density is required in the environment, which might only be given in more populated areas. Mechanical energy can also be harvested. For example, a switch may generate enough energy when activated to be able to send several radio telegrams. Another example is a thermoelectric generator, which is able to collect and transform thermal energy in form of temperature differences into electricity.

The availability of each of these forms of ambient energy depends on the environment of the use case. Not all forms might be available in all locations and the available energy might be too small to power a particular device. Besides, mobility has to be taken into account. If the device is fixed, then the availability of ambient energy can be measured and is fairly predictable. If the device is mobile, then the form and amount of available ambient energy can fluctuate widely.

Even though it might only supply a very small amount of energy, ambient energy can be used to power very energy efficient circuits and sensors and to transmit and receive small messages. An ENERGY-HARVESTING DEVICE can be powered directly if it uses very energy efficient components, but in many cases, the harvested energy will not be enough for sustained operation. In such cases, the ambient energy can be used to trickle charge a battery or capacitor. Once sufficient energy is collected, the device can then turn on and use it for a short period of operation. Another use is to supplement PERIOD ENERGY-LIMITED DEVICES to increase the intervals between recharging.

As the harvested power is often so small, it is necessary for the device to use technologies that are optimized for ultra-low energy. This includes using components, such as microchips or sensors, which are very energy efficient. It also includes using communication technologies, such as wireless modules and even protocols and payload formats, which are optimized for ultra-low energy. Often, technologies are specifically created for this in mind, for example, the ISO/IEC 14543-3-10:2012 standard. But there are also examples of existing technologies, which have been adapted to be more energy-saving, such as IEEE 802.15.4 [33], 6loWPAN [34], or CoAP [35].

Benefits:

- **Independence:** The device is independent of the electrical grid. Besides, it can be flexibly positioned because it does not require any wire.
- **Perpetual Energy:** Devices with very low energy requirements can be powered for as long as the energy-harvesting components do not fail.
- **Cost:** The total cost of ownership OF ENERGY-HARVESTING DEVICES, which includes installation, operation, and management costs, is low. No cables have to be added during installation and battery replacement or recharging are either reduced in frequency or not necessary at all. Besides, the power used by the device is also free. Because there are no special infrastructure requirements, retrofitting an ENERGY-HARVESTING DEVICE is also easy.
- **Maintenance:** Maintenance can be reduced or is not necessary at all. This is especially beneficial if the device is located in inaccessible areas or if many devices are operated.
- **Environmental Impact:** ENERGY-HARVESTING DEVICES have a low environmental impact. The energy they harvest is freely available and energy wasting is not a problem. They also do not produce as much hazardous waste in form of old batteries as PERIOD ENERGY-LIMITED DEVICES, but other components, including the energy-harvesting components, might still be hazardous.

Drawbacks:

- **Dependence:** The device depends on the availability characteristics of the ambient energy source and its environment. These might be hard to accurately predict and control. If the environment changes it might no longer provide enough ambient energy for the device.
- **Energy:** Depending on the used technology, only small amounts of energy may be harvested from the environment. To get the most out of the available energy, high energy efficiency is necessary. This requires the device to consume very little energy during idle times, which can be achieved by making it a NORMALLY-SLEEPING DEVICE. It also requires the device to be efficient when it is awake, which can be done by using low power components and technologies.
- **Fragility:** Depending on the form of ambient energy used, the components needed for energy-harvesting might be fragile and not suited for all environments.

Related Patterns:

- **PERIOD ENERGY-LIMITED DEVICE:** Energy-harvesting can be used to extend the intervals between recharging or replacing the energy source of a PERIOD ENERGY-LIMITED DEVICE.
- **NORMALLY-SLEEPING DEVICE:** Energy-harvesting may power NORMALLY-SLEEPING DEVICES if the harvested energy is only enough for short bursts of activity.

Known Uses: A common use of energy-harvesting is found in devices that use passive RFID for communication. Here, the RF signal generated by the reader also powers the device [36]. Researchers are working on extending the capabilities of RFID powered device beyond responding with fixed data. An example is the *Wireless Identification and Sensing Platform* (WISP). It allows fully programmable 16-bit microcontrollers with attached sensors to be powered by RFID [37]. A device using WISP is the *WISPCam*, a passive RFID powered camera tag [38]. *EnOcean* created a patented wireless communication technology that is now standardized as ISO/IEC 14543-3-10:2012. It uses kinetic motion, solar, and thermal converters to create enough power for transmitting wireless signals. *EnOcean* also produces modules and products (mainly in the home automation sector) that utilize this technology. Many other companies have licensed the *EnOcean* technology and offer products [39][40]. *Freevolt* is another technology that harvests energy for low power devices from radio frequencies produced by broadcast networks, such as 2g, 3g, 4g, WiFi, and digital TV. The *CleanSpace Tag* is an air quality sensor that uses this technology to generate perpetual power for its lifetime [41].

E. *ALWAYS-ON DEVICE*

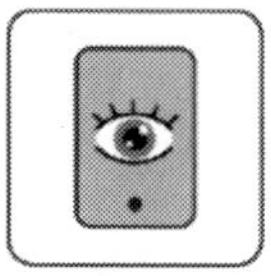

Some devices have to be available and responsive at all times. If the energy supply allows it, leave the device running and connected at all times.

Context: You have a MAINS-POWERED DEVICE or a device that has plenty of energy available, even though it is a PERIOD-ENERGY-LIMITED DEVICE, LIFETIME-ENERGY-LIMITED DEVICE, or ENERGY-HARVESTING DEVICE.

Problem: You have a device with an inexhaustible energy supply and need to have it available and responsive at all times.

Forces:

- **Energy Savings:** Saving energy is not the top priority in your situation.
- **Reachability:** The device has to be online and reachable all the time.
- **Reactivity:** The device has to react to commands instantly.
- **Functionality:** All of the device's functionality has to be available all the time.

Solution: Let the device be always on so that it is permanently connected to the network and in a state where it can receive and execute commands as soon as they arrive.

Solution Details: ALWAYS-ON DEVICES are simple. They do not have to consider a limited energy supply. Thus, they can be left running at all times with their full functionality enabled, as shown in Fig. 6. However, if their availability is a critical factor then additional precautions have to be taken to ensure availability despite possible problems. One problem might be malfunctioning or unavailable energy supply, for example, if the electrical grid is down due to a power outage. In such cases, a secondary backup power supply can be helpful, for example, in form or a backup battery. To help with a faulty communication mechanism, an ALWAYS-ON DEVICE could be equipped with multiple communication technologies to provide fallback mechanisms if necessary. To protect against failures in the device itself, multiple devices could be used to provide redundancy.

ALWAYS-ON DEVICES also benefit from an energy efficient design. As they are always running and connected, they use a lot of energy. By using energy efficient components to build these devices, the overall cost of running them can be reduced while still having them always on and connected.

Benefits:

- **Reachability:** The device will be reachable all the time as long as there are no network or power outages.
- **Reactivity:** The device will be able to react instantly because it does not have to wake up from any power saving operational states.

Drawbacks:

- **Power Consumption:** Being always on might lead to high power consumption, which could be reduced by using energy-efficient hardware.
- **Maintenance Cycles:** An ALWAYS-ON DEVICE that is also a PERIOD-ENERGY-LIMITED DEVICE or LIFETIME-ENERGY-LIMITED DEVICE will have shorter maintenance cycles than a NORMALLY-OFF DEVICE, which increases costs.
- **Feasibility:** An ALWAYS-ON DEVICE powered by Energy-Harvesting might not be feasible with current technology or only with a considerable cost.

Figure 6. Sketch of the ALWAYS-ON DEVICE Pattern.

Related Patterns:

- **MAINS-POWERED DEVICE:** Devices powered by mains power are usually a good candidate for being ALWAYS-ON DEVICES since they do not have any limitations in the power available to them.
- **PERIOD-ENERGY-LIMITED DEVICE:** ALWAYS-ON DEVICES that are MAINS-POWERED DEVICES sometimes execute critical functionality and should have high availability. Such devices may also be PERIOD ENERGY-LIMITED DEVICES and use a backup power supply, such as a replaceable battery, to guard themselves against power outages.

Known Uses: Devices that use the *Z-Wave* standard and are mains-powered are referred to as listening devices. These devices keep on their receivers at all times to extend the *Z-Wave* mesh network by acting as repeaters for messages from other devices in the network [42]. Device Gateways, such as the *Samsung SmartThings Hub* [29] or the *Wink Hub* [43], are also often permanently on so that they can effectively fulfill their function. This is also enabled by being mains-powered.

F. *NORMALLY-SLEEPING DEVICE*

Devices with a limited supply of energy have to use it wisely. Disable most of the components of the device for long periods and only enable them when required.

Aliases: Sleepy, Deep Sleep, Hibernate, Duty-cycled, Normally-Off

Context: You have a use case that comes with size, weight, cost, or energy restrictions. For example, this is the case when the use case needs mobility or wearability. You use devices optimized to fit these restrictions. These devices are LIFETIME ENERGY-LIMITED DEVICES, PERIOD ENERGY-LIMITED DEVICES, or ENERGY-HARVESTING DEVICES.

Problem: You have a device with a limited energy supply. You want to minimize the power used by the device.

Forces:

- **Limited Energy:** Having an ALWAYS-ON DEVICE is not an option since the device has a limited power source.
- **Energy Saving:** Saving energy decreases costs and is good for the environment but leads to constraints.
- **Component Use:** The device does not use every component continuously. Turning them off when not needed saves energy. However, if these components have long startup times, the responsiveness of the device suffers.
- **Communication:** Turning of the communication module when not needed saves energy. However, doing this manually takes too much effort, especially for remotely placed or large amounts of devices.

Solution: Program the device to disable its main components when they are not needed. Leave a small circuit powered which reactivates the components after a predefined amount of time has passed or when an event occurs.

Solution Details: A NORMALLY-SLEEPING DEVICE cuts power to its main components for long stretches of time, as shown in Fig. 7. Good candidates for saving energy among these components are wireless communication modules, as they drain large amounts of power. Thus, NORMALLY-SLEEPING DEVICES are not able to communicate during their off periods. Other components, from processing units to individual sensors or actuators, are also disabled to add to these energy savings.

One component has to be active continuously to wake up the device. A clock component is able to reactivate power to the other components after a predefined amount of time, shown as the first active period in Fig. 7. This time is either absolute, for example, every full hour, or relative, for example, 5 minutes after the last active period ended. Another way to reactivate the turned off components is on events, shown as the second active period in Fig. 7. One option to do this is a small circuit that monitors a sensor and reactivates power when it reaches a predefined threshold. Alternatively, a DEVICE WAKEUP TRIGGER can be used to create such an event. Once reactivated, the device resumes normal operation, as shown at the bottom of Fig. 7. For example, it saves the current sensor values and reestablishes a connection to a backend server. It uploads its state and processes messages that are waiting for it on the server. After the device has finished this process, it returns to the sleeping state until the next period of activity.

Benefits:

- **Efficiency:** The device is more energy efficient because it is active only when needed.
- **Longevity:** Sleeping for long periods saves energy. This increases the maximum lifetime of LIFETIME ENERGY-LIMITED DEVICES. Besides, it increases the interval length between replacing or recharging the power source in PERIOD ENERGY-LIMITED DEVICES.

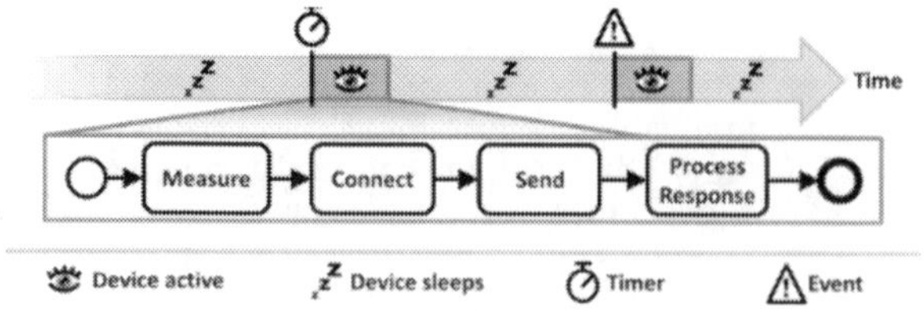

Figure 7. Sketch of the NORMALLY-SLEEPING DEVICE pattern.

Drawbacks:

- **Intermittent Connectivity:** Communication with the device is intermittent. When it is sleeping, other communication partners cannot reach it. A DEVICE SHADOW is one option to allow others to communicate with an eventually consistent version of the device. On the device itself, not every component has to be off when it is sleeping. An example is a sensor that keeps collecting measurements that need to be sent to the backend eventually. The device has to store these measurements in a queue and sends them later when it activates the next time.
- **Timing:** In important cases, for instance for critical security updates, another component has to contact the device at once. Waiting for the NORMALLY-SLEEPING DEVICE to reconnect during its next activity window is not an option. A DEVICE WAKEUP TRIGGER is one way to get the NORMALLY-SLEEPING DEVICE to reconnect at once by creating an event to which it listens.
- **Energy:** Establishing a new connection for communication needs power. Sometimes it is more efficient to sustain an existing connection than creating a large number of new ones. This point depends on the chosen technology and the required communication frequency. You have to choose sleep schedules with this in mind.

Related Patterns:

- **ENERGY-HARVESTING DEVICE:** Devices that use energy-harvesting as their source of power often also are NORMALLY-SLEEPING DEVICES. They sleep until they harvested the energy they need for a short period of activity.
- **DEVICE WAKEUP TRIGGER:** In situations when it is necessary to communicate with a NORMALLY-SLEEPING DEVICE outside of its regular communication windows, a DEVICE WAKEUP TRIGGER is one option. The DEVICE WAKEUP TRIGGER tells a disconnected device to reconnect at once.
- **PERIOD ENERGY-LIMITED DEVICE:** Being a NORMALLY-SLEEPING DEVICE extends the interval between replacing or recharging the power source in PERIOD ENERGY-LIMITED DEVICES.
- **LIFETIME ENERGY-LIMITED:** Being a NORMALLY-SLEEPING DEVICE extends the maximum lifetime of LIFETIME ENERGY-LIMITED DEVICES.
- **DEVICE SHADOW:** Using a DEVICE SHADOW allows other communication partners to retrieve the latest known state and to send commands to a currently sleeping device.

Known Uses: *Z-Wave* has so-called *sleepy devices*, which turn off to save energy and periodically wake up and reconnect. When reconnected, they inform other devices that they are listening for commands for the next seconds [42]. *Libelium's Waspmotes* support different operation modes to save power, including sleep and deep sleep modes that last from milliseconds to days. In these modes, they pause the main program and the microcontroller. Synchronous interrupts (periodic and relative programmed timers), or asynchronous interrupts (sensor readings or XBee activity) end these modes. Besides, they support a hibernation mode, where they cut power off from every part except the clock. The clock ends this mode after a predefined time with a synchronous interruption [44]. Other devices turn on for a brief moment if an event occurs. For example, the *Amazon Dash Button* turns on once a person presses the button. It connects to a WiFi network, places an order, and shuts off as soon as it receives a response [45]. The *PawTrax* pet tracker wakes up when it receives a text message, gets the current GPS position and returns it before it goes back to sleep. Besides, it has an option to return position data in set intervals [46].

G. SCHEDULE-BASED SENSING

Some situations are not well understood or require a broad overview of measurable data points. Read the sensor based on a schedule. Turn it off between readings if the interval length allows it.

Aliases: Survey-Based Sensing

Context: You have a device with sensors built into it or attached to it and need to use these sensors to acquire measurements over long periods.

Problem: You do not know what kinds of events you are looking for in your measurements or you need a general overview of the trend of the phenomenon that you are measuring.

Forces:

- **Energy Requirements:** Leaving sensors running all the time allows them to record detailed measurements but uses more energy.

- **Initialization Delay:** Sensors can be turned off to save energy but need some time to initialize and produce sensible values when turned on again.
- **Size:** Measuring and sending many values over a long period enables detailed analysis but takes up storage space and communication bandwidth.
- **Fluctuation:** Sensor measurements fluctuate but for your use case, long-term trends are more important than accurately measuring every spike.
- **Knowledge:** With some knowledge about what you want to measure, you can get better results by applying techniques specifically tailored to your use case. However, in some cases, you do not precisely know what you are looking for.
- **Relevance:** In some cases, only specific events are of relevance to you, but in other cases, you may be more interested in general long-term trends.

Solution: Define a schedule for sensor reading which fits with your use case's requirements. Program the device to power up its sensors and read their values according to this schedule. Power down the sensors after reading.

Solution Details: SCHEDULE-BASED SENSING allows you to get a general overview of the values you are measuring and how they evolve over time. Fig. 8 shows the basic process. The real state of the phenomenon that you want to measure is a continuum of values, which are constantly fluctuating over time. SCHEDULE-BASED SENSING has the device turn on its sensors based on a schedule to take measurements. Some sensors will take a certain amount of time after being turned on to initialize or calibrate before they produce sensible readings. After a certain delay, they will produce a measurement, which is stored or communicated by the device. These values can be used to interpolate an approximation of the real state. After taking a measurement, the sensor can be turned off again to safe energy.

Note that depending on the interval length between measurements some important or interesting events may be missed, as shown by the spike in Fig. 8, which is not represented in the interpolated state. By choosing a suitable sampling rate and adjusting the schedule accordingly to decrease the interval length between measurements and thereby taking more measurements per unit of time, more sampling points can be generated which lead to a more precise approximation. However, this does not solve the problem that some events might still lie outside the measurement windows. Besides, at some point the interval length may be so short that turning the sensor off between readings is no longer possible (because of the initialization delay) and you lose the energy saving benefits of SCHEDULE-BASED SENSING.

Benefits:

- **Energy Requirements:** The sensors can be turned off and the device itself can go to sleep (see NORMALLY-SLEEPING DEVICE) in the time between the sensor readings to save energy.

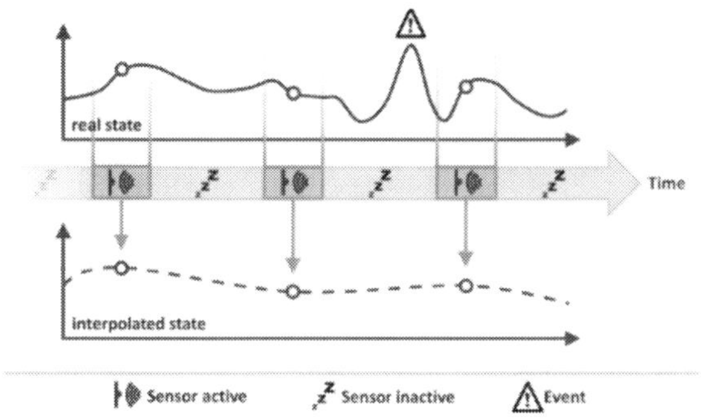

Figure 8. Sketch of the SCHEDULE-BASED SENSING pattern.

- **Knowledge:** You do not need to know anything about the values you are measuring.
- **Size:** The measuring schedule can be tuned to provide a good trade-off between accuracy, required storage space, and communication bandwidth

Drawbacks:

- **Fluctuation:** Depending on the selected schedule, the device will miss potentially interesting measurements. Use EVENT-BASED SENSING if you are interested in these spikes and know how to recognize them.
- **Size:** When a high accuracy is required and, thus, a short measuring interval is selected, many measurements will be created that have to be stored or communicated. Use DELTA UPDATE to communicate measurement values that have changed since the last measurement.
- **Relevance:** Even if you are interested in a long-term general overview of the measured event, a lot of the data collected may be not that relevant to your use case but still takes up a lot of storage space or communication bandwidth.
- **Energy Requirements:** The device has to wake up for each measurement even if nothing interesting happened, which consumes energy.

Related Patterns:

- **NORMALLY-SLEEPING DEVICE:** A NORMALLY-SLEEPING DEVICE can be programmed to wake up according to a schedule and take measurement, thus, implementing SCHEDULE-BASED SENSING.
- **ALWAYS-ON DEVICE:** Devices that are always running can also benefit from SCHEDULE-BASED SENSING as it can reduce the overall energy, storage space, and communication bandwidth required making such devices more efficient.
- **EVENT-BASED SENSING:** If certain well-defined events are more interesting than a general history of measurement values, EVENT-BASED SENSING is a good alternative to SCHEDULE-BASED SENSING.

- **Energy-Harvesting Device:** These devices can be programmed to take a measurement whenever they have gathered enough energy. Thus, they would implement Schedule-Based Sensing with an interval length that depends on environmental factors and, thus, can be irregular.
- **Period Energy-Limited Device:** The energy saved by turning the sensors off most of the time by using Schedule-Based Sensing can increase the time between replacing or recharging the batteries of these devices, which lowers their maintenance costs.
- **Lifetime Energy-Limited Device:** These devices can increase their maximum time to life by using Schedule-Based Sensing with long measurement intervals.

Variants:

- **Periodic Sensing:** A common variant of Schedule-Based Sensing uses a regular schedule with evenly spaced intervals to take the measurements.

Known Uses: Periodic sensor reading is mentioned in the *Libelium Waspmote* technical guide as an option for sensors with a high power consumption and for use cases where continuous monitoring to generate alarms is not required [44]. *NXP's MMA955xL* platform can take sensor readings at evenly spaced points in time [47]. Like many other microcontroller boards, the *Arduino* supports reading the current value of sensors attached to its analog pins in a loop [48].

H. *Event-Based Sensing*

If you are interested in specific events, reading a sensor in regular interval can be wasteful. Besides, some events may be missed if they happen outside the measurement window. Implement a low-energy event detection circuit and only generate a measurement if an event is detected.

Context: You have a device with sensors built into it or attached to it and you need to use these sensors to acquire measurement and react to certain events.

Problem: You have a use case where you are interested in irregularly occurring events that are represented in sensor values. Reading the sensor in regular intervals is wasteful because those events occur rarely and the other values are of no interest to you. Besides, it is possible that you miss an event if it falls between two sensor readings.

Forces:

- **Energy Requirements:** Leaving sensors running all the time allows them to record detailed measurements but uses more energy.
- **Sampling:** The events you are interested in can be of short duration but measuring them requires a high enough sampling rate.
- **Size:** Measuring and sending many values over a long period enables detailed analysis but takes up storage space and communication bandwidth.
- **Knowledge:** You do not always have prior knowledge about what you want to measure, but if you have, you can get better results by applying techniques specifically tailored to your use case.
- **Relevance:** In some cases, only specific events are of relevance to you, but you do not need to collect all the other uninteresting measurements.

Solution: Define the events that are of interest to you in the form of sensor values. Use low-power sensors and power them continuously. Program low energy comparator circuits to read those sensors and watch for the events. Only propagate measurements to the device if a sensor value triggers such a comparator circuit.

Solution Details: Event-Based Sensing requires that you know beforehand what events you are interested in and that you can formalize the specific features that distinguish these events from others. This allows you to implement comparator logic that can detect these events (see Fig. 9), which often can be done with very energy-efficient hardware circuits. These comparators change their output once they detect an event, which can be used to signal an interrupt pin of the device's processor. This tells the device to wake up, if necessary, and process the event at once. If the device should react to different events, it either requires multiple interrupt pins, one for each event, or the different comparator circuits have to be combined with an or gate before being put on the interruption pin. The value that triggered the comparator circuit and, thus, the interrupt should be stored in a register to allow the device to read it once it has started up.

Benefits:

- **Relevance:** You only get the measurement that you previously defined as relevant to you.
- **Size:** If the events that you are interested in do not occur very often, these measurements will not cost much storage space or communication bandwidth.
- **Energy Requirements:** The device can be turned off and is only turned on once something interesting happened, which can save a lot of energy.

Drawbacks:

- **Relevance:** You do not get a continuous history of measurement values. If you need such a history, use Schedule-Based Sensing.

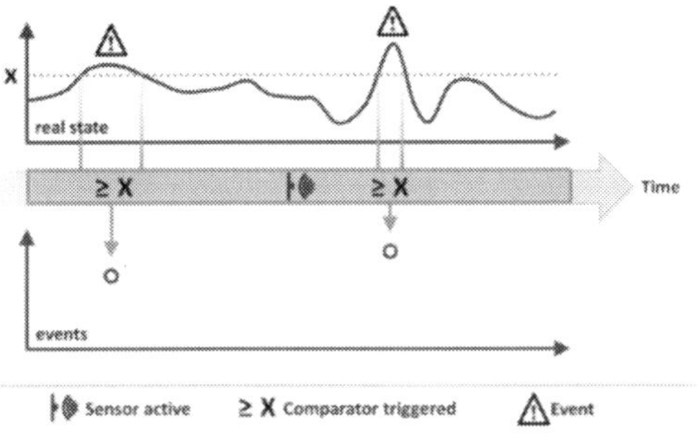

Figure 9. Sketch of the EVENT-BASED SENSING pattern.

- **Energy Requirements:** The sensors and the comparator components have to be running all the time to be able to catch the interesting events.

Related Patterns:

- **NORMALLY-SLEEPING DEVICE:** EVENT-BASED SENSING can be used to wake up a NORMALLY-SLEEPING DEVICE only when it is necessary to react to a certain event.
- **SCHEDULE-BASED SENSING:** If not only certain events are important, SCHEDULE-BASED SENSING is an alternative that provides regular sensor readings.
- **PERIOD ENERGY-LIMITED DEVICE, LIFETIME ENERGY-LIMITED DEVICE, and ENERGY HARVESTING DEVICE:** SCHEDULE-BASED SENSING is one option to lower the energy consumption of these devices by only powering the rest of the device on when an event is detected. This can increases their time between maintenance or their total time of life.

Variants:

- **CHANGE-BASED SENSING:** A common variant of the EVENT-BASED SENSING pattern is CHANGE-BASED SENSING. Here, new measurements are only propagated when the sensor value has changed by a certain significant amount, which can be configured according to the use case. Thus, messages are only sent for relevant changes. Unnecessary communication caused by small and insignificant fluctuations in the measured value is avoided.

Known Uses: *Libelium's Waspmotes* have interruption pins to which comparators can be connected. Once a comparator witnesses an event, its changing output send to the pin triggers the microprocessor to wake up and take further action [44]. *Fibaro's CO Sensor* has configuration settings to define the minimum change in sensor values that is required so that a message will be send [49]. *NXP's PCT2202* temperature sensor runs either in comparator or interrupt mode. In both modes, an alert pin is activated if the temperature remains higher than a configurable threshold for multiple readings [50]. The *Arduino*, like many other microcontroller boards, allows interrupts to be set on digital pins, to which sensors can be connected. These interrupts fire when the pin is low or high, or changes its value [51].

VI. CONCLUSION AND FUTURE WORK

Devices are a central point of any IoT system, as they link the physical with the digital world through their sensors and actuators. They are also a starting point when designing IoT systems because the particular use case and the environment directly influence them. Their selection then further influences the design of the IoT system, as it has to cater to the different device characteristics.

To help individuals to design IoT systems that work with different kinds of devices, we presented eight IoT device patterns in three categories. The energy source type patterns describe different ways a device can be powered depending on factors such as energy requirement, mobility, or the environment. The operation mode patterns explain how a device might operate under different constraints such as limited energy. The sensing patterns describe different sensing techniques that devices can use.

In the future, we want to expand this selection of patterns into a full IoT Pattern catalog and further refine their interrelations to form an IoT Pattern Language. We already added patterns for device bootstrapping and registration [52] but we will also add new patterns in several other categories, such as communication between devices and platforms, data processing, security, and more.

We also plan to do more work to support implementations based on patterns. For this, generic patterns, like the IoT Patterns presented in this work, can be refined into technology specific patterns [12]. These in turn can be linked to solution languages[53], which can provide practitioners with concrete guidance on how to implement a system based on patterns [15] and further provide implementations of the patterns [13][14]. These concepts can also be applied to IoT Patterns.

ACKNOWLEDGMENT

This work was partially funded by the projects SmartOrchestra (01MD16001F) and SePiA.Pro (01MD16013F).

REFERENCES

[1] L. Reinfurt, U. Breitenbücher, M. Falkenthal, F. Leymann, and A. Riegg, "Internet of Things Patterns for Devices," *Proceedings of the Ninth International Conferences on Pervasive Patterns and Applications (PATTERNS) 2017*: Xpert Publishing Services, pp. 117–126, 2017.

[2] L. Reinfurt, U. Breitenbücher, M. Falkenthal, F. Leymann, and A. Riegg, "Internet of Things Patterns," in *Proceedings of the 21st European Conference on Pattern Languages of Programs (EuroPLoP)*: ACM, 2016.

[3] L. Reinfurt, U. Breitenbücher, M. Falkenthal, F. Leymann, and A. Riegg, "Internet of Things Patterns for Communication and Management," LNCS Transactions on Pattern Languages of Programming, 2017. unpublished.

[4] C. Bormann, M. Ersue, and A. Keranen, "Terminology for Constrained-Node Networks," IETF, 2014. [Online]. Available from: http://www.rfc-editor.org/rfc/pdfrfc/rfc7228.txt.pdf 2017.11.14

[5] C. Alexander, S. Ishikawa, and M. Silverstein, *A Pattern Language: Towns, Buildings, Construction*. New York: Oxford University Press, 1977.

[6] G. Hohpe and B. Woolf, *Enterprise Integration Patterns: Designing, Building, and Deploying Messaging Solutions*. Boston, Massachusetts: Addison-Wesley, 2004.

[7] C. Fehling, F. Leymann, R. Retter, W. Schupeck, and P. Arbitter, *Cloud Computing Patterns: Fundamentals to Design, Build, and Manage Cloud Applications*. Wien: Springer, 2014.

[8] G. Meszaros and J. Doble, "Metapatterns: A Pattern Language for Pattern Writing," *Third Pattern Languages of Programming Conference*: Addison-Wesley, 1996.

[9] N. B. Harrison, "The Language of Shepherding: A Pattern Language for Shepherds and Sheep," in *Software patterns series, Pattern languages of program design 5*1st ed., Upper Saddler River, NJ: Addison-Wesley, 2006, pp. 507–530.

[10] N. B. Harrison, "Advanced Pattern Writing: Patterns for Experienced Pattern Authors," in *Software patterns series, Pattern languages of program design 5*1st ed., Upper Saddler River, NJ: Addison-Wesley, 2006, pp. 433–452.

[11] T. Wellhausen and A. Fießer, "How to write a pattern?: A rough guide for first-time pattern authors," *Proceedings of the 16th European Conference on Pattern Languages of Programs*: ACM, 2012.

[12] M. Falkenthal *et al.*, "Leveraging Pattern Application via Pattern Refinement," *Proceedings of the International Conference on Pursuit of Pattern Languages for Societal Change (PURPLSOC)*, 2016.

[13] M. Falkenthal, J. Barzen, U. Breitenbücher, C. Fehling, and F. Leymann, "Efficient Pattern Application: Validating the Concept of Solution Implementations in Different Domains," (Englisch), International Journal on Advances in Software, vol. 7, no. 3&4, pp. 710–726, 2014.

[14] M. Falkenthal, J. Barzen, U. Breitenbücher, C. Fehling, and F. Leymann, "From Pattern Languages to Solution Implementations," *Proceedings of the Sixth International Conferences on Pervasive Patterns and Applications (PATTERNS 2014)*: IARIA, pp. 12–21, 2014.

[15] M. Falkenthal and F. Leymann, "Easing Pattern Application by Means of Solution Languages," *Proceedings of the Ninth International Conferences on Pervasive Patterns and Applications (PATTERNS) 2017*: Xpert Publishing Services, pp. 58–64, 2017.

[16] V.-P. Eloranta, J. Koskinen, M. Leppänen, and V. Reijonen, *Designing distributed control systems: A pattern language approach*. Hoboken, NJ: Wiley, 2014.

[17] S. Qanbari *et al.*, "IoT Design Patterns: Computational Constructs to Design, Build and Engineer Edge Applications," *Proceedings of the First International Conference on Internet-of-Things Design and Implementation (IoTDI)*: IEEE, pp. 277–282, 2016.

[18] G. S. Chandra, *Pattern language for IoT applications*,

[19] Philips, *Hue White and color ambiance Single bulb BR30*. [Online]. Available from: http://www2.meethue.com/en-us/p/hue-white-and-color-ambiance-single-bulb-br30/46677468941 2017.11.14

[20] Xiaomi, *Xiaomi Mi Air Purifier 2*. [Online]. Available from: https://xiaomi-mi.com/air-and-water-purifiers/xiaomi-mi-air-purifier-2/ 2017.11.14

[21] Airboxlab, *Install & setup your Foobot*. [Online]. Available from: http://help.foobot.io/hc/en-us/articles/204713582-Install-setup-your-Foobot 2017.11.14

[22] Essence, *WeR@Home Installation Guide* 2017.01.13

[23] Afero, "Hub Secure Hub Product brief," 2016. [Online]. Available from: https://developer.afero.io/static/custom/files/HubProductBrief.pdf 2017.11.14

[24] Shortcut Labs, *Flic: The Wireless Smart Button*. [Online]. Available from: https://start.flic.io/ 2017.11.14

[25] Logitech, *POP Home Switch Simple smart home control for the whole family*. [Online]. Available from: http://www.logitech.com/en-us/product/pop-home-switch 2017.11.14

[26] Sen.se, *ThermoPeanut*. [Online]. Available from: https://sen.se/store/thermopeanut/ 2017.11.14

[27] Nest, *Nest Learning Thermostat - Install & Explore*. [Online]. Available from: https://nest.com/thermostats/nest-learning-thermostat/tech-specs/ 2017.11.14

[28] Roost, *Roost Wi-Fi battery for smoke and CO alarms*. [Online]. Available from: http://www.getroost.com/product-battery 2017.11.14

[29] SmartThings, *Architecture*. [Online]. Available from: http://docs.smartthings.com/en/latest/architecture/index.html 2017.11.14

[30] Amazon Web Services, *AWS IoT Button*. [Online]. Available from: https://aws.amazon.com/iotbutton/ 2017.11.14

[31] Tile, *What is reTile?* [Online]. Available from: https://support.thetileapp.com/hc/en-us/articles/200550678-ReTile-How-do-I-renew-or-replace-my-Tile-after-it-expires- 2017.11.14

[32] Chipolo, *Chipolo Plus Renewal Program*. [Online]. Available from: https://chipolo.net/pages/renewal 2017.11.14

[33] *IEEE Standard for Low-Rate Wireless Personal Area Networks (WPANs)*, 2016.

[34] *Transmission of IPv6 Packets over IEEE 802.15.4 Networks*, 2007.

[35] *The Constrained Application Protocol (CoAP)*, 2014.

[36] R. Want, "An introduction to RFID technology," IEEE Pervasive Computing, vol. 5, no. 1, pp. 25–33, 2006.

[37] J. R. Smith, *Wireless Identification Sensing Platform (WISP)*. [Online]. Available from: http://sensor.cs.washington.edu/WISP.html 2017.11.14

[38] S. Naderiparizi, A. N. Parks, Z. Kapetanovic, B. Ransford, and J. R. Smith, "WISPCam: A Battery-Free RFID Camera," *2015 IEEE International Conference on RFID (RFID)*, pp. 166–173, 2015.

[39] EnOcean, *EnOcean – The World of Energy Harvesting Wireless Technology*. [Online]. Available from: https://www.enocean.com/fileadmin/redaktion/pdf/white_paper/WhitePaper_Getting_Started_With_EnOcean_v1.0.pdf 2017.11.14

[40] EnOcean, *Energy Harvesting Wireless Power for the Internet of Things*. [Online]. Available from: https://www.enocean.com/fileadmin/redaktion/pdf/white_paper/White_Paper_Internet_of_Things_EnOcean.pdf 2017.11.14

[41] drayson, *RF Energy Harvesting for the Low Energy Internet of Things*,

[42] SmartThings, *Z-Wave Primer*. [Online]. Available from: http://docs.smartthings.com/en/latest/device-type-developers-guide/z-wave-primer.html 2017.11.14

[43] Wink, *Wink Hub*. [Online]. Available from: http://www.wink.com/products/wink-hub/ 2016.01.20

[44] Libelium, "Waspmote Technical Guide," 2016. [Online]. Available from:

http://www.libelium.com/downloads/documentation/waspmote_technical_guide.pdf 2017.01.13

[45] T. Benson, *How I Hacked Amazon's $5 WiFi Button to track Baby Data — Medium.* [Online]. Available from: https://blog.cloudstitch.com/how-i-hacked-amazon-s-5-wifi-button-to-track-baby-data-794214b0bdd8 2017.11.14

[46] PawTrax, *Welcome to PawTrax.* [Online]. Available from: http://www.pawtrax.co.uk/ 2017.11.14

[47] NXP, *MMA955xL Intelligent, Motion-Sensing Platform Hardware Reference Manual.* [Online]. Available from: http://www.nxp.com/docs/en/reference-manual/MMA955xLRM.pdf 2017.07.20

[48] Arduino, *analogRead.* [Online]. Available from: https://www.arduino.cc/reference/en/language/functions/analog-io/analogread/ 2017.11.14

[49] Fibaro, *CO Sensor.* [Online]. Available from: http://manuals.fibaro.com/co-sensor/ 2017.11.14

[50] NXP, *PCT2202: Ultra low power, 1.8 V, 1 deg. C accuracy, digital temperature sensor with I2C-bus interface.* [Online]. Available from: http://www.nxp.com/docs/en/data-sheet/PCT2202.pdf 2017.11.14

[51] Arduino, *attachInterrupt.* [Online]. Available from: https://www.arduino.cc/reference/en/language/functions/external-interrupts/attachinterrupt/ 2017.11.14

[52] L. Reinfurt, U. Breitenbücher, M. Falkenthal, F. Leymann, and A. Riegg, "Internet of Things Patterns for Device Bootstrapping and Registration," in *Proceedings of the 22nd European Conference on Pattern Languages of Programs (EuroPLoP)*: ACM, 2017

[53] M. Falkenthal, J. Barzen, U. Breitenbücher, and F. Leymann, "Solution Languages: Easing Pattern Composition in Different Domains," International Journal on Advances in Software, vol. 10, no. 3 & 4, 2017. in press.

A Suggested Framework for the Evaluation of e-Government Services

Maria Aristea Kalamatianou
Department of Digital Systems
University of Piraeus
Piraeus, Greece
e-mail: kalam.mar.ar@gmail.com

Abstract—**The main objective of every government is to provide efficient and effective services to citizens. Recently the Greek Government has devoted significant effort to streamlining business processes using ICT to better manage public administration resources. To this end, public sector services are designed so that they are accessed through single points, while increasing transparency and reducing cycle time for executing processes and disseminating information to civil and other agencies. To control the services provided by state agencies and to improve them continuously, it seems essential that they are continuously evaluated by users. E-government needs to be grounded on in-depth understanding of user needs, perceptions and other factors influencing its uptake. This paper focuses on the field of e-government and more precisely describes an evaluation method for investigating the success of an e-government project. Specifically, a technology adoption model is proposed and developed, which focuses on the specific characteristics of users for the on-line services of an Independent Authority. The model is essentially based on the framework of the Unified Theory of Acceptance and the Use of Technology (UTAUT2) model, which has been enhanced with four additional criteria. The findings reveal that behavioral intention and therefore usage intention are influenced by enablers, as effort expectancy, performance expectancy, social influence, price value and habit, as well as inhibitors such as privacy, profession and user satisfaction. The enhanced model furthers the discussion and development of technology adoption models and helps the government sectors regulate their strategies and future plans to facilitate successful adoption and diffusion of e-services in Greece.**

Keywords-e-government; evaluation model; unified theory of acceptance and use of technology; public administration; independed authority.

I. Introduction

This article, which is an extended version of a conference paper entitled "An Extended UTAUT2 Model for e-Government Project Evaluation", focuses on the field of Electronic Government (e-government) and more precisely describes an evaluation method for investigating the success of an e-government project, including a review of the recent developments in the e-government research field [1].

The technological revolution brought about major and rapid changes in daily human activities, providing more effective ways of communication among stakeholders, as well as more efficient working methods. Governments have been unfolding the benefits of using Information and Communications Technologies (ICT) for providing electronic public services to citizens, the government itself, public officers and businesses. Increased efficiency, information and service quality improvement, enhanced access to information, increased transparency and accountability, smoother and easier interactions between citizens and public agencies, enhanced democracy, empowered citizens and public officers, and openness are just a few of the benefits deriving from e-government for the different stakeholders [2, 3].

E-government generally presents many challenges for citizens and the community to obtain substantial benefits from it. First of all, the administration must have the traits of a democratic one and therefore should enjoy the trust of all citizens who come into contact with it. The most important elements of intervention deemed necessary refer to: meeting the needs of large population groups and avoiding exclusion for some of them; reorganizing the administration by simplifying the administrative procedures; introducing electronic authentication with digital certificates and Public Key Infrastructure (PKI); ensuring the transparency of procedures, as well as the reliability and usability of IT systems; providing access to all its services through a single one-stop gateway; ensuring multiple access to services, both through traditional methods, as well as using modern ICT (internet, telephone, transaction offices, interpersonal contact with the employees themselves), etc.

.E-government allows citizens to interact more directly with the government, transforming multiple operational and bureaucratic procedures and using a customer-centric approach to service delivery. It further allows intra-governmental communication and also offers numerous possibilities for using the internet and other web-based technologies to extend online government services [4].

Electronic government, also known as digital information services and transactions among public administration, other government agencies and the citizens of a country, has entered dynamically in the new global reality and is growing rapidly.

E-government is defined by the European Union (EU) Commission as the use of information and communication technologies in public administrations combined with organizational change and new skills in order to improve public services and democratic processes and strengthen support to public policies [5]. Interaction between e-services; provided by the government to stakeholders; may be classified into four key models, depending on who is involved. These models are: government-to-citizen /customer (G2C), government-to-employees (G2E), government-to-government (G2G) and government-to-business (G2B) [6][7]. The goal is to improve public services and streamline business processes to support public policies. Through e-government methods, civil service authorities may offer easier access to public information, upgrade operations to facilitate citizen interaction, increase productivity and competitiveness, increase transparency and accountability, combat corruption, facilitate decision-making and promote active participation of citizens, by empowering them. In order to achieve this, the supply management of goods and services must be improved. The implementation of an e-government project can have many benefits, despite the high risk of the project failing due to various factors, such as user resistance to change and their insufficient expertise [8]-[10].

For successful implementation of the e-government services and applications, criteria - such as time, cost, quality, satisfaction of e-government stakeholders and fulfillment of functional requirements - are deemed critical. E-government success means successful ICT implementation in government units in order to rebuild government processes and provide e-government services. It also means effective and efficient use of e-government by all government stakeholders (citizens, businesses and other government agencies) [11]. Citizens are the primary stakeholders and the main beneficiaries and they all are not same. To attract citizen interest, trust and aptitude towards using websites, the government needs to add value to the service delivery mechanism. On the other hand, it also needs to take a forward step by letting and allowing citizens to participate in the decision-making process, as this would help in building trust between both stakeholders [12].

User acceptance is one of the main issues involved in e-government projects; however, other issues (such as reengineering of work processes, policy changes and management commitment) need also be considered. In addition, convenience, citizen empowerment, exclusivity, choice and cost saving are parameters of utmost importance and relevance for web-based services.

From a citizen's perspective, availability and accessibility are the two critical requirements that must be met for adopting an e-government project. Services must be delivered to them in the easiest and fastest way and be available 24/7. This enables citizens to process transactions at any time, even outside government office hours [13]. It is also important for the user that the e-services offered are more user-friendly and less expensive for the taxpayer.

Therefore, the evaluation of an e-government project from the citizens' perspective is indispensable, since its success depends on their acceptance. This can be achieved by applying an evaluation model to it. Through evaluation, government agencies understand more easily what factors influence the citizens in adopting such projects. With systematic evaluation, state agencies promptly understand the users' expectations and improve their services, making them friendlier and safer.

The recent financial and economic crisis has also shown that e-government projects and realization of their benefits are important for effective crisis response. A large number of governments throughout Europe have viewed the economic crisis as an opportunity for them to speed up the implementation of their e-government services, with the aim of improving efficiency and effectiveness, increasing savings on public administration operations and enhancing trust-building with citizens.

In 2012, the European Commission estimated that all EU public administrations using e-procurement procedures could save at least €100 billion per year and that e-government (online communication between citizens and governments) could reduce costs by 15 to 20% [14]. According to the chief of UNDESA's e-Government Branch, "the fact that the European Commission's Digital Agenda forms one of the seven pillars of the Europe 2020 Strategy [for growth], provides clear evidence on how those countries have set the e-government development as one of their national priorities and how much they have been implementing" [15].

In this context, and in Greece in particular, the necessity for public services to use e-government became evident and imperative, so it may have a positive direct or indirect impact on economic recovery at this difficult point in time. This paper focuses on the field of e-government services; more precisely, on evaluating the G2C services provided by the information system (IS) of the Greek Ombudsman, an Independent Authority in Greece, and on identifying the factors, which facilitate or hinder users in using the e-government IS. The evaluation model used is based on the framework of the extended Unified Theory of Acceptance and the Use of Technology (UTAUT2) model, and has been enhanced by four additional criteria to achieve more insightful results. This study provides useful insights into the motivations underlying the user's intention to use e-government services in developed countries, that have experienced problems due to economic crisis, such Greece, and helps gain a better understanding of the factors that influence the user to adopt such systems.

This paper is structured as follows: In Section II, the relevant theories and the background research are described, along with the main point that this research aims to achieve. In Section III, the case study is presented, and the developed research model and hypotheses are proposed. In Section IV, the study results are presented and analyzed. Finally, in Section V, the conclusions of the study and the future projects are discussed.

II. BACKGROUND

There are several models and theories in the literature aiming at studying the success of an e-government project based on user acceptance. Many studies focus on examining the various factors that might influence the decision of users/citizens to adopt and use such systems. Earlier evaluation models focused on behavioral intention and attitude of the users towards the use of technology, using as main criteria the perceived usefulness and perceived ease of use [16][17]. Due to the enormous development and evolution of digital technology, these models had to be extended to give more accurate results, by adding new factors (criteria) for evaluation.

Because e-government is a technology-based solution for government institutions to provide services to citizens, it is important for behavioral studies to focus specifically on the diversity of citizens in terms of age, language, norms and ethics. As noted in recent literature, many research studies have proved that factors - such as demographic characteristics, social influence, trust, risk perception, quality of information, user characteristics and user satisfaction - may be instrumental in adopting e-government services [18]-[21]. Also, the national culture of the population may influence the citizens' intention to use government-offered digital services [22]-[25]. Hence, new integrated models that combine independent and dependent variables have emerged, which use variables such as gender, age, experience and the willingness to use in an attempt to examine whether they significantly affect digital technology use [26]-[28].

Among the most widely accepted evaluation models for e-government services are the following: the Technology Acceptance Model (TAM) [29] and its expanded versions models TAM2 [30] and TAM 3 [31]; the Information System Success Model (IS Success Model) [32] and its refined version [33]; the Unified Theory of Acceptance and Use of Technology (UTAUT) [34] and its extended Unified Theory of Acceptance and Use of Technology 2 (UTAUT2) [35]; the Integrated Success Model (ISM) [36]; the Model for Mandatory Use of Technologies (MMUST) [37]; and the Diffusion of Innovations Model (DOI) [38].

Venkatesh et al. (2003) argue that the situation and context of ICT acceptance and use differ widely from organizational setup to consumer setup. As such, researchers are allowed to add and remove determinants and moderator variables to suit different circumstances [34].

To investigate and analyze factors that influence the adoption and use of an e-government project, researchers have most often adopted various forms of the TAM and UTAUT models. For instance, the TAM has been extended with the self-efficacy measure, to evaluate the use of an e-government website and more specifically, to investigate and understand the fundamental factors that influence the citizens' continued intention to use it. The results of the analysis reveal that TAM, together with computer self-efficacy, can be applied to better understand the citizens' continuous intention to use e-government websites [39].

Furthermore, the use of an amended version of the UTAUT model in the adoption of e-government services has been investigated in Kuwait and it was found that performance expectancy, effort expectancy and peer influence determine the students' behavioral intention for use. Moreover, facilitating conditions and behavioral intentions determine the students' use of e-government services [40].

Additionally, an extended version of UTAUT was used to investigate a number of factors that affect the Kuwaiti citizens' adoption of the traffic violation e-payment system (TVEPS). The results showed that effort expectancy and social influence affect the use intention, and the users' internet experience moderated such a relationship. However, results revealed that performance expectancy did not influence the intention to use TVEPS. Also, facilitating condition, trust and use intention were found to influence the actual use of the system. It is also stated that, while gender moderated the relationship between facilitating conditions and actual use of the system, awareness moderated the relationship of trust and use intention with the actual use of the system [41].

To explore the citizens' behavioral intention to adopt e-government services and the factors affecting e-government adoption in Qatar, a UTAUT model has been used. The findings indicate that there is a significant positive relationship between performance expectancy, effort expectancy, social influence and behavioral intention to use e-government services for the citizens of Qatar [42][43].

A model that is essentially a blend of TAM, TAM2 and DOI has been used in Greece, along with trust and perceived risk as factors, for describing teachers' behavioral intentions to adopt e-government services. The research findings revealed that cognitive and intrinsic factors have significant effects on the intention to use e-government websites. Out of both attitudinal (trust and perceived risk) and operational variables (compatibility, advantage and job relevance), it is the second set that had a significant effect on the users' intention [44].

A more recent study aims at investigating citizen behavior and the role of Citizen Service Centers in e-government adoption in Greece. Since trust and culture cannot be considered with TAM, an extended UTAUT model was deemed more suitable. The findings revealed that performance expectancy, effort expectancy, trust of intermediary, trust of the government, trust of the internet and finally, social influence are key drivers, influencing directly or indirectly the users' intention. In addition, all the demographic variables that were included in the study (age, gender, educational level and internet experience) were found to be related to the adoption of e-government in Greece [45].

To examine the perspective of trust towards e-government initiatives in a study in Sri Lanka, trustworthiness was included as an additional construct to TAM. The results showed that the model is well suited to investigate the adoption and use of e-government services from the perspective of trustworthiness [46].

A framework that combines TAM, Theory of Planned Behavior (TPB) and Information System Success (ISS) was introduced as a foundation to examine factors that affect the intention to use e-government services. The proposed model assumes that personal innovativeness, perceived usefulness, perceived ease of use, attitude, subjective norm, perceived behavior control and system quality should be the predictors of user satisfaction over e-government services [47].

To investigate the influence of six determinants on taxpayer intention to adopt e-file systems in the USA, a model, which integrates technology adoption factors from the UTAUT model with personal perceptions on trust, efficacy, and security was applied. The findings of this study revealed that theoretical constructs from the UTAUT model are well suited in explaining intentions to use multiple e-government services. Specifically, the results indicate that three factors from the UTAUT model (performance expectancy, effort expectancy and social influence) play a significant role in predicting the e-filing intentions of taxpayers [48].

Among a multitude of models, researchers face difficulties in finding the most appropriate and suitable model for the evaluation of e-government systems that would improve their adoption by the end users. That is because the users' behavioral intention is determined by factors that may vary along with the situation studied, such as groups in different cultures, level of use and interaction, money constraints, and time [19][45][49][50]. In fact, many authors propose the UTAUT model as an ideal choice for e-government evaluation because it has a well-established theory in the field of e-government, it is the most comprehensive model, it has been extensively used in many empirical studies on ICT adoption and utilization, and it offers a better understanding of the factors, which determine the citizens' intention to adopt [40][51]-[55].

Based on previous studies, although the UTAUT model seems appropriate to evaluate the adoption of e-government in Greece, there are factors that have not been explored and have a direct impact on the Behavioral Intention of the Greek citizens. Recent studies by the Hellenic Statistical Authority and the Greek Information Society show that there are many factors in Greece that may affect the citizens' intention to adopt e-government systems, including digital technology culture, social influence, face-to-face interaction, gender, age, etc. In light of these - and in view of analyzing the influence of social and demographic characteristics, profession, user satisfaction, privacy and continuous usage on the adoption of an e-government service in Greece - an in-depth study must be conducted using an enhanced adoption model. In what follows, an extended version of the UTAUT2 model was used, which was enriched with four additional criteria, as determinants of user behavioral intention.

III. CASE STUDY

A. *The Independent Authority of the Greek Ombudsman*

The Greek Ombudsman is an Independent Authority sanctioned by the Constitution, which provides its services to the public free of charge. The Authority mediates between public administration and citizens to help citizens exercise their rights effectively. As a mediator, the Greek Ombudsman makes recommendations and submits proposals to the public administration (ministries, regions and municipalities, social insurance funds, tax offices, hospitals, schools and universities, prisons, the police, public utility companies and organizations). The Greek Ombudsman's guiding principle and drive as a mediator is its commitment to the win-win approach, i.e., visualizing solutions from which both the citizens and the administration can benefit. Additionally, the Authority's mission is to safeguard and promote children's rights and the rights of vulnerable groups; to promote equal treatment and fight discrimination based on race, ethnicity, religious or belief, disability, age or sexual orientation; and to monitor and promote the application of equal opportunities and treatment between men and women in matters of employment, as well as in matters of access of men and women to goods and services [56][57]. Anyone facing a problem with a Greek public service, anywhere in Greece or abroad, can submit a complaint to the Greek Ombudsman, regardless of their nationality.

The Independent Authority stands by the citizens affected by the financial crisis; it investigates problems caused by legislation or administrative acts or omissions and undertakes targeted initiatives, building on the expertise it has developed so far and the enhanced competences it enjoys. Until 2009, a complaint to the Greek Ombudsman could be submitted to the Ombudsman Office in person, by post or by fax.

From the beginning of its operation, the Authority had a modern IT system installed. This was updated in 2009 to capitalize on modern technology, by improving its services to the citizens. The new Integrated Information System (IIS) aimed at providing a more effective and efficient operation for citizens, employees and stakeholders, by promoting the automation of the Authority's processes to cope with the increased workload created by the citizens. To facilitate and expedite the services offered to complainants on its website, besides general information about the Ombudsman, the system enables a secure two-way communication between the Authority and the users. An on-line form is available by following a link, to submit a complaint [58]. Through this process, citizens/complainants are able to monitor the progress of their complaint online and receive updates about it. Thus, each complainant is able to submit complaints and send additional information regarding his/her case electronically from anywhere, using their personal e-mail.

B. *Evaluation Model Selection*

Given the diversity of the Authority's complainants (Greek and foreign citizens, refugees, children, prisoners), it is hypothesized that complainant behavior on using the Authority's website is affected by demographic characteristics (gender, age, nationality), culture, friends or relatives, habits and their skill/experience in using IT services. Also, other parameters might determine the users' behavioral intention for the Authority's website. Thus, it was decided to examine the following factors: user privacy, satisfaction, profession and continuous usage [59].

User privacy: In the era of automated profiling and electronic surveillance, citizens face a serious threat against their right to privacy and informational self-determination, especially when using the internet and mobile services. The lack of transparency regarding the functionality and interconnection of such services increases the risk of uncontrollable processing of personal data. Data protection regulation would be a useful instrument to protect the privacy of individuals. [60].

A wide variety of users use the Authority's services (Greek or foreign citizens, children, disabled people, immigrants, refugees). Hence, the level of trust between the users and the Authority may be crucial, since it is widely recognized as very important that the user feels safe and protected when registering personal data. Private data protection is an important issue in the evolving relationship between digital technology and the legal right to privacy when collecting and sharing data. The need for state computerization has led to a greater demand for personal information from citizens. Concerns about privacy arise when sensitive personal data are collected and stored in digital form. These concerns relate to how these data are collected, stored, modified, transmitted, become available (open data) and connected. There are European and national obligations for personal data protection and there is also a specific legal and regulatory framework on data protection in place, based on a European Commission regulation [61]. In January 2012, the European Commission adopted a proposal for regulation on data protection that would replace the existing data protection directive. The proposal for the new regulation contains specific provisions relevant to the collection and storage of personal data. [62]. On 15 December 2015, the European Parliament, the Council and the Commission reached an agreement on the new data protection rules, establishing a modern and harmonized data protection framework across the EU [63].

User satisfaction: E-government adoption requires that citizens show higher levels of satisfaction with the online service provided by the government [64]. Citizen satisfaction with e-government service is related to the use of an e-government website and it is positively associated with trust in the government [65]. A satisfactory project offers users the ability to complete their tasks successfully. By asking them to reply if they are satisfied by a service, it can provide a measure of all the parties' contribution to the overall user experience, such as ease of use, navigation and design.

User profession: The influence of profession significantly helped explain differences between adopters and non-adopters of new technology and especially e-services [66]. Through this factor, one can specify the types of users, in terms of occupation, who consider the e-government service friendlier due to the same occupation.

Continuous usage: Most internet users are reluctant to use online methods to interact with public authorities. It is remarkable to see, that people participate in social networking sites, use e-commerce applications, perform their banking transactions online, but hesitate to use the internet to communicate with public authorities [67]. This factor determines whether users would be willing to use the services at a future time. The more satisfied they are by the e-government services the more likely it is that they may use them. Furthermore, it is interesting to note that according to the United Nations e-government survey, there is an indirect effect of social media on e-service usage. It seems that greater social media usage (through increased transparency) may increase trust, and thus also increase e-service take-up [68].

Figure 1 shows a conceptual model that was created by extending the traditional UTAUT2 model with these four additional criteria. Gender, age and experience are factors, which are already included in the UTAUT2 model, and, as has been determined, have a direct impact on behavioral intention towards e-government services [69] and play an important role to the evaluation of the Authority's e-services.

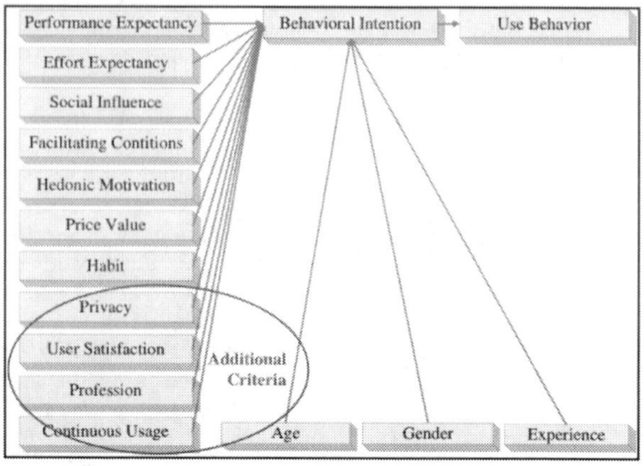

Figure 1. The proposed evaluation model.

C. *Research Hypotheses*

To improve the quality of the results, the research was focused on several hypotheses between these variables and the behavioral intention:

H1: Age: Differences in citizen ages have a significant effect on e-services adoption. Younger people are more inclined to use e-government services compared to older ones.

H2: Gender: Gender of respondents plays an important role in influencing behavioral intention and how an individual perceives the usefulness of e-government services. It is important to understand how gender roles may affect participation in e-government, encouraging or deterring women and men from e-participation. Gender differences affect the opportunities and challenges in connectivity and access. Due to the fact that women and men have different needs vis á vis public information and e-services, the content and use of public information should be tailored to their needs to empower both men and women to use such services.

H3: Experience: There is a significant positive relationship between internet experience and behavioral intention in the use of e-government services. Internet experience is found to significantly predict the perceived usefulness of e-services because higher and satisfactory level of internet experience increases the rate of e-government adoption.

H4: Privacy: Privacy determines the influence of behavioral intention and moderates individual behavior towards e-government services.

H5: User satisfaction: User satisfaction can affect the user's behavioral intention and how an individual perceives the usefulness of e-government services.

H6: Profession: Profession may possibly moderate the individual's influence on behavioral intention to use e-government services.

H7: Continuous Usage: The continuous use of electronic services and internet positively affects the intention of a person to use e-government services.

D. Method – Data Collection

Given that this study examines how end-users perceive the usefulness of an Independent Authority's online services, it has been considered necessary that they have already visited the Authority's site at least once, but without necessarily having submitted a complain.

To this end and in view of enabling users to provide their feedback in a smooth and effective manner, a questionnaire was created in April 2015 and was posted online, on the Authority's home page, for completion on a voluntary basis. To maintain confidentiality, individuals responded anonymously. For the purpose of speed and convenience, a method of multiple choice questions was chosen. Likert's five-point scale was chosen for the answers. With this scale, the respondent indicated the degree of his/her agreement or disagreement to the questions. The questionnaire was developed through free online software, specialized for specific routing, supplementing and monitoring on-line forms-questionnaires [70]. After data submission by users, the software stored the collected information in a special database, which was processed by the researcher (collector).

The questionnaire was divided into two main parts. The first part contained the individual elements of the user associated with the factors of gender, age and profession, as well as three additional questions related to the original topic. The second part contained general questions referring to applying factors for evaluating the model. The individual factors are presented as follows:

Performance Expectancy: The degree to which a person believes that using the system will help them benefit professionally.

Effort Expectancy: The degree of convenience associated with the use of the system.

Social Influence: The extent to which an individual perceives that important others (family and friends) believe they should use the new system.

Facilitating Conditions: The degree to which a person believes there is an organizational and technical infrastructure in place to support their use of the system.

Price Value: The pricing method based on the perceived value of the new system was intended.

Hedonic Motivation: Pleasure or happiness from the use of a technology may play an important role in determining its adoption.

Habit: The degree of influence of habit through behavioral intention.

Experience: The acquired experience of someone when using technology.

Additional Factor 1 – Privacy: The degree of safety through behavioral intention for technology use.

Additional Factor 2 - User Satisfaction: How pleased the user is with the technology.

Additional Factor 3 - Continuous Usage: The intention of the user to continue using the technology.

IV. RESULTS

Data from the perspective of users was collected and analyzed the. The survey findings of the data analysis show that the majority of respondents (81%) believe that using the authority's website helps increase performance and view this program positively.

Most of the respondents (44%), although they use the internet extensively and often visit public service websites, do not often visit the websites of independent authorities.

Additionally, the majority of respondents (79%) stated that the online services of various authorities contribute greatly to saving time because they help users fulfill their obligations in the shortest possible time. In particular, lodging e-complaint and monitoring its progress online is an important factor in saving time and money. They were also open to the usefulness of these services because they believe that they greatly facilitate the lives of citizens. End-users felt satisfied to very satisfied with the navigation of the authority's website and furthermore felt satisfied with the use of its electronic services. Moreover, the provision of e-services by the authority through mobile applications seems very user-friendly to them, as most users use their smart phones to access the internet. With regard to performance expectancy, the findings revealed that the citizens' intention to use e-services was influenced by their expectations of their usefulness. Finally, the results proved that behavioral intention is strongly associated with privacy, profession, user satisfaction and continued use.

Table I depicts the descriptive statistical data (percentage) of this study, obtained through the survey of 97 users/total respondents to the Authority's online system.

TABLE I. CHARACTERISTICS OF STUDY SUBJECTS N=97

Characteristics	%	Characteristics	%	Characteristics	%
		Effort Expectancy		***Hedonic Motivation***	
		Not at all	1	Not at all	1
		Slightly	5	Slightly	7
Gender		Moderately	24	Moderately	35
Male	43	Very	48	Very	38
Female	57	Extremely	22	Extremely	19
		Performance Expectancy		***Habit***	
		Not at all	0	Not at all	5
Age		Slightly	3	Slightly	8
Up to 18	1	Moderately	16	Moderately	27
19-29	21	Very	43	Very	38
30-39	31	Extremely	38	Extremely	22
40-49	36	***Social Influence***		***User Satisfaction***	
50-59	6	Not at all	5	Not at all	1
		Slightly	8	Slightly	5
		Moderately	31	Moderately	30
Experience		Very	34	Very	51
Not at all	0	Extremely	22	Extremely	13
Slightly	4	***Facilitating Conditions***		***Privacy***	
Moderately	17	Not at all	0	Not at all	12
Very	43	Slightly	4	Slightly	14
Extremely	36	Moderately	17	Moderately	26
		Very	52	Very	28
		Extremely	27	Extremely	20
Profession		***Price Value***		***Continuous Usage***	
Private Employee	44	Not at all	0	Not at all	0
Public Servant	23	Slightly	5	Slightly	7
Freelancer	12	Moderately	28	Moderately	24
Unemployed	8	Very	39	Very	42
Else	13	Extremely	28	Extremely	27

These are the main findings of the study:

- Gender has no specific impact. The difference in percentage is relatively small and does not display preference of a specific gender group of users.
- Age shows strong impact between the ages of 19 to 49. If these percentages are associated with the "experience" rates, it is concluded that experience is very high among these groups.
- Most respondents were private employees, as they believed that e-government services help them save time and money. The next high percentage are public servant users, maybe because they are already working in public administration and want to reinforce the e-Government project in this way.
- The majority of respondents positively accepted the system and believed that the Authority's online services help increase performance. Only a small percentage considered that the objective was not achieved. It is worth mentioning that a significant percentage (16%) had a "moderate" stance towards the Authority's website and web services, which questions the need for further improvement.
- Most of respondents believed that the website was comprehensible and well organized, provided clear information material to guide users and, to a large extent, met the needs of its users. Again, there was a high percentage of users (24%), who described the degree of the Authority's "ease of use" as "moderate", which means that the Authority must examine certain details that will enrich the content and image of the website.
- According to the factor of "social influence", 34% of users considered that using the Authority's web services enhanced their status in their social system. Furthermore, they would recommend the Authority's web services to other people.
- Referring to facility conditions, over half of the respondents believed that the Authority's website facilitated citizens, and that the information provided was accurate and compatible with other technologies they use.
- In relation to "price value", 39% of users believed that using the online services significantly decreased cost and considered that the cost for providing the services was mostly justified.
- As to "hedonic motivation", while citizens were "very" satisfied with the navigation environment on the Authority's website and felt satisfaction with the use of electronic services, 35% had a "moderate" view on this. This rate may mean that users might not have the required free time to navigate through the Authority's website. Alternatively, the content of the offered services may not correspond to their interests or they may not have yet identified the benefits that they may gain from the use of e-governance.
- Regarding the users' "habit", most of them felt very familiar to website navigation and they considered it very important to expand its use through mobile equipment.
- The "user satisfaction" from the Authority's website and the perceived usefulness of the e-services provided were significant. The users appeared "very" satisfied with the overall service system, which indicates a positive view for the service and obviously reinforces the attitude that they will continue using it in the future.
- Concerning "citizen privacy" and the "sensitive data protection", users seemed to have a more "moderate" view associated with the security of the e-services when a complaint was submitted to the Authority.
- 69% of the respondents were positive to the factor of "continuous usage" and only 24% continued to have "moderate" intent to use.

V. Conclusion And Future Work

An e-government project was evaluated to extract descriptive statistical data and to deal with any problems regarding specific features of an e-government system. Since citizens are the primary stakeholders and the main beneficiaries, the importance of citizen feedback regarding e-government evaluation is indisputable.

The study aimed at producing better products and services, as well as at enhancing the existing situation and the intention of the end users. By increasing the productivity and effectiveness, the project evolves towards quality and success. This study used a specific evaluation framework/model (an extended UTAUT2) to evaluate the design and effectiveness of an e-government project owned by an independent Greek Authority - specifically, the Greek Ombudsman service. The study also made an initial attempt towards understanding the adoption of on-line web services from the users' perspective.

The proposed model proved to be a well-fitted model, which fully met the evaluation requirements of the Authority's online services.

Amongst the adoption factors considered, performance expectancy, effort expectancy, facilitating conditions, age, Internet experience, profession, privacy and continuous usage had a significant impact on user behavior for use. On the contrary, factors such as gender, social influence and hedonic motivation did not seem significant predictors of behavioral use.

The results show that the above-mentioned e-government project largely covers the success criteria of people saving time and money. User satisfaction - through their navigation on the Authority's website, the convenience of the services offered, but also the familiar and secure environment offered by the specific website- was the driving force and seemed to meet initial expectations and needs. The respondents' answers showed that citizens consider the system beneficial with regard to the e-services and consequently encouraged e-government adoption. It is worth mentioning that most of the website users assessed positively the usability of the system, as well as the security offered to them and had a positive attitude towards encouraging others to use it. However, formal statistical methods must be implemented so as to examine the significance of the factors considered. The results of this study should only be considered as indications of factor significance.

Finally, user satisfaction increases the intention for future use of the system. This puts an extra key to the concept of success of this project and is related to the sustainability of the Independent Authority's website. Moreover, the success of the project is characterized by its complete acceptance by the complainants and end users, through the satisfaction of their initial expectations, the cost savings and the protection of their personal data. The fact that the specific Authority project and the practices implemented are considered successful encourages administrators to further enhance the functional and technical design of system.

The findings of this study can be further extended to cover more e-government projects in the Greek Public Administration.

We believe that the proposed extended UTAUT2 model covers a wide range of evaluation models for e-government evaluation. It can also be used for the evaluation of any e-service, which may not necessarily belong to an e-government sector, but is citizen-focused.

A future research study may be undertaken, which would expand on this one, by thoroughly and extensively analyzing additional crucial independent variables, which may affect the citizens' intention to use e-government services. Some of the key factors that future research work must focus on include natural culture, subjective norm, user attitude and trust in the government. In addition, e-government accessibility for people with disabilities is another factor that must be investigated in future studies, to ensure the inclusive access of these people to information.

REFERENCES

[1] M. A. Kalamatianou and F. Malamateniou, "An extended UTAUT2 Model for e-Government Project Evaluation," ICDS 2017 : The Eleventh International Conference on Digital Society and eGovernments (ICDS 2017), IARIA, Mar. 2017, pp. 48-54, ISSN: 2308-3956, ISBN: 978-1-61208-537-1.

[2] J. Rowley, "e-Government stakeholders—Who are they and what do they want?," International Journal of Information Management, 31 (1), pp. 53-62, 2011.

[3] R. D. Atkinson, and D. Castro, "Digital Quality of Life. The Information Technology and Innovation Foundation," 2008, pp. 137–145.

[4] D. B. Gant, J. P. Gant, and C. L. Johnson., "Enhancing e-Service Delivery," E-government series, state web portals: delivering and financing e-service, 2002.

[5] Communication from the Commission to the Council, the European Parliament, the European Economic and Social Commttee and the Committee of the Regions – The role of eGovernment for Europe's Future, 2003, Available: http://balkantenderwatch.eu/btw/uploaded/EU%20eng/Documents/com2003_0567en01.pdf, [retrieved: December, 2017].

[6] D. G. Garson, "Public Information Technology and E-governance," Sudbury, MA: Jones and Bartlett Publishers, The vision of e-governance, 2006, pp. 23.

[7] M. M Brown and J. L. Brudney, "Achieving advanced electronic government services: An examination of obstacles and implications from an international perspective," Paper presented at the National Public Management Research Conference, Bloomington, IN, October 2001.

[8] OECD E-Government Task Force, The Case for E-Government: Excerpts from the OECD Report "The E-Government Imperative," 2003 Available from: https://www.oecd.org/gov/budgeting/43496369.pdf, [retrieved December, 2017].

[9] United Nations E-Government Survey, "Expanding usage to realize the full benefits of e-government," chapter Six, 2012.

[10] J. Nograšek, "Change Management as a Critical Success Factor in e-Government Implementation," Business Systems Research, Vol.2, No.2, 2011, pp. 1-56.

[11] E. Ziemba, T. Papaj, and M. Jadamus-Hacura, "E-government Success Factors: A Perspective on Government Units," Issues in Information Systems Volume 16, Issue II, 2015, pp. 16-27.

[12] M. Butt, "Result-oriended e-government evaluation: Citizen's perspective," Webology, Volume 11, Number 1, June 2014. http://www.webology.org/2014/v11n2/a124.pdf [retrieved: December, 2017].

[13] T. Almarabeh and A. AbuAli, "A General Framework for E-Government: Definition Maturity Challenges, Opportunities, and Success," European Journal of Scientific Research, ISSN 1450-216X Vol.39 No.1, © EuroJournals Publishing, Inc., 2010, pp. 29-42

[14] European Comission, Digital Agenda for Europe. Available from: http://europa.eu/rapid/press-release_IP-12-1389_en.htm [retrieved: December, 2017].

[15] United Nations, United Nations Public Administration Network (UNPAN), United Nations, e-Government Survey 2016, E-governmetn in support of sustainable development, Available from: http://workspace.unpan.org/sites/Internet/Documents/UNPAN96407.pdf. [retrieved: December, 2017].

[16] N. M. Suki and T. Ramayah, "User Acceptance of the E-government Services in Malaysia: Structural Equation Modelling Approach," Interdisciplinary Journal of Information, Knowledge, and Management, Volume 5, 2010.

[17] F. D. Davis, "Perceived usefulness, perceived ease of use, and user acceptance of information technology," MIS Quarterly 13 (3), 1989, pp.319–340, doi:10.2307/249008.

[18] M. Alruwaie, "The role of social influence and prior experience on citizens' intention to continuing to use E-government systems: A conceptual framework," International Journal of Electronic Government Research, 2014, pp. 1-20.

[19] T. D. Susanto, "Individual Acceptance of e-government: A Literature Review," The Second International Conference on Informatics Engineering & Information Science (ICIEIS), 2013, pp. 334-342.

[20] A. - A. Al Athmay, "Demographic Factors as Determinants of E-governance Adoption: A Field Study in the United Arab Emirates (UAE)," Transforming Government: People, Process and Policy, 9 (2), 2015, pp. 159-180.

[21] V. Kumar, B. Mukerji, I. Butt, and A. Persaud, "Factors for Successful e-government Adoption: a Conceptual Framework," The Electronic Journal of e-government, Volume 5, Issue 1, 2007, pp. 63-76.

[22] O. Al-Hujran, M. Al-dalahmeh, and A. Aloudat, "The Role of National Culture on Citizen Adoption of eGovernment services: An Empirical Study," 2011, pp. 93-106.

[23] K. Bagchi, R. Cerveny, P. Hart, and M. Peterson, "The Influence of National Culture in Information Technology Product Adoption," Ninth Americas Conference on Information Systems, 2003, pp. 967-965.

[24] Z. J. Kovačić, "The Impact of National Culture on Worldwide eGovernment Readiness," Informing Science Journal Volume 8, 2005, pp. 143-158.

[25] A. Aida and M. Majdi, "National Culture and E- Government Services adoption Tunisian case," International Journal of Business & Economic Strategy (IJBES), Vol.1, 2014.

[26] S. A. Alateyah, R. M. Crowder, and G. B. Wills, "Towards an integrated model for citizen adoption of E-government services," International Journal of Information Technology & Computer Science (IJITCS), (ISSN No : 2091-1610), Volume 6 : Issue on November / December, 2012, pp. 47-57.

[27] R. Raudah and A. Akilah, "User's Satisfaction on E-government Services: An Integrated Model," International Conference on Accounting Studies 2014, ICAS, 2014, pp. 18-19 .

[28] S. Alateyah, "An integrated model for citizens to adopt e-government services in the Kingdom of Saudi Arabia," University of Southampton, Physical Sciences and Engineering, Doctoral Thesis, 2014, pp. 225.

[29] F. D. Davis, R. P. Bagozzi, and P. R. Warshaw, "User acceptance of computer technology: A comparison of two theoretical models," Management Science 35, 1989, pp. 982–1003, doi:10.1287/mnsc.35.8.982.

[30] V. Venkatesh and F. D. Davis, "A theoretical extension of the technology acceptance model: Four longitudinal field studies," Management Science 46 (2), 2000, pp. 186-204, doi:10.1287/mnsc.46.2.186.11926.

[31] V. Venkatesh and H. Bala, "Technology Acceptance Model 3 and a Research Agenda on Interventions," Decision Sciences 39 (2), 2008, pp. 273–315, doi:10.1111/j.1540-5915.2008.00192.x.

[32] W. H. DeLone and E. R. McLean, "Information systems success: the quest for the dependent variable," Information systems research, 3(1), 1992, pp. 60-95.

[33] W. H. DeLone and E. R. McLean, "The DeLone and McLean Model of Information Systems Success: A Ten-Year Update," Journal of Management Information Systems, 19(4), 2003, pp. 9-30.

[34] V. Venkatesh, M. G. Morris, G. B. Davis, and F. D. Davis, "User acceptance of information technology: Toward a unified view," (PDF), MIS Quarterly 27 (3), 2003, pp. 425–478.

[35] V. Venkatesh, J. Y. L. Thong, and X. Xu, "Consumer acceptance and use of information: extending the unified theory of acceptance and use of technology," MIS Quarterly 36(1), 2012, pp. 157- 178.

[36] B. H. Wixom and P. A. Todd, "A Theoretical Integration of User Satisfaction and Technology Acceptance," Information Systems Research 16 (1), 2005, pp. 85 – 102.

[37] C. E. Koh, V. R. Prybutok, S. D. Ryan, and Y. A. Wu, "A Model for Mandatory Use of Software Technologies: An Integrative Approach by Applying Multiple Levels of Abstraction of Informing Science," Informing Science: the International Journal of an Emerging Transdiscipline, 13, 2010, pp. 177-203..

[38] E. M. Rogers, "Diffusion of innovations," 4th ed. New York: Free Press, pp. 1-453, 1995.

[39] S. Wangpipatwong, W. Chutimaskul, and B. Papasratorn, "Understanding Citizen's Continuance Intention to Use e-government Website: a Composite View of Technology Acceptance Model and Computer Self-Efficacy," The Electronic Journal of e-government, Volume 6, Issue 1, pp. 55 – 64, 2008.

[40] S. Al Awadhi and A. Morris, "The use of the UTAUT model in the adoption of e government services in Kuwait," 41st Hawaii International Conference on System Sciences, 2008, pp. 219-230.

[41] O. Khalil and A. Nasrallah, "The Adoption of the Traffic Violation E-payment System (TVEPS) of Kuwait," The Electronic Journal of Knowledge Management, 12 (1), pp. 3-22, 2014.

[42] S. Al-Shafi, and V. Weerakkody, " Understanding citizens' behavioral intention in the adoption of e-government services in the state of Qatar," 17th European Conference on Information Systems - EMCIS, 2009.

[43] S. Al-Shafi and V. Weerakkody, "Factors Affecting E-government Adoption in the State of Qatar," European and Mediterranean Conference on Information Systems - EMCIS, 2010, pp. 1-23.

[44] I. Karavasilis, K. Zafiropoulos, and V. Vrana, "Assessing the Adoption of e-Government Services by Teachers in Greece," Future Internet, 4(2), 2012, pp. 528-544, doi:10.3390/fi4020528

[45] A. Voutinioti, "Determinants of user adoption of e-government services in Greece and the role of citizen service centres," Procedia Technology 8, 6th International conference on ICT in agriculture, food and environment (HAICTA 2013), pp. 238–244, 2013.

[46] H. Ranaweera, "Perspective of trust towards e-government initiatives in Sri Lanka," SpringerPlus. 2016, 5(1), pp.1-11, 2016.

[47] R. Danila and A. Abdullah, "User's Satisfaction on E-government Services: An Integrated Model," Procedia-Social and Behavioral Sciences, vol. 164, pp. 575-582, 2014.

[48] L. Carter, L. C. Shaupp, J. Hobbs, and R. Campbell, "The role of security and trust in the adoption of online tax filing," Transforming Government: People, Process and Policy, 5 (4), pp. 303-318, 2011.

[49] M. Alshehri, S. Drew, and R. AlGhamdi, "Analysis of Citizens' Acceptance for E-government Services: Applying the UTAUT Model," International Conference Internet Applications and Research, Lisbon, Portugal: IADIS, 2012, pp. 95-105.

[50] H. Al-Khatib and H. Lee, "E-government Systems Success and User Acceptance in Developing Countries: The Role of Percieved Support Quality," International Journal Of eBusiness and eGovernment Studies, Vol 3, No 2, pp. 69-78, 2011. ISSN: 2146-0744.

[51] I. B. Hassan and M. A. A. Murad, "Acceptance of Health Information Application in Smart National Identity Card (SNIC) Using a New IP Framework," World Academy of Science, Engineering and Technology International Journal of Social, Behavioral, Educational, Economic, Business and Industrial Engineering, Vol:8, No:12, pp. 3767-3775, 2014.

[52] N. P. Rana, Y. K. Dwivedi, B. Lal, M. D. Williams, and M. Clement., "Citizens' adoption of an electronic government system: towards a unified view," Inf Syst Front, pp. 1-20, 2015. doi:10.1007/s10796-015-9613-y.

[53] M. A. Mahfuz, L. Khanam, and W. Hu, "Examine Website Quality on M-Banking Services Adoption in Bangladesh," International Journal of Computer Science & Information Technology, 8 (2), pp. 33-50, 2016.

[54] J. Tavares and T. Oliveira, "Electronic Health Record Patient Portal Adoption by Health Care Consumers: An Acceptance Model and Survey," Journal of Medical Internet Research, 18 (3), pp. 49-55, 2016.

[55] Y. H. Al-Mamary, M. Al-nashmi, Y. A. G. Hassan, and A. Shamsuddin, "A Critical Review of Models and Theories in Field of Individual Acceptance of Technology," International Journal of Hybrid Information, Technology, 9 (6), pp. 143-158, 2016.

[56] The Greek Ombudsman site, Available from: http://www.synigoros.gr/?i=stp.en/2017.12.01

[57] The Greek Ombudsman- Department of Children's Rights and the Institute of Child Health site, Available from: http://www.0-18.gr/paidikiprostasia/statement-of-principles-for-child-protection-in-greece/ 2017.12.01

[58] The Greek Ombudsman, Complaint Submission, Available from: http://www.synigoros.gr/?i=submission-system.en/2017.12.01

[59] A. Omari, "Technology Adoption in the Arabian Gulf Countries: The Case of E-government," International Journal of Computer Science and Information Technology (IJCEIT), vol.3, No 3, 2013, pp. 1-8, DOI : 10.5121/ijcseit.2013.3301.

[60] The European Union Agency for Network and Information Security (ENISA), [Online]. Available from: https://www.enisa.europa.eu/topics/data-protection/2017.12.01

[61] European Commission – Justice, [Online]. Available from: http://ec.europa.eu/justice/data-protection/2017.12.01

[62] European Comission, Proposal for a regulation of the European Parliamnet and of the Counsil. Available from: http://ec.europa.eu/justice/data-protection/document/review2012/com_2012_11_en.pdf [retrieved: December, 2017].

[63] European Comission, Justige, Data Protection, Reform of EU data protection rules. [Online}. Avalable from: http://ec.europa.eu/justice/data-protection/reform/index_en.htm/2017.12.01

[64] M. M. Komba and P. Ngulube, "An Empirical Application of the DeLone and McLean Model to Examine Factors for E-Government Adoption in the Selected Districts of Tanzania," Emerging Issues and Prospects in African E-Government, pp. 118, 2014.

[65] H. AlShibly and R. Chiong, "Customer empowerment: does it influence electronic government success? a citizen-centric perspective," Electronic Commerce Research and Applications, Volume 14, Issue 6, pp. 393-404, 2015.

[66] Y. K. Dwivedi and B. Lal, "Socio-economic determinants of broadband adoption," Industrial Management & Data Systems, vol. 107, pp. 654-671, 2007.

[67] C. Akkaya, M. Obermeier, P. Wolf, and H. Krcmar, "Components of trust influencing e-government adoption in Germany," In M. Janssen, H. Scholl, M. Wimmer and Y.-h. Tan, eds., Proceedings of IFIP EGOV Springer Verlag, 2011, pp. 88- 99.

[68] United Nations Public Administration Network (UNPAN), United Nations e-Government Survey 2012, E-governmet for people. Available from: https://publicadministration.un.org/egovkb/Portals/egovkb/Documents/un/2012-Survey/unpan048065.pdf [retrieved: December, 2017].

[69] A. Touray, A. Salminen, and A. Mursu, "The Impact of Moderating factors on Behavioural intention towards internet: A transnational perspective," International Journal of Computer and Information Technology, vol. 2(6), 2013, pp. 1035-1041.

[70] https://www.jotform.com/ [retrieved: December, 2017].

Activation Mechanism for Recommending Appropriate Users and Comments on Wedding Community Sites

Toshinori Hayashi*, Yuanyuan Wang†, Yukiko Kawai‡, and Kazutoshi Sumiya*
*Kwansei Gakuin University,
2–1 Gakuen, Sanda, Hyogo 669–1337, Japan
Email: den82687@kwansei.ac.jp, sumiya@kwansei.ac.jp
†Yamaguchi University,
2–16–1 Tokiwadai, Ube, Yamaguchi 755–8611, Japan
Email: y.wang@yamaguchi-u.ac.jp
‡Kyoto Sangyo University,
Kamigamo Motoyama, Kita-ku, Kyoto 603–8555, Japan
Email: kawai@cc.kyoto-su.ac.jp

***Abstract*—In this paper, we present an active communication mechanism based on a user behavior analysis on wedding community websites. To this end, we propose a novel mechanism for the activation of user communications, which suggests other users and their related comments by detecting knowledge and interests from archived comments. Such information on a community website evokes conversations among users. We focus on a wedding community website in this study. The proposed mechanism consists of the following three components: 1) the profiling of user login information, such as users' ages and locations, and extraction of user characteristics, such as their interests and intentions to communicate; 2) the detection and recommendation of users who are likely to communicate with each other; and 3) the recommendation of comments that may be of interest to a user. Through the proposed activation mechanism, users on a wedding community website can easily find other users who share similar experiences, and engage in active communication with them. We discuss our proposed user characteristic extraction and user recommendation methods using actual users' posts from a wedding community website, and also discuss applications for e-learning. In addition, we evaluated the activation of user communications using our proposed system through interviews.**

Keywords–user behavior analysis; wedding community site; communication.

I. Introduction

In recent years, research has been conducted using data from social networking services (SNSs). In this context, it is important to collect as much data as possible from SNS community websites, such as Facebook, LINE, and other Q&A sites. However, such services that focus on data collection cannot activate user communications on community websites, because of differences in human values. In this paper, we focus on conversations on a wedding community website. Moreover, we focus on the problem that users cannot find appropriate users to communicate with. We aim to evoke user communications by recommending appropriate users and comments, considering human values. Our proposed system analyzes users' situations from user login information and user preferences by extracting user characteristics, because we assume that human values consist of situations and preferences. This research constitutes an extension to the work in [1], which we presented in Venice in April 2017.

Wedding community websites are community sites for sharing and obtaining information regarding wedding planning, and are completely distinct from dating websites, the purpose of which is to meet a partner for dating. We focus on a wedding community site that shares the same concept as other kinds of bulletin board systems (BBSs). On this community site, users can post their opinions and experiences on a conversation thread created by an administrator. Each conversation thread has questions that ask about weddings as discussion themes, such as "how did you choose your wedding location?" Thus, users post their opinions and experiences in response to these questions, and exchange information. However, conversations between users are not active in these threads, because it is difficult for users to find others to communicate with. Our proposed system solves this problem by finding appropriate users based on user login information and characteristics.

Specifically, we propose a novel active communication mechanism that shares comments of users considering their knowledge and interests by analyzing their behavior on community websites. To this end, we first extract all posts for each user, and extract their feature words using the term frequency–inverse document frequency (*TF-IDF*) method. Next, we calculate the similarities between users to detect appropriate users. Finally, we recommend their comments by generating links to them in posts (see Figure 1). Through this mechanism, users can communicate with other users that are recommended to them about wedding planning. Furthermore, this promotes communications among users on a wedding community website.

We also propose an active communication mechanism for e-learning, in order to confirm the possibility of applying our proposed system to other community websites. According to some studies regarding online discussions [2][3], active communications among users on e-learning is an effective mechanism for students to learn knowledge efficiently. To extend the effect of our proposed method, we aim to apply it to e-learning.

To evaluate this system, we use the actual data from a wedding community website. This is sorted and processed to provide recommendations to users for evaluation, in order to verify whether this mechanism is successful. Then, we interview five users to ask how helpful the proposed system is. Although we could not interview many actual users, we performed a qualitative evaluation through these interviews.

The remainder of this paper is organized as follows. Section

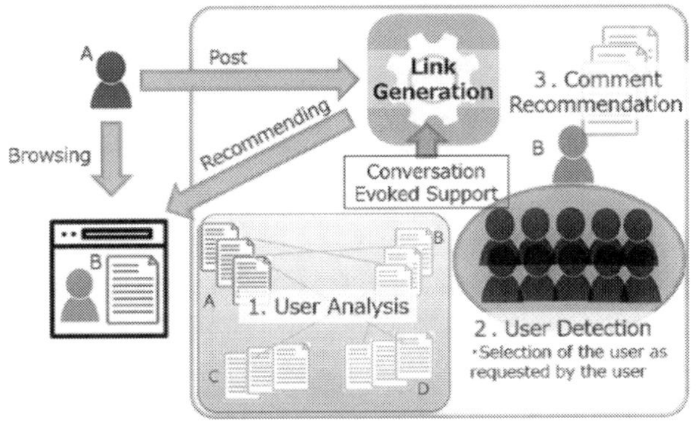

Figure 1. User and comment recommendations for the activation of user communications based on a user behavior analysis.

II provides an overview of our system and reviews related work. Section III explains how users and their comments are recommended on a wedding community website. Section IV explains the application of our proposed methods to e-learning. Section V presents the experimental results obtained using a real dataset from a wedding community website. Finally, Section VII concludes the paper, and Section VI outlines our future work.

II. System Overview and Related Work

A. Active Communication Mechanism

We present an active communication mechanism based on user behavior analysis on wedding community websites. This mechanism consists of the following three steps (see Figure 1):

1) User login information and user characteristic extraction.
2) User detection and recommendations.
3) Comment recommendations.

To use this mechanism, users are required to install a toolbar (a browser plug-in) on an existing wedding community website in Japan. Wedding community websites are generally utilized by people who plan to hold a wedding, and are intended to assess a couples' requirements regarding the wedding. On the website we focus on in this study, there are conversation threads for wedding planning for various marriage statuses, and users can freely post their comments on each thread. The website addresses users' anxieties and troubles. For example, a user can create a post such as "I do not know what I should be careful about in planning for a wedding." Users can also share their experiences, such as impressions and enjoyments. For example, a user could post "I had an amazing wedding overseas."

The only way to communicate with other users is by posting comments as replies to other users' comments on threads. However, users rarely post replies on other users' comments, because they cannot find appropriate users to communicate with. To raise the number of replies, we propose a method that recommends both users and their comments by analyzing user behavior and profile information on a wedding community website to activate conversations.

A wedding community website is not a "question & answer" site; rather, it is a website where users can share their opinions and experiences regarding weddings. The proposed system will recommend other users who have been in similar situations or have shared values regarding marriage, in order to evoke communications between users. This system can also be adopted on other community websites. However, because the proposed system is considered on a wedding community website, it uses user login information entered by a user during their initial registration regarding their ideal wedding ceremony.

Figure 1 presents an overview of our proposed mechanism. After a user posts, the mechanism analyzes their behavior and recommends other users by calculating the similarities between them. After a user posts information, it will pass through the link generation system. This system will generate information to evoke conversations. First, it extracts all of the posts of users, and analyzes user behavior through feature words. Then, it detects recommended users by performing selections as requested by the user. To detect a recommended user, we categorize each user by three kinds of profile information. These methods are explained in Section III.

B. Related Work

Issac et al. [4] noted that communication is important for discussing various topics and working with others as a group. They mentioned that communication makes people more willing to contribute to society. Moreover, communication on websites is also effective, not only face-to-face communication. Ellison et al. [5] focused on SNS communities. L. H. Shaw et al. found that Internet communication decreases loneliness and depression significantly [6]. According to these studies, communicating with others on SNSs makes people feel happier.

In our previous work, users communicated with each other when searching for web pages [7]. In this work, we extend our previous work to recommend users and comments based on link generation for a wedding community site.

Knowledge extraction from online communities [8] have also been researched. Park et al. [9] confirmed that the knowledge users obtain through online communications is connected to their purchasing behavior. They proved that online communities provide users with important information regarding purchase behavior. Randhawa et al. [10] improved the utility of knowledge collaboration between organizations and online communities for open innovation (OI). There have been many studies concerning the use of data from online communities [11][12][13][14] to discover new knowledge.

Our proposed system activates communications on online community websites. Akihiro et al. [15] conducted an experiment concerning active communication in e-lectures through a chat system. However, this did not work very effectively, because it was a burden for students to chat with others during the lectures. In this paper, we propose a new active communication mechanism by recommending appropriate users to other users with various marriage statuses.

Some researchers [16][17][18] analyzed effects of conversation from online community. Hemmings-Jarrett et al. [19] measured the effect of online communications with a focus on political topics, comparing before and after the event. They assumed that the activity levels of users on online conversations were related to their opinion. However, this research was not intended to activate conversations.

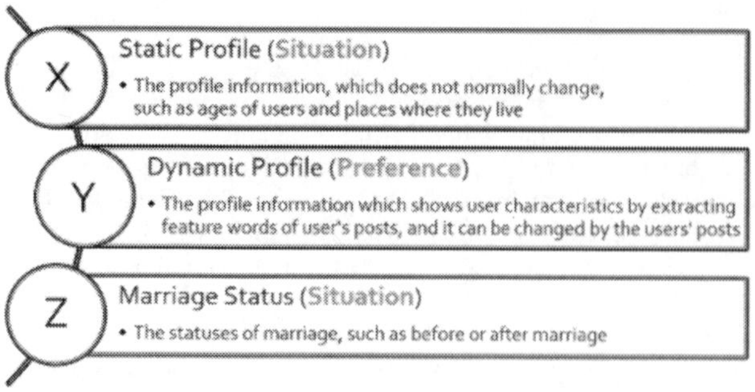

Figure 2. Profiling based on user aspects.

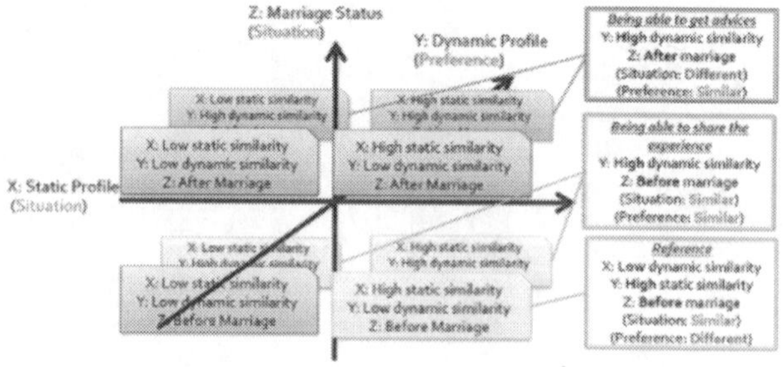

Figure 3. User detection when the original user is not yet married.

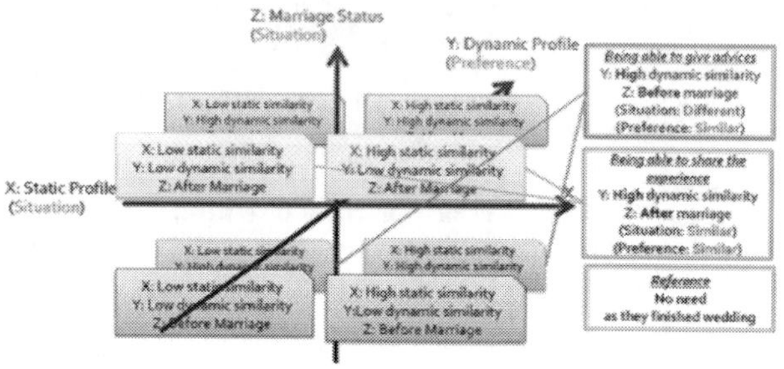

Figure 4. User detection when the original user is already married.

Other studies that have recommended analyzing user behavior on news websites [20][21] did not consider the relationships between users. In this paper, we first extract user posts to analyze user behavior, and then detect users to recommend by extracting the relationships between users.

Our proposed method involves activating user communications by recommending appropriate users and their comments. Xu et al. [22] proposed a novel user recommendation system based on users interests and networks of relationships. However, there have not been many studies regarding user recommendation systems that focus on specific community websites.

Although several automatic link generation methods for websites have been studied [23][24], these have primarily focused on web pages for knowledge support only; they did not consider communications among users. To address this deficiency, our proposed method recommends users in order to evoke communications.

III. Active Communication Mechanism for Wedding Websites

A. *User Behavior Analysis on a Wedding Community Website*

To evoke communication among users, our active communication mechanism recommends users and their comments by analyzing user behavior on a wedding community website. According to our previous work in [7], users can help other users when they search for the same web pages. Furthermore, in general users can communicate with each other easily when they share similar statuses or situations and have similar preferences. Therefore, in order to recommend users we analyze users' humans values by considering three kinds of profile information based on aspects of a wedding community website (see Figure 2). In particular, we consider the axes of "Static Profile Information," "Marriage Status," and "Dynamic Profile Information."

"Static Profile Information" and "'Marriage Status" indicate a user's situations. "Dynamic Profile Information" indicates a user's preferences. This system analyzes users' human values based on their situations and preferences. Static profile information is generated from user login information, such as age and location, which does not normally change. Marriage status implies a user's position regarding a wedding, such as before or after marriage. Dynamic profile information is generated from the extraction of user characteristics. This uses the data from posts from each user, and so this information often changes.

On wedding community websites, marriage status is the most important factor in analyzing users, because this implies a big difference in the purpose of use. The purpose of using this website for users who are preparing for a wedding is to obtain information regarding weddings. On the other hand, for users who have already finished their wedding, the purpose is to share information and their experiences of their wedding to provide advice and help others. Thus, "Marriage Status" is the most important factor in the user analysis for categorizing users.

1) User Login Information Extraction: We extract user login information by acquiring the information that users input during registration on a wedding community website. Users input information such as their age, area where they live, and marital status. We divide this user login information into user static profile information and marital status.

2) User Characteristic Extraction: We extract user characteristics by extracting all posts for each user. Next, we calculate the term frequency and document frequency based on the *TF-IDF* method. Specifically, we use the following formulas:

$$TF_{i,j} = \frac{n_{i,j}}{\sum_k n_{k,j}}, \quad (1)$$

$$IDF_i = \log \frac{|D|}{df_i}, \quad (2)$$

where *TF* indicates term frequency, *IDF* indicates inverse document frequency, and $n_{i,j}$ denotes the term frequency of the word t_i in document d_j. In this work, d_j denotes the document that is integrated all posts of one user. Therefore,

TABLE I. FIVE USER PATTERNS FOR RECOMMENDATION.

Pattern	User (Who)	Marriage Status (to who)	Static Profile Information	Active Profile Information	Purpose
1	After marriage	Before	Neutral	Similar	Give advice
2	After marriage	After	Neutral	Similar	Share
3	Before marriage	Before	Similar	Different	Reference
4	Before marriage	Before	Neutral	Similar	Share
5	Before marriage	After	Neutral	Similar	Get advice

TABLE II. RECOMMENDATION SITUATION FOR EACH USER PATTERN.

Pattern	Purpose	When	How
1	Give advice	Links are generated in the comments	XX needs some advice from you
2	Share	After Login	XX is on the same status as you
3	Reference	Links are generated in the comments	You can refer to XX
4	Share	After Login	XX is on the same status as you
5	Get advice	Links are generated in the comments	XX can be a good adviser for you

the number of documents is equal to the number of users on the wedding community site. Furthermore, $\sum_k n_{k,j}$ denotes the sum of the term frequencies of all words in document d_j, and $|D|$ denotes the total number of documents, which is also equal to the number of users. Finally, df_i denotes the number of documents that include the word t_i.

Based on the above, we use the obtained *TF-IDF* values and feature words for each user to determine a user's active profile information. This information changes every time a user posts on a thread on the wedding community site, and so users' dynamic profile information is normally changed by user posts.

B. User Detection and Recommendation

1) User Detection: "Marriage Status" takes an absolute value of either "preparing for wedding" or "finished wedding." Therefore, there are only two kinds of value. However, "Static Profile Information" and "Dynamic Profile Information" are represented by relative values. These will vary depending on each user.

To detect a recommended user, the system needs to calculate the similarity for each axis. First, the method of calculating the "Static Profile Information" depends on the dataset. We will explain this in Section . Second, the similarity for "Marriage Status" is very simple, as this consists of only two kinds of status, so that the relationship between users for "Marriage Status" must either be the same or different. Third, we calculate the similarities for "Dynamic Profile Information" between users using cosine similarity as follows:

$$Sim(\overrightarrow{x}, \overrightarrow{y}) = \frac{\sum_{i=1}^{|V|} x_i \cdot y_i}{\sqrt{\sum_{i=1}^{|V|}(x_i)^2} \cdot \sqrt{\sum_{i=1}^{|V|}(y_i)^2}}, \quad (3)$$

where $\overrightarrow{x}$ denotes the feature vector of user x and $\overrightarrow{y}$ denotes the feature vector of user y, and $|V|$ is the number of dimensions for the feature vector.

Thus, this system calculates the similarities between users by using three kinds of profile information. Based on these similarity values, the system detects recommended users for each original user.

2) User Recommendation: We recommend users to evoke communications with others by considering users who are in similar situations. Such users may easily relate to each other and share their experiences or advice. As mentioned in the previous section, we use three kinds of profile information: "Static Profile Information," "Marriage Status," and "Dynamic Profile Information." Considering the relationships between users, each type of profile information has a high or low similarity. However, we assume that "Marriage Status" has four possible combinations: "preparing for wedding" and "preparing for wedding," "preparing for wedding" and "finished wedding," "finished wedding" and "preparing for wedding," and "finished wedding" and "finished wedding." A total of 16 kinds of user can be extracted by the system. We separate these into two cases: where the original user is preparing for a wedding and where the original user has already finished a wedding.

Figure 3 illustrates the case in which the original user is preparing for a wedding. There are eight kinds of user that the system can detect in this case, based on three kinds of profile information. The idea of recommending users is to suggest an appropriate user who is able to provide advice or share related experiences, or could be a reference for a different style of wedding.

For a user to be recommended who can provide advice, they should have a high dynamic similarity, which means that their preferences should be similar. Because they have similar preferences, the recommended user can provide advice if they have already finished their wedding.

For a recommended user to be able to share their experiences, they should have high similarity for dynamic profile information, which means that their preferences are similar. In addition, the marital status should be the same for the users to be in the same situation. We assume that users who are in a similar situation with similar preferences can communicate easily to share their experiences.

To recommend a user who could be a reference, that user should be in a similar situation and have different preferences. To activate communications among users, recommending similar users is important, but users are also interested in others who are different. For instance, even though a user has an ideal style of wedding in mind, this might be changed by referring to others. A user recommended to another for reference has to have a low similarity for dynamic profile and high similarity for static profile information.

Figure 4 illustrates the case in which the original user has already finished their wedding. There are eight kinds of users in this case, based on three types of profile information. The idea of recommending users is the same as in 3; however, we assume that a user who has finished their wedding does not use this website for reference, because the motivation of these users is to provide advice or share experiences with other users.

Based on the three axes described in the previous subsection and the theory of recommending users, we classify five useful patterns of users on a wedding community website (see Table I).

For each user, we detect the other user that is most similar to them for Patterns 1, 2, 4, and 5. Moreover, we detect the user that is most different for Pattern 3. Based on the above procedure, we propose recommendations to users.

C. Comment Recommendation

1) Comment Extraction: In the previous subsection, we explained how to detect users and make recommendations in order to stimulate communications on a wedding community website. To recommend user comments, we calculate the most closely related comments from the recommended users that are derived using Eq. (3). The recommended comments suggest why the recommended user is relevant for the original user.

2) Recommendation Interface: Our active communication mechanism recommends other appropriate users and their comments in different scenarios corresponding to each user pattern in Table II.

This mechanism has two methods of recommending users. The first method recommends users in the comments by generating links to them. The second method recommends users on the top page following login.

For the first method, the interface provides recommendation for Patterns 1, 3, and 5. The recommended users for these patterns have similar preferences. We expected that recommending other users using generated links in the comments would be an effective way to raise the interest of the original user, because the recommended users are detected by their preferences, which are extracted from their comments on threads.

This mechanism generates links in the comments. To generate links in the comments after users have posted, we attach the links to user information or comments to related words by extracting user characteristics (feature words).

In the second method, the interface provides recommendations for Patterns 2 and 4, and the mechanism presents users on the top page of the website following login. This mechanism also recommends users on the top page that are likely to share similar experiences. We assume that users prefer to see more users on the top page than in the links generated in the comments, because this method focuses on recommending users.

IV. Active Communication Mechanism for e-Learning

In previous section, we discussed how to activate communication among users on wedding community websites. However, we expect that this method for recommending other users based on user characteristics in order to evoke communication will also be effective on other community websites, such as e-learning community sites. To enhance the user community on e-learning websites, we discuss an active communication mechanism for e-learning in this section.

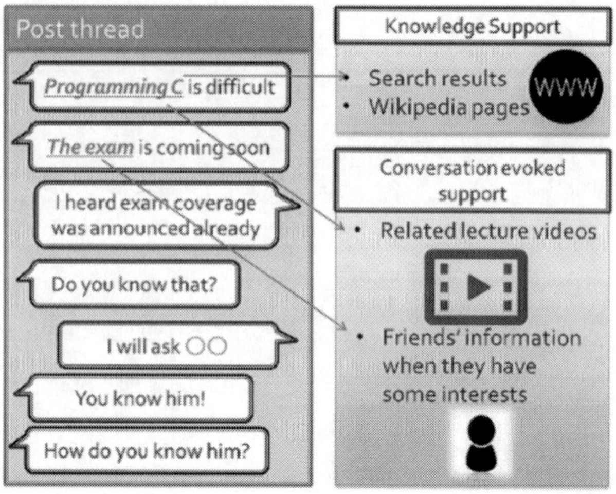

Figure 5. Conceptual diagram of automatic link generation.

A. System Overview for e-Learning

In recent years, massive open online courses (MOOC) have emerged as a new form of education for students who wish to attend courses at any level or cannot access traditional education because of constraints on time, location, or other factors. However, it is difficult to maintain students' motivation for self-learning. Currently, many students can collaborate during online courses through SNS, such as Facebook and Twitter. Liao et al. [25] and Chen et al. [26] investigated the use of SNS in online education. Students can communicate with each other when they use post threads on SNS. Because of the different levels of knowledge between students, communications cannot proceed smoothly. This is a problem that we aim to solve in this research. Therefore, it is necessary to extract user characteristics from SNS user behavior, which indicate users' knowledge and interests, and supplement users' posts with related information (e.g., search results, Wikipedia pages, lecture videos, or information on other friends) in the post thread.

In this work, the goal is to develop a novel automatic link generation method by analyzing SNS user behavior from user posts in e-learning. The proposed method generates two kinds of links: 1) knowledge support for receivers who receive posts from senders, and 2) conversation evoked support for receivers to give information to senders (see Figure 5).

Although several automatic link generation methods for websites have been studied [27][28], these have focused on web pages for knowledge support only, and they do not solve the abovementioned issues regarding user communication in e-learning. Other studies regarding user behavior on news websites [29] have not considered the relationships between users.

In this paper, we first extract user characteristics by analyzing SNS user behavior in e-learning from their posts. Then, we can detect users' relationships based on user characteristics. Thus, 1) links for knowledge support are attached to posts by using search results or Wikipedia pages for unknown vocabulary words for receivers, and 2) links for conversation evoked support for receivers to offer information regarding

TABLE III. TOP 15 FEATURE WORDS OF USERS A, B, C, AND D.

User \ Method	1)	2)	3)
A	of, a, ceremony, wedding ceremony, to, sister, I will, heart, family, after, because, to, did, et al., that	sister, wedding ceremony, **earthquake disaster, Fukushima**, bata, fireplace, chaya, sister, attendance, column, heart, family, safety, stop, name	wedding ceremony, sister, **Earthquake disaster**, bata, attendance, heart, **Fukushima**, chaya, fireplace, family, sister, column, 11, safety, influence
B	of, did, better, object, pull, a marriage, I will, he, now, a student, generation, learning, Toyama, now, chestnut	**fish paste**, Toyama, red snapper, gift, girlfriend, object, luck, a student, surprised, age, pull, mountain, form, chestnut, happiness	Toyama, red snapper, **fish paste**, object, gift, girlfriend, luck, a student, surprised, age, mountain, form, happiness, chestnut, woman
C	did, of, better, reach, day, that, friend, friends, ceremony, wedding ceremony, while, a, before, first, good	it seems intriguing, eve, **limousine**, the eve, first meeting, face to face, a van, friend, the other day, reach, move, the previous day, festival, the best	eve, it seems intriguing, **limousine**, first meeting, friend, face to face, the best, a van, move, the previous day, festival, the other day, Hawaii, fellow, reach
D	a, of, did, one, this, now, better, "", to, about, place, et al., yo, filtration, meeting	reserved, **snow board**, lending, no, alternating current, table, **hair style**, comment, firing, male, rooftop, development, release, frank	reserved, **snow board**, alternating current, male, hair style, table, board, **BGM**, rooftop, firing, girlfriend, in Tokyo, development, comment

senders are attached to posts by using related lecture videos for topics of posts or other information on other friends with the same interests. Thus, the proposed novel method encourages users to communicate with each other during conversations on e-learning platforms. This method activates communication not only by recommending other users, but also by generating links to relevant knowledge for users' studies.

In this section, we describe the proposed link generation method for active communications in e-learning. The proposed method extracts user characteristics by analyzing user behavior from their posts, selects vocabulary words as links based on user characteristics from their posts, and selects vocabulary words as links based on user characteristics. We first extract feature words for each user from their posts as user characteristics. Then, low or high weight vocabulary words are selected as link candidates based on users' relationships. The link information is classified into two categories: 1) knowledge support and 2) conversation evoked support.

B. Analysis of SNS User Behavior

To analyze SNS user behavior, we first extract high-frequency words from each post of each user using the Yahoo! Web API[1]. Next, we calculate the average weight of each extracted high-frequency word. Then, we extract user characteristics by extracting feature words for each user. We calculate the weight of each word i that appears in each user's posts using the following formula:

$$\frac{\text{weight of } i \text{ by Yahoo!Web API}}{\text{\#posts with } i} \times \frac{\text{total \#posts}}{\text{\#posts with } i} \qquad (4)$$

The left part of Eq. (4) calculates the average weight of i that appears in each post. The right part of Eq. (4) gives an *IDF* value of i in all posts of each user. In addition, "Like" and "Share" options are available on SNS, to respectively mark interests or spread a post. Therefore, we can improve the calculation method by adding the numbers of "Like" and "Share" actions to the weight of each word.

C. Generation of Links in Chats

To generate links in chats between users, we attach link information to vocabulary words in posts based on users' relationships by using user characteristics (feature words). The link information for knowledge support is intended to supplement unknown vocabulary words for the receiver. We select the low weight words as unknown vocabulary words to

[1]http://developer.yahoo.co.jp/webapi/jlp/keyphrase/v1/extract.html

TABLE IV. NUMBERS OF COMMENTS.

#posts	#users
1 - 10	440 users
11- 20	64 users
21 - 30	37 users
31 - 40	14 users
41 - 50	1 user
51 - 60	1 user

be as link candidates in the post from the extracted feature words from the receiver's characteristics. Then, we attach search results and Wikipedia pages for the low weight words to the post. In Figure 5, it is determined that the receiver has a lack of knowledge regarding "C Programming," and "C Programming" is generated as a link in the post to the receiver.

The link information for conversation evoked support is intended to promote user communication for receivers by offering information regarding the senders. We select the high weight words from extracted feature words of the receiver's characteristics, and detect information on other friends (linked with the receiver through the network) related to the post as link candidates using cosine similarity the high weight words through the formula given below. In Figure 5, it is determined that a friend is similar to the sender and mentions "the exam", and "the exam" is generated as a link in the post to the receiver.

$$Sim(\overrightarrow{x}, \overrightarrow{y}) = \frac{\sum_{i=1}^{|V|} x_i \cdot y_i}{\sqrt{\sum_{i=1}^{|V|} (x_i)^2} \cdot \sqrt{\sum_{i=1}^{|V|} (y_i)^2}}, \qquad (5)$$

where $\overrightarrow{x}$ denotes the feature vector of user x, and $\overrightarrow{y}$ denotes the feature vector of user y. Furthermore, $|V|$ is the number of dimensions of the feature vector.

V. EVALUATION

In this section, we first extract the actual data from a wedding community website, in order to verify the user characteristic extraction method by extracting feature words for all posts of each user. Next, we detect similar users by comparing the cosine similarity with collaborative filtering. The dataset consists of 6,361 posts by 588 users during six months. Table IV shows the distribution of the numbers of comments for each user.

A. Experiment 1: Verification of User Characteristic Extraction on a Wedding Community Website

To evaluate our user characteristic extraction method, we extracted feature words from all posts of each user. We

TABLE V. COSINE SIMILARITY AMONG 588 USERS.

Value	#user combinations
0 - 0.1	154,132
0.1- 0.2	16,158
0.2 - 0.3	2,022
0.3 - 0.4	209
0.4 - 0.5	46
0.5 - 0.6	7
0.6 - 0.7	4
0.7 - 1.0	0

compared the following three methods:

1) *TF*
2) *TF-IDF* (*DF* = all of users)
3) *TF-IDF* (*DF* = the users before or after marriage)

We extracted 7,728 terms from 588 user posts.

Table III shows the top 15 feature words for users A, B, C, and D for each method. Bold words indicate that feature words are related to these users. We found that many feature words are proper nouns for methods 2 and 3, such as "fish paste" and "limousine." However, for method 1, we found common words that all users often use, i.e., there are no effective words that can be considered as feature words. We determined that calculating using *IDF* is a more effective way of extracting feature words. However, there are no differences between methods 2 and 3. The *IDF* values imply how the words are generally used by many users. If the *IDF* value is high, then the word is rarely used among users, and similarly if it is low the word is common among users. Therefore, there are no differences between the posts of users before marriage and the posts of those after marriage. Thus, we considered different definitions of document groups, which are not limited to the marital status.

Our results suggest that in the future we need to remove common words, because some generally used words were identified using methods 2 and 3.

The above discussion confirms that many feature words of users are effectively extracted using *TF-IDF* methods, namely methods 2 and 3. To detect user characteristics with feature words, more advanced methods are required.

B. Experiment 2: Verification of User Detection on a Wedding Community Website

In our active communication mechanism, the similarities between users constitute the key aspect for recommending users. In the previous section, we described our classification scheme that classifies users based on similarities of three axes. In this manner, we choose the most suitable users to promote communication.

To evaluate the similarities between users, we compared two calculation methods. The first is the proposed method, specifically the content-based recommendation method using the cosine similarity with active profile information. The second method is an item-based recommendation method that uses collaborative filtering with static profile information and marriage status. As mentioned previously, we calculated the cosine similarity based on user characteristics, which consist of feature words for each user. Therefore, each user has feature vectors of *TF-IDF* values. In Experiment 1, method 2 is the most useful method for extracting feature words. We also calculated the cosine similarity based on the feature words produced by method 2. Collaborative filtering is also a method used to calculate similarities between users. This method calculates similarities using user login information as items for each user. This is mainly used to recommend other items to users according to the following formula:

TABLE VI. COLLABORATIVE FILTERING AMONG 30 USERS.

Value	#user combinations
-1.0 - -0.9	0
-0.9 - -0.8	0
-0.8 - -0.7	2
-0.7 - -0.6	4
-0.6 - -0.5	5
-0.5 - -0.4	8
-0.4 - -0.3	8
-0.3 - -0.2	15
-0.2 - -0.1	23
-0.1 - 0	26
0 - 0.1	35
0.1- 0.2	39
0.2 - 0.3	40
0.3 - 0.4	38
0.4 - 0.5	41
0.5 - 0.6	41
0.3 - 0.7	44
0.7 - 0.8	31
0.8 - 0.9	26
0.9 - 1.0	9

$$Sim(X,Y) = \frac{\sum(x-\bar{x})(y-\bar{y})}{\sqrt{\sum(x-\bar{x})^2\sum(y-\bar{y})^2}}. \tag{6}$$

This equation calculates the similarity between users X and Y. On a wedding community website, users create individual accounts by answering questions regarding their wedding planning. For example, "Do you agree with a simple style marriage?" For each question, a user may choose from one of the following responses: "Strongly disagree," "Disagree," "Neither disagree nor agree," "Agree," or "Strongly agree." Each of these responses was assigned a numerical value ranging from 1 to 5, for calculation purposes. We then calculated the similarities using these numbers. Note that $\bar{x}$ and $\bar{y}$ denote the averages of the chosen answers. For example, if a user chose answer 1 and 5, the average value would be 3.

The users evaluated for our proposed user characteristic extraction method are shown in Table III. For this evaluation, we calculated 172,578 combinations from 588 users. The value of the cosine similarity ranges between 0 and 1.

Table V shows the distribution of results for the cosine similarity. The average value of all combinations is 0.045. We found that many results of user combinations are below 0.1. This can be attributed to the fact that most users talk about different topics relating to their wedding planning. However, some user combinations induce a high cosine similarity.

Table VI shows the distribution of results of collaborative filtering. The value of collaborative filtering should be between -1 and 1. For this method, the values are calculated based on the answers from the questions regarding wedding planning

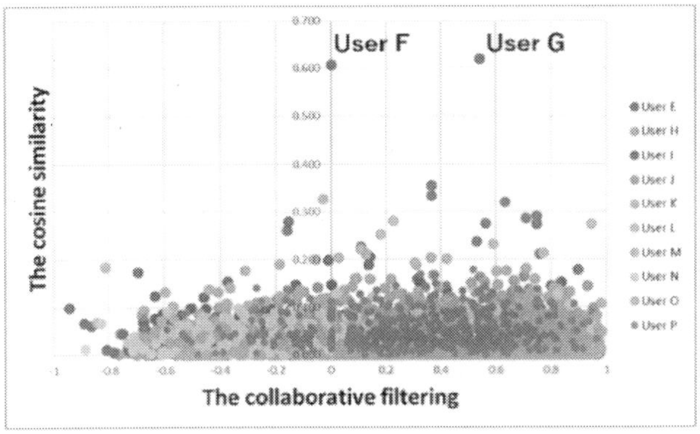

Figure 6. Distribution of the cosine similarity and collaborative filtering 1.

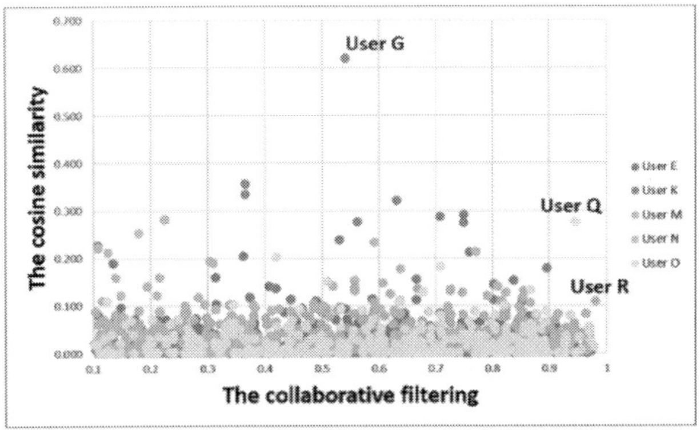

Figure 7. Distribution of the cosine similarity and collaborative filtering 2.

when users are creating accounts on the wedding community website. A high value implies that the users have similar wedding planning ideas. For this evaluation, we calculated 435 combinations of 30 users. The average value of all combinations was 0.304, which confirms that many users have similar wedding planning tastes.

Based on these results, we compared two similarity calculation methods. Here, we focused on user E, who has a high cosine similarity with other users and often posts on the wedding community site as a main user. We calculated all combinations with user E. Therefore, there were a total of 588 values for the cosine similarity and 588 values for collaborative filtering.

Figure 6 shows the distribution of the cosine similarity and collaborative filtering for 10 users, specifically users E, H, I, J, K, L, M, N, O, and P. Each dot corresponds to one user and has two values: the cosine similarity with each user and the collaborative filtering with each user. The vertical axis corresponds to the values of the cosine similarity, and the horizontal axis corresponds to the values of collaborative filtering. We focused on two users for user E, specifically F and G. Both of these users have high cosine similarity values of over 0.6, but their values of collaborative filtering are 0 and 0.54, respectively.

First, we compared the posts of users E and F. A post by user E describes their cousin's impressive wedding and the groom's tears. On the other hand, a post of user F describes how their cousin's wedding was organized. Even though common words were used in their posts, the meanings of these sentences and their topics are different.

Second, we compared the posts of users E and G. The post from user E is the same one as mentioned above. A post from user G describes their cousin's wedding, with tears resulting from a letter about a grandmother who has passed away. These posts both mention the same type of wedding and their cousin's weddings with tears, even though the content of these posts is slightly different.

As a result, we found that only calculating the cosine similarity is not effective for detecting similar comments. However, we found that calculating both the cosine similarity and collaborative filtering is effective. Therefore, these two methods can help to detect similar user comments in order to evoke communications among users. However, we must still evaluate different situations for a user by considering other users' axes and marriage statuses.

Figure 7 shows the distribution of the cosine similarity and collaborative filtering for users E, K, M, N, and O. We found several users that are particularly similar to these users, such as users Q and R. In the future, we plan to propose methods for clustering using the cosine similarity and collaborative filtering.

C. *Experiment 3: Verification of Recommendation Effect*

We interviewed five users to evaluate effect of our proposed recommendation system. On experiments 1 and 2, we verified that our proposed methods work effectively to detect recommended users. For this experiment, we evaluated the similarities for comments and the communication desire through interviews.

We interviewed five users of the wedding community website. On this community website, majority of users want to communicate with others to share their experiments, and want to obtain information from other users. The purpose of using this community website for the five users is same as for the majority. Therefore, these five users' opinions should reflect the opinions of the majority on this website.

The interviewer evaluated the two questions below regarding the users ' own comments and those of recommended users.

1) Similarity of comments
2) Communication desire

As mentioned in Section III, this system is able to recommend five patterns of different users (see Table I). For this evaluation, we considered two kinds of comments: 1) comments of recommended users whose preferences are similar according to one of the patterns 1, 2, 4, and 5; and 2) recommended users' comments whose situation is similar, but whose preferences are different, corresponding to pattern 3.

1) Other users' comments
whose preferences are similar,
(corresponding to one of the patterns 1, 2, 4, 5)
2) Other users' comments
whose situation is similar,
but whose preferences are different,
(corresponding to pattern 3)

TABLE VII. VERIFICATION OF RECOMMENDATION EFFECTS.

Recommended user	Comments similarity (adv)	Communication desire (adv)
1. High posting similarity (users with similar preferences)	3.00	3.33
2. Low posting similarity, but high static similarity (different preferences and similar situation)	2.89	3.56

TABLE VIII. EFFECTIVE RECOMMENDED USER FOR ACTIVATING CONVERSATION.

	Similar Situation	Different Situation
Similar Preference	Good	Good
Different Preference	Very Good	—

Figure 8. An example of recommender system.

Table VII presents the results of the interview experiments. The five users answered using the numbers between 1 and 5. The number 1 indicates strong disagreement, and 5 means strong agreement. According to the results, we can see that recommending other users is effective for activating communication, as the users want to communicate with others.

However, we could determine whether recommending a user who has a similar situation and different preferences is more effective than recommending similar users. We assume that recommending a similar user would activate communication, but this turned out not to be true at all (see Table IV).

Through this experience, we created one example of our proposed recommendation system (see Figure 8). In this example, based on the original user, the recommended user's situation is similar, but their interests, which also correspond to preferences, are different. We could determine that their conversations will be activated through this experiment by interviews.

D. Experiment 4: Verification of User Characteristics on SNS

The purpose of this evaluation is to verify whether our proposed method is useful for extracting user characteristics based on SNS user behavior. We acquired posts for public online course pages using the Facebook API[2] as follows:

- A: the latest 50 posts of "Exciting Programming Starting from Elementary School"
- B: the latest 50 posts of "Online Programming Learning Service on APP Development"

A is an online course for programming beginners, and B is an online course for advanced learners in programming. In this evaluation, we extracted feature words as user characteristics of A and B by using the following four methods:

1) The weight of word i given by Eq. (1)
2) 1) $\times$ #likes of posts with i
3) 2) $\times$ #shares of posts with i
4) 3) + 1) for each reply $\times$ #likes for each reply

Here, #likes and #shares for A or B were normalized to fit within the range of 0 to 1. As described above, we proposed the following methods to test: 1) *TF-IDF*, which was calculated using only the text that the user has posted; 2) integrating the value of 1) with the number of likes, which was normalized as the weight; and 3) integrating the value of 2) with the number of shares, which was normalized as the weight. In addition, 4) we verified user characteristics (feature words) by adding the value of 3) to the value obtained by integrating 1) *TF-IDF* for each comment with the number of likes for each comment. Table IX shows the top 15 feature words for A and B obtained using each method. Bold words denote feature words that are related to A or B.

We found that many feature words are proper nouns, such as "Graduate School of Information Science and Technology, The University of Tokyo" and "jQuery UI." In all methods, the ranking orders of the same feature words are different, and several feature words are different. For example, the feature word "Kenichirou Mogi" of A ranked highest for method 1, and does not occur in the top 15 for methods 2-4. In this work, high weight feature words representing user characteristics are used to extract the relationships between users. Therefore, these feature words for generating feature vectors for each user are useful for both receivers and senders in conversations. According to the correlations between the method 1 and other methods found by comparing the rankings of the top 15 feature words based on Spearman's rank correlation coefficient, the correlation coefficient for methods 1 and 2 is 0.77, that for methods 1 and 3 is 0.76, and the value for 1 and 4 is 0.72. Although the correlations between method 1 and the other methods are similar, method 4, which considers #likes, #shares, and replies, is different from method 1. In addition, the correlations between method 1 and the other methods are not high, and we could confirm that the feature words obtained using these four methods are different.

As discussed above, many proper nouns occur that do not require knowledge assistance. Conversely, common words are widely used, and they are not useful for our proposed system. In the future, we need to improve the calculation method in order to remove common words when extracting user characteristics.

E. Future Work

We verified the validation of our proposed system by evaluation, however, we still need to consider several points of our proposed methods as future work. In the future, we plan to enhance the proposed method based on our experimental results, and evaluate the effects of user recommendations. Furthermore, we plan to extract the relationships between users

[2]https://developers.facebook.com/

TABLE IX. TOP 10 FEATURE WORDS OF A AND B.

Method	A	B
1)	**Kenichiro Mogi**, **Nikkei software**, **debate**, **Graduate School of Information Science and Technology**, **The University of Tokyo**, **Kuramoto Daishi**, innovation, self-expression, **industrial competitiveness conference**, **robot programming teaching materials**, **programming compulsory subject**, **Newsweek Japanese version**, **trilingual**, **study Roh**, **Mitsuru Sugaya**, account every single	**CSS3**, **EdTech JAPAN Pitch Festival vol.4**, **go to jappan**, **Higher or Lower**, **IE KMD Venture Day Tokyo**, **jQuery UI**, **Tech academy**, **u-note**, **parallax**, Engineering, good, **SF JAPAN NIGHT semi Finals team**, learning, **Now we're hiring a great web designer**, **SF JapanNight**
2)	**Hour of Code Japan**, **Graduate School of Information Science and Technology**, **The University of Tokyo**, **programming compulsory**, **scratch Di**, **Prof. Yoshiaki Hashimoto**, **PC away**, a few lines, **study Roh**, **Show&Tell**, **Touch& Try**, **Code.org**, **World Business satellite**, self-expression, **Minecraft EDU**, **robot programming**	**CSS3**, **jQuery UI**, **Thanks for Five Thousand Fans**, learning, u-note, **Higher of Lower**, feedback, **SF JAPAN NIGHT semifinalists decision**, **intern**, **we'll launch a radical web wervice which**, **Trello**, **Pyhonista**, **Now we're hiring a great web designer**, **SF Japan Night**, This new service has already decided
3)	**scratch Di**, **Graduate School of Information Science and Technology**, **The University of Tokyo**, **Show &Tell**, **Touch &Try**, **Prof. Yoshiaki Hashimoto**, **Hour of Code Japan**, **PC away**, **study Roh**, **robot programming**, **Code.org**, **World Business Satellite**, **programming a compulsory subject**, **Nikkei style**, the former, co-workers	**Yukihiro Matsumoto**, learning, **object-oriented scripting language**, **jQuery UI**, **server-side scripting language**, tab, **SF JAPAN NIGHT semi fainalists decision**, **Higher or Lower**, **the three-column layout**, already learned, inquiry, voice, learning situation, **Mats**, **CSS3**
4)	nowadays, **education**, **scratch Di**, **faculty side**, **Graduate School of Information Science and Technology**, **The University of Tokyo**, **Show &Tell**, **Touch &Try**, **compulsory**, **high school**, **Nikkei BP booth**, challenge, **Prof. Yoshiaki Hashimoto**, maximum, case, **Hour or Code Japan**	very, sue, **Yukihiro Matsumoto**, learning, **Koushou Kawasoe**, **object-oriented scripting language**, **jQuery UI**, **server-side language ban**, tab, **SF JAPAN NIGHT semifinalists decision**, Higher or Lower, **three-stage assenmbly layout**, already learned, inquiry, voice

by constructing a matrix based on user behavior, as in our previous work [30].

Our proposed method has only been applied to users of an existing wedding community website in Japan. It should also be considered for intercultural communications. Furthermore, we are planning to verify this mechanism on other community websites.

Moreover, we are planning to propose a more effective user interface that considers the security implications of sharing and combining the information. Some users may feel annoyed to be suggested to other users, and so this system requires additional options to protect privacy. This problem should be discussed more in future research.

VI. CONCLUSION

In this paper, we proposed an active communication mechanism for a wedding community website. This mechanism recommended users who may potentially evoke communications, as well as their comments. To detect users, this mechanism classified all users according to three axes, specifically "Static Profile Information," "Marriage Status," and "Dynamic Profile Information." We then calculated the similarities between users using the cosine similarity. To extract comments that were posted on a wedding community website by recommended users, our mechanism detected the most closely related comments. We also proposed an activation mechanism for e-learning. Finally, we evaluated the method for extracting user characteristics from posts by comparing *TF-IDF* methods, and evaluated the similarity calculation methods using the cosine similarity and collaborative filtering. Moreover, we verified the extraction of user characteristics using data from Facebook.

ACKNOWLEDGMENT

This work was partially supported by JSPS KAKENHI Grant Numbers 15K00162, 16H01722, and 17K12686.

REFERENCES

[1] T. Hayashi, Y. Wang, Y. Kawai, and K. Sumiya, "A Proposal of Activation Mechanism for User Communication based on User Behavior Analysis on Wedding Community Sites," in Proceeding of The Ninth International Conference on Advances in Multimedia (MMEDIA 2017). IARIA, APR 2017, pp. 67–72, ISBN: 978-1-61208-548-7.

[2] M. Rathakrishnan, R. Ahmad, and C. L. Suan, "Online discussion: Enhancing students' critical thinking skills," AIP Conference Proceedings, vol. 1891, no. 1, 2017, p. 020120.

[3] F. Abel, I. I. Bittencourt, E. Costa, N. Henze, D. Krause, and J. Vassileva, "Recommendations in online discussion forums for e-learning systems," IEEE transactions on learning technologies, vol. 3, no. 2, 2010, pp. 165–176.

[4] R. Isaac and J. Walker, "Communication and free-riding behavior: The voluntary contribution mechanism," Economic Inquiry, vol. 26, no. 4, 1988, pp. 585–608.

[5] N. B. Ellison, C. Steinfield, and C. Lampe, "The benefits of facebook "friends:" social capital and college students' use of online social network sites," Journal of Computer-Mediated Communication, vol. 12, no. 4, 2007, pp. 1143–1168.

[6] L. H. Shaw and L. M. Gant, "In defense of the internet: The relationship between internet communication and depression, loneliness, self-esteem, and perceived social support," Cyberpsychology & behavior, vol. 5, no. 2, 2002, pp. 157–171.

[7] Y. Mastsui and Y. Kawai, "Social search system for retrieval and communication based on networks of pages and users," Computer Software, vol. 28, no. 4, 2011, pp. 196–205.

[8] J. Preece and D. Maloney-Krichmar, "Online communities: Design, theory, and practice," Journal of Computer-Mediated Communication, vol. 10, no. 4, 2005, pp. 00–00.

[9] E. Park, R. Rishika, R. Janakiraman, M. B. Houston, and B. Yoo, "Social dollars in online communities: The effect of product, user and network characteristics," Journal of Marketing, 2017.

[10] K. Randhawa, E. Josserand, J. Schweitzer, and D. Logue, "Knowledge collaboration between organizations and online communities: the role of open innovation intermediaries," Journal of Knowledge Management, no. just-accepted, 2017, pp. 00–00.

[11] P. Grace-Farfaglia, A. Dekkers, B. Sundararajan, L. Peters, and S.-H. Park, "Multinational web uses and gratifications: Measuring the social impact of online community participation across national boundaries," Electronic Commerce Research, vol. 6, no. 1, 2006, pp. 75–101.

[12] J. Preece, "Sociability and usability in online communities: Determining and measuring success," Behaviour & Information Technology, vol. 20, no. 5, 2001, pp. 347–356.

[13] P. J. Batterham and A. L. Calear, "Preferences for internet-based mental health interventions in an adult online sample: Findings from an online community survey," JMIR mental health, vol. 4, no. 2, 2017.

[14] C. Liang, C.-C. Chang, W. Rothwell, and K.-M. Shu, "Influences of organizational culture on knowledge sharing in an online virtual community: Interactive effects of trust, communication and leadership," in Organizational Culture and Behavior: Concepts, Methodologies, Tools, and Applications. IGI Global, 2017, pp. 972–992.

[15] H. Akihiro, Y. Madoka, T. Hiroyuki, and K. Yahiko, "Experimental chat sessions to encourage active communication in lectures," IPSJ SIG Notes, vol. 2000, no. 45, 2000, pp. 61–66.

[16] D. Godes and D. Mayzlin, "Using online conversations to study word-of-mouth communication," Marketing science, vol. 23, no. 4, 2004, pp. 545–560.

[17] J. M. Kayany and P. Yelsma, "Displacement effects of online media in the socio-technical contexts of households," Journal of Broadcasting & Electronic Media, vol. 44, no. 2, 2000, pp. 215–229.

[18] P. K. Chintagunta, S. Gopinath, and S. Venkataraman, "The effects of online user reviews on movie box office performance: Accounting for sequential rollout and aggregation across local markets," Marketing Science, vol. 29, no. 5, 2010, pp. 944–957.

[19] K. Hemmings-Jarrett, J. Jarrett, and M. B. Blake, "Evaluation of user engagement on social media to leverage active and passive communication," in Cognitive Computing (ICCC), 2017 IEEE International Conference on. IEEE, 2017, pp. 132–135.

[20] J. Liu, E. Pedersen, and P. Dolan, "Personalized news recommendation based on click behavior," Proceedings of the 15th International Conference on Intelligent User Interfaces, 2010, pp. 31–40.

[21] L. Li and T. Li, "News recommendation via hypergraph learning: encapsulation of user behavior and news content," in Proceedings of the sixth ACM international conference on Web search and data mining. ACM, 2013, pp. 305–314.

[22] K. Xu, Y. Cai, H. Min, X. Zheng, T. Wong et al., "Uis-lda: a user recommendation based on social connections and interests of users in uni-directional social networks," in Proceedings of the International Conference on Web Intelligence. ACM, 2017, pp. 260–265.

[23] D. Zhou, M. Truran, T. Brailsford, H. Ashman, and A. Pourabdollah, "Llama-b: Automatic hyperlink authoring in the blogosphere," in Proceedings of the Nineteenth ACM Conference on Hypertext and Hypermedia, ser. HT '08. New York, NY, USA: ACM, 2008, pp. 133–138. [Online]. Available: http://doi.acm.org/10.1145/1379092.1379119

[24] R. D'souza, A. Kulkarni, and I. A. Mirza, "Automatic link generation for search engine optimization," International Journal of Information and Education Technology, vol. 2, no. 4, 2012, pp. 401–403, ISSN: 2010-3689.

[25] H.-C. C. Yi-Wen Liao, Yueh-Min Huang and S.-H. Huang, "Exploring the antecedents of collaborative learning performance over social networking sites in a ubiquitous learning context," Computers in Human Behavior, vol. 43, 2015, pp. 313–323.

[26] R. Cheng and S. K. Sharma, "Learning and self-disclosure behavior on social networking sites: the case of facebook users," European Journal of Information Systems, vol. 24, no. 1, 2015, pp. 93–106.

[27] R. D ' souza, A. Kulkarni, and I. A. Mirza, "Automatic link generation for search engine optimization," International Journal of Information and Education Technology, vol. 2, no. 4, 2015, pp. 401–403.

[28] Y. Aoki, R. Koshijima, and M. Toyama, "Automatic determination of hyperlink destination in web index," Proc. of IDEAS 2015, 2015, pp. 206–207.

[29] J. Liu, P. Dolan, and E. R. Pedersen, "Personalized news recommendation based on click behavior," Proc. of IUI 2010, 2010, pp. 31–40.

[30] Y. Wang, Y. Kawai, S. Miyamoto, and K. Sumiya, "An automatic scoring system for e-reports based on student peer evaluation using groupware," DBSJ Journal, vol. 13, no. 1, 2015, pp. 71–76.

Semiotic Annotation of Narrative Video Commercials: Bridging the Gap between Artifacts and Ontologies

Elio Toppano
Dipartimento di Scienze Matematiche,
Informatiche e Fisiche (DMIF)
Università di Udine, Italy
e-mail: elio.toppano@uniud.it

Vito Roberto
Dipartimento di Scienze Matematiche,
Informatiche e Fisiche (DMIF)
Università di Udine, Italy
e-mail: vito.roberto@uniud.it

Abstract—**Drawing on semiotic theories, the paper proposes a new concept of annotation – called semiotic annotation – whose goal is to describe the multilayered articulation of meaning inscribed within narrative video commercials by their designers. The approach exploits the use of a meta-model of the narrative video genre providing the conceptualizations and the vocabulary for analysis and annotation. By explicating design knowledge embodied in the video, semiotic annotation plays the role of intermediate level knowledge between the meta-model (an informal ontology) and practice (the concrete video artifact). In order to assess the feasibility of the approach, a test bed is presented and results are reported. A final discussion about the potential contribution of semiotic annotation in the fields of Research Through Design, Technological Mediation, and Interface Criticism concludes the study.**

Keywords-video; content annotation; ontology; semiotics; advertising; semantic web.

I. INTRODUCTION

This paper is about representation and semantic-based content annotation of narrative video commercials during production. It is an elaboration and extension of previous work presented in the IARIA Fifth International Conference on Building and Exploring Web Based Environments [1]. Narrative video commercials are multimodal artifacts used in the domains of marketing and advertising to communicate a product's features, a public service announcement (PSA), or abstract concepts such as a brand personality [2] or brand identity [3] through a story-like format. The intention is to persuade people to buy the product or, in the case of brand communication, to resonate with brand meanings (e.g., brand core values) [4].

Nowadays, video advertising covers a wide range of products differing in production quality, time length, and distribution. Standardization activities made by the IAB (Interactive Advertising Bureau) have provided several formats and guidelines to improve the development process of this genre of artifacts and to enhance the viewer experience [5][6].

A number of reasons motivate the use of stories in advertising. First, humans are storytellers. They use narratives as a natural and effective way to understand, structure, and communicate their experiences. This is because narratives evoke more meaning and emotions than bare facts. Narratives are also crucial for our understanding of time and time-based events as well as for understanding own identities and self [7]. Second, narratives have an intrinsic persuasive potential that is related to the extent that viewers/readers are "transported" into the world of the narrative and become involved with its protagonists [8]. Strong immersion into a story reduces counterarguments against story assertions, creates a lifelike experience, and provides strong connections with characters, all of which facilitate *narrative persuasion* [9][10]. Third, studies show that recall of narrative information is twice as likely as recall of expository information [9].

Narrative video commercials demand a careful design activity. A critical decision is, for example, how to integrate the persuasive message (e.g., information intended to influence the audience) with the story told by the video. Another decision is how to combine narrative persuasion with other non-narrative persuasive mechanisms such as reasoned arguments, statistical evidence, celebrity endorsement, etc. in order to achieve maximum effectiveness. Yet, another problem arising in brand communication concerns the development of a *brand-specific design language*, i.e., to decide how to communicate abstract meanings such as brand values and personality by a systematic and consistent use of expressive features (e.g., visual shapes, color scheme, auditory timbres and leitmotifs). This process - called *semantic transformation* - has been extensively studied in the field of industrial design [11] but has received much less attention in the field of multimedia design [12].

It should be evident from the above discussion that describing and annotating the (semantic) content of narrative video ads during the design process poses several problems due to the density and complexity of meanings that are inscribed into these kinds of artifacts. The annotation can be reduced neither to the description of what is depicted in the video nor to the specification of the general theme/claim of the video or the description of basic visual and auditory features. Rather, it should be possible to capture the entire range of meanings inscribed within the product including deep values, narrative structure, figurative and plastic meanings, rhetorical and persuasive mechanisms, to name only a few. Most importantly, the annotation should be able to capture the relationships existing among all these meanings, i.e., their articulation in different conceptual layers within the artifact and their distribution across representation modalities (i.e., written words, images, sound objects).

In this paper, we address this problem by exploiting contemporary semiotic theories. We wish to evaluate whether a semiotic perspective provides a useful meta-model for the analysis and annotation of audio-visual resources and narrative video commercials in particular. Semiotics studies signs, meaning, and sense-making. It addresses processes of signification by investigating the ways meaning arises from mappings among sign structures. Therefore, it can be used to model the content and expression of a narrative video commercial intended here informally as "the sum of meanings that the designer intends to communicate through the space/time composition of the audio-visual resources that constitute the video presentation".

An important assumption is that the content of the video commercial is the result of an intentional act of designing intended as meaning-making or rhetorical argumentation [13][14][15]. This assumption does not hold - or only partially holds - for other types of audio-visuals such as surveillance videos, home videos, documentary and scientific videos, news videos, etc. where the content is largely determined by what happens in the reality and its structure depends on the nature of events being recorded rather than on high control over screenplay, editing, and filming. In narrative artifacts, in particular, the meaning is strictly related to experience and its constitutive components namely the sensorial, cognitive and affective component [16]. Therefore, designing a narrative video ad means embedding, within the artifact, the conditions for affording in the viewer an intended experience. The artifact, thus, plays the role of *mediator* (of experience) between the intentions of a sender (intended, here, metonymically to represent all parties involved in the development of the video including sponsors, client, designers, producer) and the interpretation of a receiver (the user, consumer) [17].

We are interested in the production side of this framework: how meaning (e.g., projected experience) is intentionally constructed and articulated during the message construction process, how it is embedded in the video and gives form to it. Consequently, by semantic annotation, we refer to a kind of "serious" annotation performed by trained professionals in the course of video development [18][19]. Its aim is to capture the intended and inscribed meanings in order to exploit them not only for retrieval, filtering, and browsing tasks but also for explanation, critical evaluation, and content (i.e., meaning) reuse. We shall not address online user' annotation or social tagging although they obviously represent an important contribution to the development of the field.

The paper is organized as follows. In Section II we review related work about multimedia semantic-based content annotation. Section III introduces the concept of Semiotic Annotation that is at the core of our approach. This kind of annotation exploits a semiotic compliant informal ontology (i.e., a meta-model) of the artifact under consideration. A critical discussion of available ontologies of narrative videos is presented as well as some basic requirements the design of an ontology supporting the proposed approach should satisfy. In Section IV, we illustrate the meta-model we have developed for semiotic annotation. It specializes our previous work on hypermedia [20][21] for the narrative video commercial genre. An example of application is presented in Section V while possible uses and implications for research are discussed in Section VI. Finally, Section VII summarizes the strengths and limitations of the approach and draws the conclusions.

II. Related Work

The term "annotation" can denote both an activity (i.e., the process by means of which additional data - *metadata* - are attached to existing data) and the result of that activity.

Models and technologies for annotation have been studied within many communities, with different goals and perspectives. In the digital library community, for example, metadata is seen as a way of supporting cataloging and retrieving information in a large collection of documents [22]. In the knowledge representation community, the focus is, instead, on representing the underlying content of a document rather than describing the document that contains the content [23]. In the semantic web community, an annotation is viewed, first of all, as a tool for representing and linking resources together in order to support information retrieval, filtering, and browsing [24].

Figure 1 represents a basic model of an annotation A in terms of a tuple, i.e., $A = < a_s, a_o, a_r, a_c >$ where a_s denotes the *annotated data* (i.e., the subject or target of the annotation), a_o the *annotating data* (i.e., the object or body of the annotation), a_r the *annotation relation* (i.e., a predicate that defines the type of relationship existing between annotated and annotating data) and a_c the *context* in which the annotation is made [25], [26]. The context includes several facets such as, for example, *who* makes the annotation (e.g., a single individual, a group, an automatic system; an expert annotator of a casual user); *when* (e.g., during different phases of the development process of a resource; during its use); *why* (e.g., for classification, description, retrieval, filtering, explanation, browsing, reuse); *how* (e.g., manually, semi-automatically, fully automatically; using free text, controlled vocabularies, taxonomies, ontologies); and *application domain* (e.g., entertainment, news, marketing, brand management).

The two most widely known approaches towards machine processable and semantic-based content annotation are the Semantic Web Activity of the W3C [27] and the ISO efforts in the direction of complex media content modeling, in particular, the Multimedia Content Description Interface (MPEG-7) [28].

The Semantic Web approach provides a structured set of cooperating languages (e.g., RDF, RDFS, OWL) and processing tools to define ontology vocabularies. It supports reasoning with ontologies but does not specify any collection of specific metadata for multimedia products. Andrews, Zaihrayeu, and Pane [24] surveying various

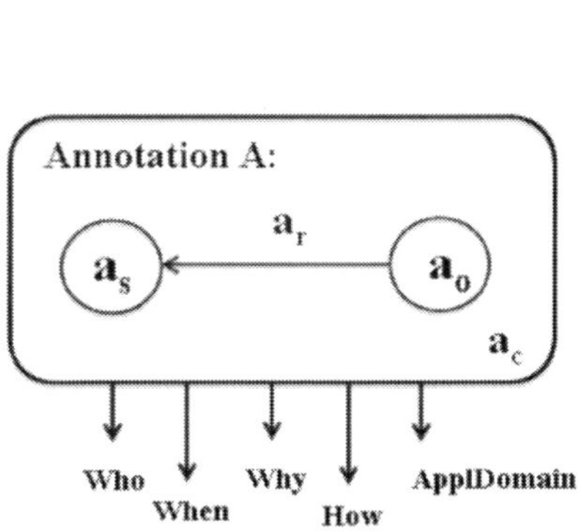

Figure 1. Annotation model: a_s is the target of the annotation, a_o the body, a_r the annotation relation and a_c denotes contextual information (i.e., who makes the annotation, when, how, and the application domain).

annotation systems for the web, investigate existing models for representing annotations and analyze their different characteristics, forms and function. Based on this analysis a classification scheme for annotation models was developed that distinguishes three main dimensions namely: i) the structural complexity of annotations (e.g., simple labels, attribute/value pairs, structured collections of concepts and relations), ii) the type of vocabulary used (e.g., free text, controlled vocabulary, taxonomies, ontologies), and iii) the level of user collaboration in sharing and reusing semantic annotation, and in the collaborative construction and evolution of the underlying vocabulary or ontology.

MPEG-7 is aimed at providing standardized means for describing audio-visual data content in multimedia environments [29]. The standard provides a set of descriptors and description schemes specifying the structure of the metadata elements, their relationships and the constraints a valid MPEG-7 description should adhere. It does not incorporate formal semantics and it is based on XML encoded metadata. As a consequence MPEG-7 is not open to standards that represent knowledge and make use of existing controlled vocabularies for describing the subject matter. Moreover, its XML schema-based nature has led to design decisions that leave the annotations conceptually ambiguous and, therefore, prevent direct machine processing of semantic content descriptions. In order to overcome these limitations, several approaches have been published providing a formalization of MPEG-7 as an ontology. A survey of these initiatives is provided by [30] where a detailed comparison of MPEG-7 compliant ontologies - such as Hunter's ontology, AceMedia, SmartWeb, Boemie, Rhizomik and COMM - is made on the base of three main dimensions namely: 1) low-level descriptors covering visual and audio features; 2) structural descriptions pertaining to the decomposition and localization of content parts; 3) subject matter descriptions expressing the semantic conveyed by a multimedia resource.

What emerges from the analysis is that most of the approaches use a modular architecture to mainly represent structural issues and low-level features, using OWL DL formal languages. Subject matter descriptions are usually demanded to external top ontologies such as SUMO or DOLCE or domain-specific conceptualizations. The COMM ontology (Core Ontology for MultiMedia) [31] constitutes one of the more recent approaches to the formalization of MPEG-7 descriptions semantics. It extends the Description&Situation pattern (D&S) and Ontology of Information Objects (OIO) of DOLCE by re-engineering the MPEG-7 description tools in order to provide a common foundational framework for describing multimedia documents.

A comparison between MPEG-7 and several other multimedia metadata standards is discussed in [32][33]. The analysis is made according to several dimensions including the specific media production process - e.g., premeditate, capture, archive, query, message construction, organize, publish and distribute [34] - during which the metadata are intended to be used.

What emerges from the comparison is that a support for describing semantic content linked to premeditate, message construction, and organization processes is generally missing. The premeditate process is where initial ideas about media production, e.g., goals, intentions, target audience, subject, genre, deep values are established; the message construction and organization processes are where the author/designer specifies the message he/she wishes to convey and media assets are organized according to the message.

MPEG-7, for example, supports premeditation in the CreationInformation description scheme and in the Classification scheme [29]. The former allows the annotator to represent date, place, action, material, staff involved in the creation of the content entity. The latter allows the annotation of the artifact with information about the subject, genre, purpose, and market segment. However, these data are completely disconnected with respect to content structure and semantics. As an instance, the genre is a label that is associated to the entire multimedia product; it cannot refer in any way to discourse structure or to expressive characteristics that are used to materialize that genre in the artifact. As a consequence, it is difficult to understand *how* the genre is intentionally constructed and articulated within the message during the design process, *how* it shapes the message and *how* users can infer the designer's intentions – both informative and persuasive. A similar argument can be stated for product purpose, intended audience and so forth. It is not possible to explain *how* a purpose is achieved in that artifact, *how* an intended audience is inscribed within the artifact itself, or *why* a specific design decision has been made.

As far as message construction and organization processes are concerned, the MPEG-7 standard provides very high flexibility by introducing general-purpose descriptor schemes for representing a wide collection of story-related semantic entities such as objects, people, events, concepts, states, places, and time together with their properties and relationships [29]. In practice, this flexibility is hindered by the fact that the annotator is left alone in using these descriptors to model a narrative.

The problem is that to be a true narrative, a text must exhibit a specific quality called *narrativity* [35]. This quality, that may be present in various degrees, is the result of a set of interrelated structural factors (e.g., clear structure, genre typicality, affective structure, dramatic mode) [36], that are not taken into account by MPEG-7 and the other multimedia metadata standards alike.

In other words, to build a narrative, it is not sufficient to have the main ingredients, it is necessary to know how to put these ingredients together in order to reflect the specific qualities of this kind of genre. MPEG-7 and other standards provide the What but do not support the How.

For the genre of narrative video commercials that are the scope of the present article, what is needed is a vocabulary (and a conceptualization) that is able to bridge the gap existing between abstract concepts such as purpose, narrativity, narrative structure, discourse structure, intended values, affective states of the story's characters, etc. and perceptual qualities such as basic visual and auditory features. The aim of the research described in this paper is to explore how it is possible to represent this kind of meanings and use them to annotate the message in order to exploit it for content retrieval, explanation, and reuse.

III. Semiotic Annotation

In this section, we introduce the concept of *semiotic analysis* and *annotation* that is at the core of our approach [1]. This process exploits a meta-model (i.e., an informal ontology) of the narrative video genre. Therefore, we first review some relevant conceptualizations that have been proposed in the past to describe or annotate narrative videos. The analysis and comparison of these conceptualizations allowed us to identify a set of requirements for the development of our meta-model that will be illustrated in Section IV.

A. Semiotics

Semiotic studies cover a wide range of theories, models, and conceptualizations according to the specific intention they try to achieve and the unit of inquiry they address. Classical semiotics assumes the concept of *sign* as the main unit of signification and studies languages as sign systems [37]; interpretative semiotics focuses on processes of *interpretation* (i.e., semiosis) [38]. Contemporary semiotics extends its scope to the *text* construct intended as a unit of interrelated sign structures while Social Semiotics investigates human signifying practices in specific social and cultural circumstances [39]. More recent developments studies *mediated experiences* [40], *technical artifacts* and *design* [41][42].

What is common to all these approaches, regardless the variety of perspectives, is a focus on meaning, meaning construction (sense-making) and communication. As stated by Scolari [43]: "Semiotics studies objects (texts, discourses) to understand processes (sense production and interpretation)". From this point of view, semiotics appears as a methodology. What it actually does is to reflect on the more appropriate *methods* that can be used to perform the *analysis* of communicative and physical artifacts viewed as kind of multimodal texts. As a consequence, it elaborates tools (e.g., conceptualizations, models, grids of focal queries) for making the analysis and tests the effectiveness of these tools with concrete artifacts.

B. Semiotic analysis and annotation

By *semiotic analysis*, we mean a process of knowledge acquisition based on decomposition and re-composition of a given communicative artifact. Its aim is to unfold the *articulation of meaning* inscribed within the artifact by its designer/author. The basic assumption is that the *intended meaning* is spread over different interconnected *forms* - understood, here, as structured sets of relationships among content or expression entities - deployed within the artifact. The decomposition and re-composition processes are always based on some idea or conceptualization - a meta-model or (informal) ontology - of the genre of artifact under consideration. To be effective, such a conceptualization should be capable to capture the internal articulation of interconnected forms that are inscribed within the artifact. The result of the semiotic analysis is a partial or complete instantiation of the meta-model, i.e., a description (model) of the artifact that is then used for the annotation. The process can be detailed as follows (Figure 2):

- Step-0. An object - e.g., a clip video in the current case - is selected and regarded as a text, i.e., an autonomous, multilayered and organic unity having a goal/purpose: to produce effects by means of signification processes.
- Step-1. A meta-model of the type of object under consideration is selected as a reference guide to individuate main parts and relationships. The text object is *decomposed* accordingly.
- Step-2. Constituent parts and relationships are investigated, in turn, in order to understand how they may contribute to the functioning of the whole. To this end, a *re-composition* of the parts into the whole is mentally attempted and a description (model) of the artifact is produced. Again, the meta-model is used to build the description. This step involves a back-and-forth movement between pointing out material particulars and relating them to interpreted wholes.
- Step-3. The result of the analysis is used to annotate the object.

As shown in the figure, several meta-models of the type of object under consideration may be available, at a certain time, for supporting analysis and annotation; so the selection of an appropriate one depends on specific purposes and interests of the analysis. If we assume that the considered artifact is an organic unity and we seek to explain this unity, not all meta-models are equally appropriate for the task. We need a meta-model that embodies a hypothesis about the general organization and internal coherence of the elements that constitute the artifact. This coherence may have several sources, including the existing relationships between the artifact's structure and its function, the artifact's genre, author's style, the cultural meanings associated with multimodal materials. In this way, the annotation is not simply used for classifying the artifact elements into categories; we want to relate the elements and their respective categories in order to explain its organic unity. Moreover, meta-models may change over time reflecting the interests and tastes of mainstream research communities. As a consequence, also the aspects of an object that are deemed relevant change. In the field of multimedia design, for example, we have witnessed a shift of interest from pragmatic issues related to technology, product utility, usefulness, and performance to hedonic aspects that are related to the whole human experience such as aesthetics, pleasure, fun, values. The meta-models have evolved accordingly.

It should be stressed that the process of semiotic annotation does not occur in the vacuum but within a specific pragmatic situation and a social and cultural context. The result of analysis and thus the annotation are simultaneously personal and inter-subjective. The annotation is personal because it is particular to the individual analyst, his/her knowledge, and experience. It is inter-subjective because the analysis is driven by a meta-model that represents a shared conceptualization within a community of practice, i.e., it is socially constructed. In this way, the personal dimension is balanced both by the qualities found in the object itself, and the characteristics of the meta-model. The interpretation must start from empirical qualities but is completed by the experience of the analyst and the knowledge embedded into the meta-model.

Finally, the process of semiotic analysis and annotation is also a process of evaluation of the meta-model itself that may be modified and enriched in order to better represent concrete artifacts.

C. Ontologies of narrative videos

Quoting Gruber [44] an Ontology is an: "explicit and formal specification of a shared conceptualization about a given domain of interest". We are interested in the *knowledge level* (conceptualization and vocabulary) of an ontology rather than its *symbolic level* (formal representation). At this level Ontologies are *meta-models*. They provide the *concepts* (of entities, properties, and relationships) and the *vocabulary* that can be used to build models (e.g., descriptions) of specific things belonging to the considered domain of interest. By specifying the conceptual primitives, a meta-model implicitly defines the set of questions (called *competence questions*) that can be answered using the conceptualization. Ontologies are always incomplete and perspectival, i.e., they partially represent the domain of interest and they do it from a specific point of view that is related to the intended purpose of the ontology.

In this subsection, we briefly review some relevant conceptualizations of digital video with specific attention to those models aimed at annotation or indexing tasks or including narrative features. Before doing that it is worth attempting to characterize the nature of a narrative video viewed as a cultural artifact (e.g., a semiotic text) rather than a technological object featuring specific digital data structures, video format, compression algorithms and so forth [45]. Therefore, in this paper, a *video* is conceived of as a tangible object, a space-time dynamic configuration (a

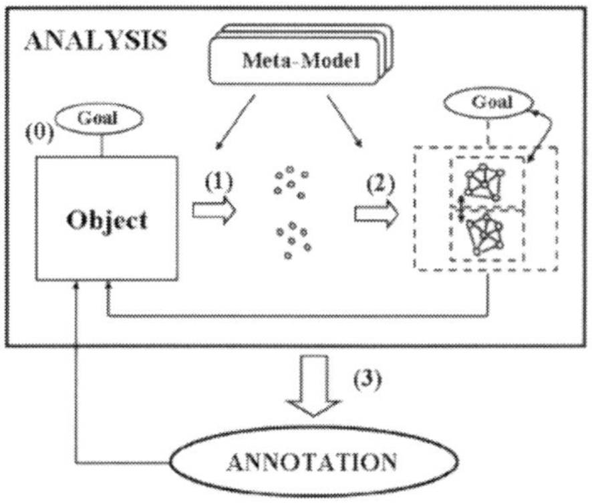

Figure 2. Analysis and annotation processes: 0) object selection, 1) decomposition, 2) re-composition, and 3) annotation steps. Object decomposition and re-composition are driven by a meta-model of the genre of object under analysis.

presentation) of visual and auditory signs that are inscribed within a material support using specific techniques, and are, therefore, available for an activity of visual and aural exploration and interpretation by a subject (the user or viewer/listener). A narrative video is a video that satisfies the conditions of narrativity stated by Ryan [35] or, alternatively, that is compliant with one of the definitions of narrative proposed by Grimaldi [46].

Attempts to exploit narrative theory for describing and annotating audio-visual resources date back to the early 90s. An example is the research work by Davis [47] at MIT who proposed a set of base categories for narrative video representation including action, character, object, mis-en-scene, cinematography. Davis explores annotation for video repurposing. More recently [48] illustrates a multilayered conceptualization of digital videos for indexing tasks that distinguishes among three main levels of analysis: layout, content and semantic index. For each level, a core set of descriptive concepts has been introduced. A similar proposal is the meta-model discussed in [49]. In this paper, video analysis and description is articulated into three dimensions: a spatiotemporal dimension representing the artifact at different levels of structural aggregation; a semantic dimension focusing on content (e.g., objects, events, plot structure) and an interpretative dimension inspired to film semiotics featuring different levels of interpretation (e.g., perceptual, cinematic, diegetic, connotative and sub-textual). Other relevant contributions are the research work by Stakelberg [50] and by Lombardo et al. [51] in the field of transmedia production and storytelling. The former contribution represents a very rich conceptualization (not yet an ontology) of transmedia narratives. The latter, developed within the CADMIO project, is focused on semi-automatic annotation of narrative artifacts and illustrates two computational ontologies devoted to characters and story respectively. Generative Theory by Greimas [52] is actually one of the most widely used frameworks - in the field of contemporary semiotics - for the analysis of commercials video [53]. The framework distinguishes four interrelated levels of analysis: i) the textual level representing the concrete/physical manifestation of narrative content in terms of audio-visual features ii) the discourse level referring to thematic, figurative, rhetorical aspects iii) a shallow narrative level describing a story in terms of abstract roles (called actants) and narrative schemas (e.g., the narrative canonical schema) and iv) a deep narrative level that uses a specific tool called semiotic square to articulate deep semantic meanings such as narrative values (axiology). Signification unfolds by crossing these levels from shallow features of a video to the most abstract and deep ones. Although this framework is highly popular in the field of semiotic studies there are few attempts to transfer it (or parts of it) in the technical fields of multimedia analysis, design, and annotation. A notable exception is represented by the work illustrated in [54]. The authors exploit a framework of consumers' values proposed by Floch [55] within generative semiotics for automatic classification of videos and retrieval. Finally, the work by Bateman [56] and Tseng [57], although not strictly related to annotation tasks, are important contributions focusing on the application of Metz's semiotics of film and social semiotics, respectively, to the analysis of audio-visual artifacts.

What emerges from the analysis of relevant literature can be summarized as follows. A common objective of the considered works is the attempt to represent the complex and multilayered syntactic and semantic structure of video artifacts at different abstraction and aggregation levels. However, the number of layers, their meaning, the links existing between layers, and the conceptualizations proposed to describe the semantic content of each layer vary from one approach to another. There are differences and ambiguities in the use of core terms such as for example, narrative, narrativity, discourse, plot, story, as well as their conceptual meanings. As an instance, the concepts of story and narrative are often used interchangeably and defined in various ways along a continuum ranging from the easiest definition (e.g., a narrative is a representation of one or more events) to the hardest one (e.g., a narrative is an emotion-evoking and value-laden representation of one or more characters in a series of chronological events that are connected by causality or agency and which progress through conflicts toward a climax). As a consequence, meta-models of video artifacts vary in complexity and expressive power. The same concept of "event", which recurs in all definitions of story or narrative, is actually intended in different ways. Sometimes the term is used as a synonym of action or happening, i.e., something that - intentionally or unintentionally - occurs in time and space and produces a state transformation; other times it refers to the effect of an action (e.g., the state transformation itself); or to a state of affairs. These conceptual ambiguities hinder the development of usable and shared conceptualizations as the basis for interoperable ontologies.

It seems that no one of the forenamed approaches is able to exploit the benefits of contemporary semiotic conceptualizations in their full potentiality. This is the aim of the present work as discussed in the next sections.

D. Requirements for Semiotic Annotation

That said, we present a list of requirements for the design of a semiotic compliant narrative video annotation. Our aim is to integrate concepts belonging to the MPEG-7 standard with concepts that are drawn from contemporary semiotic fields, namely, visual semiotics, social semiotics, and generative semiotics. We have taken inspiration from classical theoretical papers in order to provide a conceptualization that is widely shared among experts in these fields. To this end we have aggregated the requirements into three main classes namely: syntactic, semantic and pragmatic requirements.

At the *syntactic level*, the conceptualization should enable the annotator:

- to structurally decompose the video presentation using different spatiotemporal *aggregation levels*. As an instance it should be possible to focus on single regions within a representative frame; on moving regions crossing a sequence of adjacent frames; or look at the video as a temporal sequence of more aggregated entities such as shots, scenes, sequences, and episodes. We need specific mechanisms for the univocal identification of the anchor of annotating data;

- to describe the video using multiple structural decompositions. As an instance, a decomposition representing the video as a sequence of shots, another as a sequence of scenes and another one representing the same video as a sequence of homogeneous sound objects (e.g., music, silence, speech, effects) or combination of sound objects;

- to relate together structural entities belonging to the same or to different decompositions (e.g., to represent the relationships existing between adjacent shots; between shots and scenes or between scene boundaries and sound objects);

Structural decompositions constitute the scaffolding for the semantic level. They allow the annotator to represent compositional (or organizational) meaning that tells us what goes with what, what smaller units belong to what larger unit, how parts are related together, and how semantic meanings are distributed across the whole video.

At the *semantic level*, the conceptualization should enable the annotator:

- to associate basic kinetic and plastic features (e.g., shapes, colors, positions, textures, sizes, cinematic movements, visual contrasts, rhythm) to visual regions or structured groupings of regions within a frame or across frames [58]. To describe spectro-morphological features of sound objects (e.g., time features such as amplitude, envelope, loudness, tempo, and spectral ones such as pitch, timbre, harmony) [59].

- to associate a semantic construct (e.g., a figurative sign such as an object, subject, action, event, or abstract concepts such as goals, deep values, emotions) to visual or auditory fragments, and, indirectly to the plastic or spectro-morphological features that characterize them [60]; to link the semantic constructs by several types of relationships (e.g., spatial, temporal, logical, rhetorical, typological, mereological, causal, teleological relationships);

- to associate dramaturgical patterns (e.g., the canonical narrative schema by Greimas [61], the Hero's Journey by Campbell [62], the Dramatic Arc or Three Acts Model [63]) to visual or auditory segments of the video, and, indirectly, to the semantic constructs and expressive features that represent these segments at the syntactic and semantic/figurative levels;

Semantic annotation allows the annotator to describe representational (or ideational) meaning that tells us what recognizable existents are represented, who is doing what, to whom, and with what means, what is happening and what is related to what and how.

At the *pragmatic level*, the conceptualization should enable the annotator:

- to identify the images, called simulacra, of all the participants involved in the production and use of the video (i.e., addresser, addressee, narrator, observer, actor) that are inscribed within the artifact and specify their interrelationships [64];

- to describe the kind of relationship the designer/author of the video wants to evoke between the various subjects inscribed within the video and the intended user.

Pragmatic annotation allows the annotator to represent interpersonal (or orientational) meaning that refers, for example, to social distance and intimacy, image acts and gazes, narrative engagement and power relationships [65].

Table I exemplifies focal questions that can be used to direct the attention of the analyst to key perspectives and issues related to the three main types of meanings taken into account by social semiotics [39][66].

Finally, the conceptualization should provide the annotator with a set of relationships that can be used to link all the above aspects together in order to build the desired means/ends ladder: deep values with the storyline, the elements of the story with discourse segments and expressive qualities; expressive qualities with interpersonal meanings.

TABLE I. EXAMPLES OF FOCAL QUESTIONS RELATED TO TYPES OF MEANING AND LEVELS OF ANALYSIS

Type of meaning	Focal questions (examples)
Compositional (Syntactic level)	What constitutes the whole video text under analysis? How do you know what is and what is not a part of it? What is the most salient visual/auditory element? Which parts are related together? Which parts are separated? How are parts related together?
Representational (Semantic level)	What recognizable actors or participants in actions and relationships are presented? Persons? Concrete things? Abstract ideas, qualities? What relationships are presented among these participants? In what common or shared action, event, happening are they presented? What are le locations, settings, causes of, temporal location of, these relationships, actions, and events? How are actions, events synchronized or sequenced in time? What logical, rhetorical relationship among actions, are presented? What emotions are described? How emotions evolve over time? What values drive the story?
Interpersonal (Pragmatic level)	Who is the intended viewer/receiver of this video text? What internal features index anticipated qualities of the receiver? What qualities of the sender/author of the video are indexed by internal features? How does the video position the sender relative to the receiver? In a relation of power? Dominance? Intimacy? Formality? What does the video request or demand of the receiver? How? How does the video index the stance of the sender (or any voice it projects) toward the text itself? Toward the receiver? Toward its own representational content?

IV. THE META-MODEL

We propose an informal conceptualization - a meta-model not yet a formal ontology - that provides a core set of basic descriptors that can be used to perform a semiotic annotation according to the above requirements. It has been organized into four main related modules (called boxes): the text, discourse, story, and agent boxes. Figure 3 (left) shows a conceptual schema of the modules and their inter-relationships. In this schema, and in the following ones, we use different graphical representations (i.e., types of arrows) to denote three main relationships: hyponymic (i.e., *sub-class-of* relation), meronymic (i.e., *part-of* relation) and generic etherarchical (e.g., associative) relationships between core concepts.

A. The Text Model

By Text we mean a concrete manifestation of a narrative, i.e., a complex fabric of signs belonging to different semiotic modalities (e.g., moving images, sounds, written words) and conveying narrative content to the user's interpretation.

The text model is a key issue of our conceptualization since it relates *content* with *expression*, according to the schema reported in Figure 3 (right). A Text has a T-Structure composed by T-Segments and relations (T-SegmentRel). Segments have been classified into several classes following MPEG-7 [29]. Relations include spatial and temporal relationships as described by Allen [67] and Galton [68].

A text segment is linked to a discourse segment representing its content and points to a set of sensory qualities and quality relations representing its expression. As sketched in Figure 4 (left), we distinguish between tonal - static, persistent - and rhythmic - dynamic, transient - qualities. Qualities may have associated facets and quantity spaces, i.e., domains of possible values. Color, for example, has hue, saturation and lightness as facets, and values in YCbCr or RGB color spaces. Sensorial qualities can be related together by several kinds of relationships such as contrast, affinity, and completion producing higher aesthetic effects such as salience, separation, connection, balance,

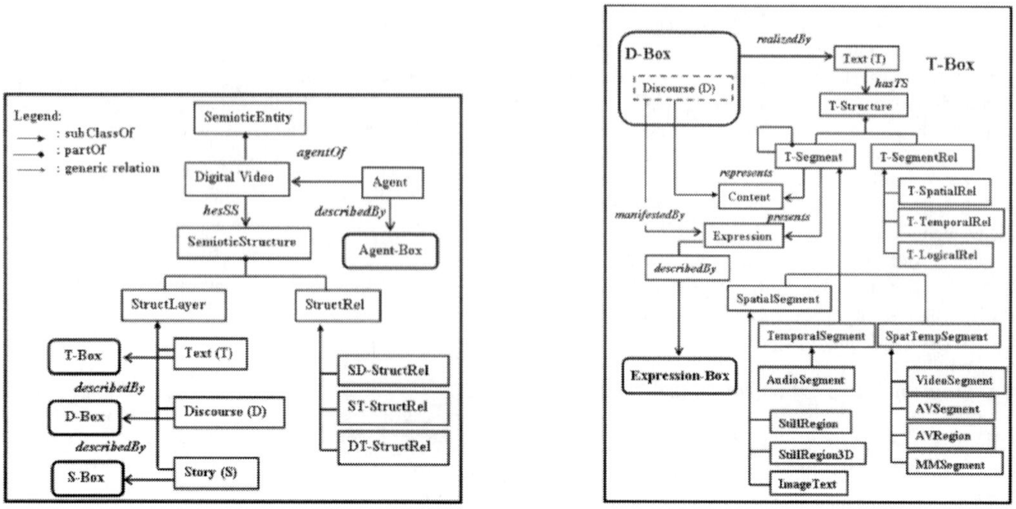

Figure 3. An overview of the proposed meta-model (left); the Text module (right).

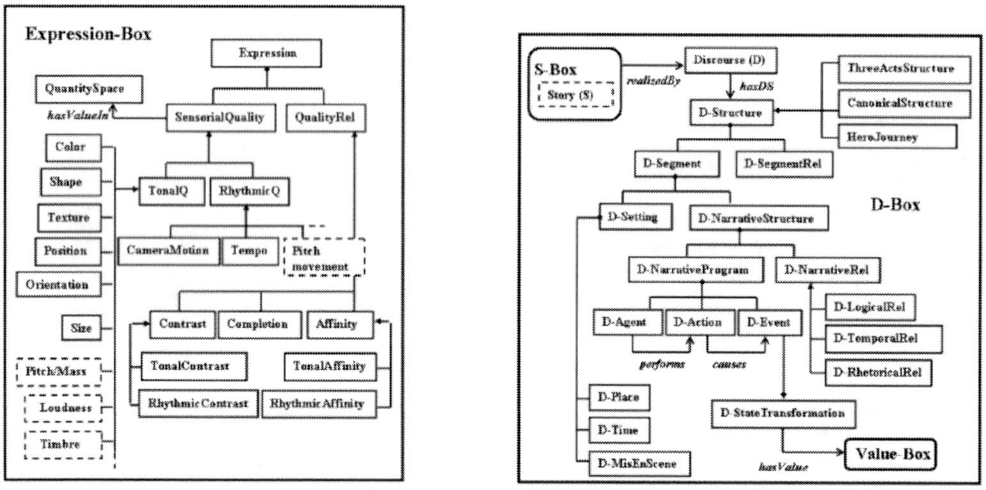

Figure 4. Expression (left) and Discourse (right) modules.

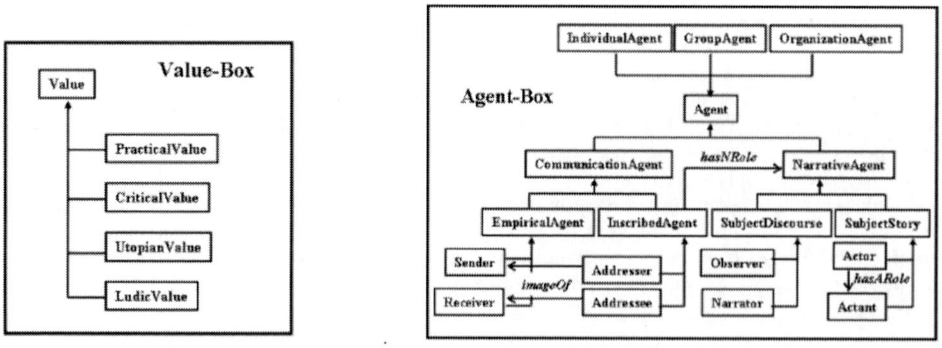

Figure 5. Value module (left) and Agent module (right).

symmetry, order, complexity or affective states (e.g., emotions, feelings, mood or atmospheres).

From an experiential point of view, the text module is intended to capture the sensorial experience the user has when viewing/hearing a narrative video. This experience is strongly related to the visual and auditory qualities of semiotic materials. Plastic forms, in particular, represent an autonomous level of signification of the video that can be used to make sense [58].

B. The Discourse Model

Discourse (also "syuzhet") represents the content of a narrative, i.e., *what* is narrated by the text (e.g., the events of a story) and *how* it has been done (e.g., plot, rhetorical structure, stylistic choices). As shown in Figure 4 (right), a Discourse has a D-Structure composed of D-Segments and relations (D-SegmentRel). A D-Segment consists of D-Setting and D-NarrativeStructure, the former specifying place, time and mis-en-scene; the latter specifying a structured set of narrative programs. A *narrative program* is defined in terms of D-Agent performing a D-Action and causing a D-Event intended here as a kind of state transformation. Narrative programs are related by logical, temporal or rhetorical relationships [69]. The concept of narrative program is a key concept of the proposed conceptualization. It is borrowed from Greimas [52][61]. It allows the annotator to represent "who does what": how actions are distributed among agents (see Figure 5, right) as well as the effects produced by the actions be they external physical changes, or internal cognitive, or affective transformations of subjects. As an instance, the effect of an action can be the acquisition or loss of a concrete object or person or of a more abstract entity such as freedom, knowledge, happiness. In any case, transformations can be interpreted as conjunction or disjunction processes of a subject with an object charged with values (object of value). Values have been classified according to Floch [55] into four classes namely, practical, critical, utopian and ludic values (Figure 5, left). Practical values refer to utility, usefulness; critical values to convenience, performance, quality; utopian values to identity, reflection, social relations, and ludic values to surprise, madness, astonishment, irony and pleasure including aesthetic pleasure. The selection of specific values in the construction of the story allows the author to realize specific marketing strategies. The discourse model is flexible enough for allowing the modeler to represent single actions, aggregates of actions occurring simultaneously or in sequence, and aggregates of aggregates (an entire story). Actions may be performed by the same agent or by different agents; they may occur in the same setting or in different settings. For narrative texts, several discourse structures have been proposed in literature such as [62][63]. Each of them decomposes a story in phases that are bounded by specific kinds of events and imposes a set of specific constraints on the narrative structures constituting each phase. As an instance, each dramatic arc of a Dramatic Arc model is strictly related to specific rhetorical relationships as discussed in [70]. Further constraints exist between discourse and text. Major events of a dramatic discourse structure such as the inciting incident, climax, resolution, etc. should be expressed, at the textual level, by appropriate sensorial qualities. Dramatic tension evolution as well as affective events (i.e., internal state transformations of main characters) should be sensed first, through appropriate visual images or melodic contour, then conceptualized. This imposes an internal coherence between narrative content and expression that is at the core of the semantic ladder we want to establish between different forms of meaning articulation.

From an experiential point of view, discourse is intended to capture cognitive and affective aspects of the interaction. This experience is strongly related to figurative features, narrative structures and their spatial and temporal configuration. Figurative forms (formants), in particular, represent another level of signification of the video that is superimposed to plastic qualities [58].

C. The Story Model

Most of the literature [71] understands "story" (also "fabula" or "histoire") to be the events that constitute the content of a narrative. Since the story is embedded within discourse we do not specify a new model for it but use the conceptualization provided by MPEG-7 with minimal variations [29]. This conceptualization represents basic components of stories namely, existents (Object DS, AgentObject DS), events (Event DS), abstract concepts and states (Concept DS, SemanticState Ds), and settings (SemanticPlace DS, SemanticTime DS).

D. The Agent Model

The agent model takes inspiration from Enunciation Theory [64]. This theory suggests that every communicative artifact contains, inscribed within it, an image or simulacrum (i.e., a constructed representation) of the actual sender and receiver. These images are called the *addresser* and *addressee* respectively. They are embodied in the artifact in the sense that they are analytically available to the critic by means of a close analysis of the artifact itself.

The agent model is aimed at representing the addresser e addressee and their relationships with the subjects of the story and discourse as they are prefigured by the product. More specifically, agents - individuals, groups or organizations - have been classified into two main classes: communication agents and narrative agents (see Figure 5, right). The former class includes the actual sender/receiver (called empirical agents) and their simulacra, the addresser and the addressee. The latter comprises the subjects of the story (e.g., actors and actants) and the subjects of discourse (e.g., observers and narrators). An *observer* is an agent responsible for physical focalization. It establishes the spatial position of the viewer with respect to the story world, for example, by selecting, at the expressive level, specific shot sizes, camera angles, lighting conditions. A *narrator* is an agent responsible for the cognitive and affective focalization. Actually, the viewer/spectator is invited not only to perceive what is told by the video from a spatial position but, more importantly, to interpret what is happening from a specific conceptual point of view (cognitive perspective taking) and to emphasize with some characters of the story (i.e., to understand and share their perceptual, cognitive, and affective status). Notice, that the D-Agent concept belonging to the discourse box can be equated to the NarrativeAgent of the Agent-Box (e.g., to an Actor or Narrator) thus realizing a connection between these two conceptualizations. The agent box is intended to capture relational experience, that is, possible relationships (e.g., social distance, power relationships, engagement) between the sender/receiver of the advertising message and narrative/discourse agents arising from their images within the text. As an instance, a company (a sender) may be associated with a visual or auditory segment that represents the company visual or auditory logo within the text. The logo plays the role of the addresser. An actor of the story may represent the user (addressee) playing a specific actantial role (e.g., the hero of the story). An observer may adopt the physical position of an actor of the story thus showing the story world through the eyes of that actor. Analogously, an actor may be associated with a narrator (a storyteller) and so forth. The "distance" between the actual receiver (the viewer) and the actors of the story is a function of two main factors: i) the distance existing between the receiver and the observer, and ii) the distance between the observer and the actors. The former can be reduced, for example, by letting the viewer play the role of an observer, i.e., by giving him/her the control of the camera such as in interactive videos; the latter by letting the observer represents the story world and events from the vantage point of an actor of the story. Seeing events from the point of view of a story's character makes the viewer aware of the character's perspective and his or her interpretation of events, and moreover, of the character's motives in relation to events and other characters. By adopting a character's perspective the viewer can understand and relive the character's emotions. This is essentially empathy, a viewer's mirroring of a character's emotional experience. Relational experience is strongly related to processes of narrative engagement such as cognitive perspective taking, empathy, presence, flow, and involvement [11]. Narrative experiences that are more engaging should result in more enjoyment, i.e., fun and pleasure. Therefore, it is important to represent these features in order to be able to compare products and evaluate their respective hedonic effectiveness.

V. The Case Study

We illustrate an example of manual annotation of a narrative commercial video clip. The aim is evaluating the feasibility of semiotic analysis and annotation. To this end, we start by illustrating the annotation tool we have chosen, then the procedure we followed and obtained results.

A. The annotation tool

A critical comparison of annotation tools has been presented in [72]. Among them, the EUDICO Linguistic Annotator (ELAN) shows several advantages including its relatively shallow learning curve and user-friendly interface [73].

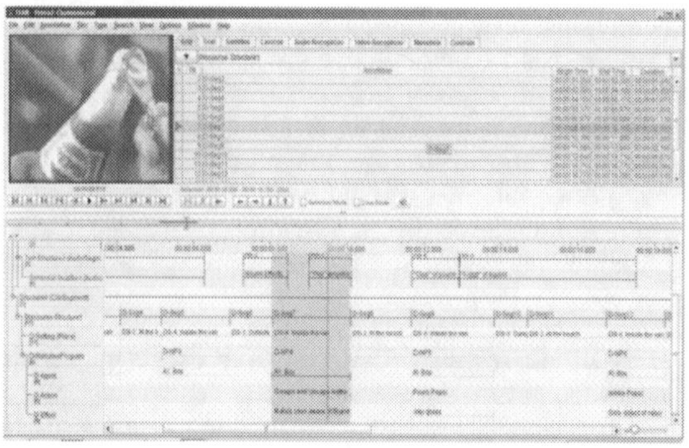

Figure 6. A screenshot of the ELAN annotation tool.

Figure 6 shows a screen shot of the ELAN interface. Annotations in ELAN can be grouped into multiple layers (called tiers) that are part of tier hierarchies. Annotation values are Unicode characters, and the annotation document is saved in an XML format based on the ELAN XML Schema. The tool can be easily connected with the *Praat* software for the analysis of the audio component of the video in the temporal and spectral domains [74].

ELAN allows the annotator to define a vocabulary of descriptors at the beginning of the process; a more recent version of the environment, called ONTO-ELAN, is capable of importing an ontology to be used in the analysis and annotation [75]. A limitation of the tool is that is not possible to annotate single regions within frames.

B. Annotation of a Pepsi Cola clip

The clip produced in the late 1980's is based on the body copy "Pepsi Cola. The choice of a new generation". It lasts 29.4 s at a frame rate of 30fps [76]. The story can be summarized as follows:

A delivery van of Pepsi–Cola reaches a crowded beach. The young driver gets out, opens the side door and switches an amplifier on; two loudspeakers emerge from the roof. The boy brings a bottle of Pepsi close to the microphone; uncaps it; pours the liquid into a glass and drinks emitting an "Ahhhh" of pleasure. People attracted by the puffing of gas and boy's expression rush to the van to quench their thirst (and buy the product!).

A characteristic of this clip that makes it a candidate for semiotic annotation is that it stages a narrative telling "the process itself of advertising and persuasion". The process includes three steps (see Figure 7): 1) insert the potential viewer into a familiar situation (the delivery van of the Pepsi Cola reaches the crowded beach); 2) draw viewer's attention on a positive, euphoric experience of consumption (loudspeakers attract people; the experience of the boy drinking Pepsi is communicated both visually and auditory); 3) activate into the viewer a desire to live a similar experience assuming a purchase behavior (people rush to the van to buy the Pepsi).

The procedure followed for the analysis and annotation of the clip consists of the following basic stages:

Stage-0. *Annotation of the whole video with its genre and purpose.* The whole clip is represented by an alignable annotation tier linked to a single segment (ClipSegment) representing the root of a hierarchical multi-tiers decomposition. Alignable tiers in ELAN are directly linked to the time axis of the audio-visual and can be further segmented. This tier is annotated with the multimedia genre (video commercial) and intention/purpose: "To advertise Pepsi Cola; to represent a persuasive process".

Stage-1. *Textual decomposition of the video: identification of the visual and auditory textual structures in terms of audio and video segments and their relationships.* The ClipSegment is represented by several text structures (T-Structure): some of them are associated to the visual modality, others to the aural one. A structure (T-Structure1) decomposes the ClipSegment into a sequence of T-Segments representing individual visual shots. A further text structure (T-Structure2) annotates special transitional effects/edits like fades, dissolves, overlayed text. Another structure (T-Structure3) decomposes the ClipSegment based on continuous sequences (T-Segments) of homogeneous sound objects (called Audio Segments, AS). The sequences include silence, speech, environmental sound, and effects. In more complex cases it may be necessary to devote a separate text structure to each constituent of a complex audio sandwich. Notice how the sonic effect "Frzzzz" of the liquid while the boy uncaps the bottle covers several adjacent shots of the video, i.e., the two structures are not aligned in time.

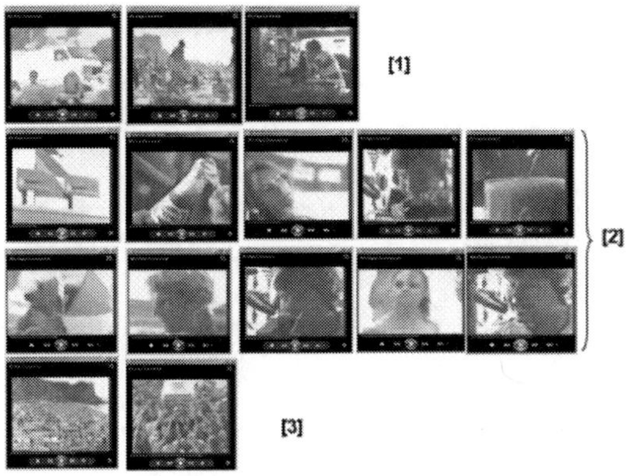

Figure 7. Main steps of the process of advertising and persuasion: 1) insert the viewer into a familiar situation; 2) draw attention on a euphoric experience of consumption; 3) activate a purchase behavior.

Stage-2. *Textual annotation: association of expressive descriptors to the structures found in the previous stage.* During this stage, a set of referring annotation tiers are introduced and associated to previous visual and aural structures to annotate single shots, transitions, and sound objects with tonal and rhythmic sensorial qualities according to the conceptualization shown in Figure 4 (left).

Stage-3. *Discoursive decomposition of the video: identification of the discourse structure of the video in terms of discourse segments and their relationships.* The ClipSegment is represented by one or more discourse structures (D-Structure), based on scene analysis. A scene (D-Segment) is defined as a - not necessarily continuous - sequence of frames representing a narrative situation characterized by a stable setting (i.e., place, time and mise-en-scene). In the case under consideration, we use a single discourse structure (D-Structure1), which is decomposed into 17 D-Segments. Scene boundaries correspond to changes in settings from outside to inside the Pepsi Cola van and vice-versa.

Stage-4. *Narrative segmentation: each discourse segment is further analyzed in terms of a setting and a narrative structure.* Each scene (D-Segment) is annotated by a narrative structure composed of narrative programs and their logical and temporal relationships.

Stage-5. *Annotation of narrative programs.* A set of referring annotation tiers are introduced and associated with previous narrative structures to annotate single narrative programs. For each narrative program, a set of tiers is used to separately describe the main components of the program namely the actor, the action, and the event. The event is further elaborated in terms of state transformation and value. In the example under consideration, D-Segment7 and D-Segment9 (a scene inside the van) is annotated by a narrative structure composed by the temporal sequence of two narrative programs. The first program (D-NP4) refers to the boy (D-Agent) grasping the bottle of Pepsi (D-Action) thus making the user aware of the brand (D-Event). The second narrative program (D-NP5) refers again to the boy (D-Agent) who uncaps the bottle and pours drinks content (D-Action) thus getting the object of value, i.e., the product (D-Event).

Stage-6. *Relational analysis and annotation.* The root segment (ClipSegment) is analyzed in order to identify the markers of addresser and addressee. In the Pepsi Cola clip, the bottle including logo and trademark represents the addresser (i.e., the brand Pepsi Cola). The boy and the people approaching the van represent the addressee. Three types of relationships are shown: i) between the viewer (represented by the boy) and the product/brand ii) between the viewer (represented by people in the beach) and the boy that is consuming the product and iii) between the viewer (represented by the real user) and the people on the beach who are experiencing a growing desire to drink a Pepsi. A set of further tiers have been introduced and linked to the

ClipSegment to implicitly represent relational analysis by annotating actors' gazes, kind of shot, vertical and horizontal camera angle. As already said, these features are related to engagement, social distance, power and involvement relationships, respectively [65]. In the same way, the tone of voice in speech, sound perspective, volume, can be used to represent various degrees of intimacy or distance between the characters of the story (and indirectly the brand) and the user.

Several temporal relationships among annotations belonging to different tiers are implicitly described through the relations existing between their corresponding tiers. As an instance, all referring tiers associated with the same alignable tier inherit its time decomposition. As a consequence, their annotations are automatically time aligned. Figure 8 summarizes the resulting decomposition and annotation structures. The figure also shows the articulation of meaning across the various tiers of the annotation hierarchy. Compositional meaning is represented by the decomposition of the video in terms of shots and sound objects and their associated visual and auditory qualities. Representational meaning is represented by scenes and their associated narrative structures (i.e., settings, narrative programs, relationships between narrative programs). Finally, interpersonal meaning is represented by relational annotations (e.g., social distance, engagement, simulacra) associated to video shots.

VI. Discussion

In this section we view semiotic annotation in a broader context by relating it to research work made within Research through Design (RtD) [77][78], Philosophy of Technology [79] and Interface and Interaction Criticism [80][81][82][83]. The aim is to highlight connections with these fields and potential contributions.

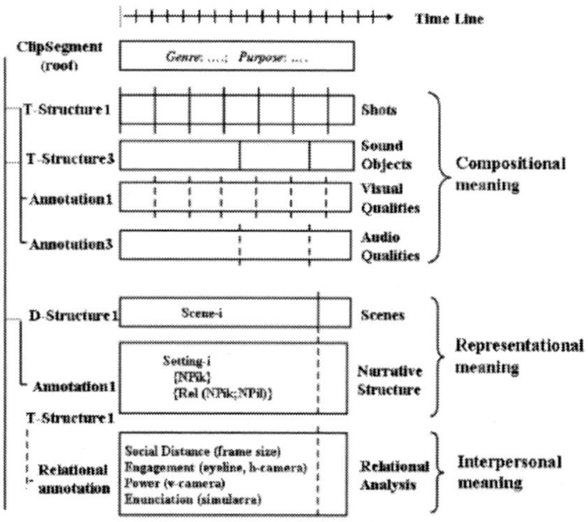

Figure 8. The hierarchy of decomposition tiers used in the Pepsi Cola example and their associated meanings.

A. Semiotic annotation and design knowledge

Semiotic annotation represents a kind of *intermediate level knowledge* [84] (see Figure 9). It is *in-between* the annotated object (the video) and a conceptualization of the object (the meta-model or ontology of the video). On the one hand, the annotation, using the concepts of the meta-model as descriptors $\{d_{ij}\}$, explicates the conceptual model adopted by the designer and, indirectly, the aspects that are implicitly deemed important and relevant for the design of that artifact according to that meta-model. On the other hand, the annotation, by indexing specific parts of the concrete artifact, shows how the descriptors - and thus the concepts of the meta-model - have been instantiated $\{v_{ij}\}$ in *that* particular artifact. As a consequence, the annotation reveals the specific point in the *design space* (i.e., the space of all possible alternative instantiations associated to the adopted conceptualization) occupied by that artifact $\{(d_{ij}=v_{ij})\}$. In this sense, we can say that the design knowledge embedded in the video is unfolded by the annotation that can be seen as a particular type of interpretation of the object made according to a meta-model (e.g., an ontology) of the object itself.

The availability of design knowledge provides several benefits for the designers and the users as well. It allows explaining the way a specific video works from a communicative point of view: how meaning is constructed - in *that* video - by the interplay of several elements located at different levels of the means-end semiotic ladder. For designers, in particular, the annotation affords extraction of design knowledge in order to reuse it, evaluate its internal coherence or take inspiration from it in developing new products.

They can exploit the annotation to compare two or more videos during the phase of competing analysis in order to understand *why* they are designed the way they are and *how* they differ from one to another. They may search for redundancies and variations; or aggregate videos on the base of similarities in the way they function (i.e., how they instantiate the meta-model) with the goal of constructing

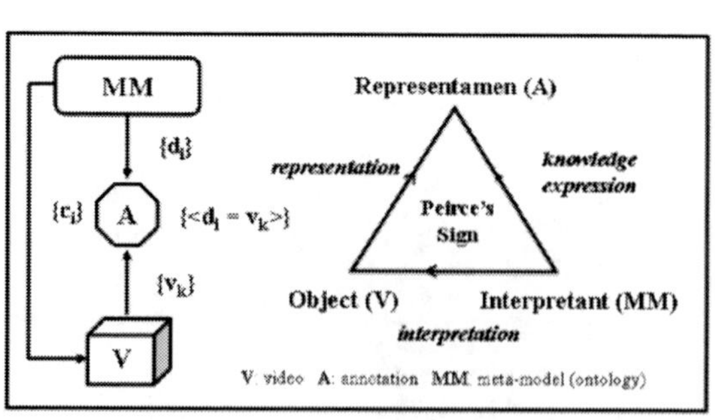

Figure 9. Annotation A is in-between the video V and the metamodel MM. The metamodel provides concepts {ci} and descriptors {di} for interpretation and annotation. The video provides specific values {vi} to instantiate descriptors. The model echoes Peirce's concept of sign [38].

portfolios [85]. Consider, as an instance, the following production scenario.

Scenario-1. Samantha is a video producer. She has to design and develop a narrative video commercial for a client. The main requirement is that the video advertises a new line of products and communicates the core set of values that constitute the brand identity of the client's firm in a way that is innovative with respect to the videos of previous ad campaigns. Different issues are involved in this kind of design problem. First, Samantha has to know what does it means to design a narrative text and the various ways a product can be included in a narrative (e.g., as a prop in the setting, as the main character of the story, as an helper/instrument that can be used to achieve some abstract object of value or as the object of value by itself). Second, she must be able to understand how existing videos communicate the brand identity through their expressive and narrative features. More specifically, how values have been inscribed into the videos. To address these issues it is important to make explicit the brand design language used in the various products.

Therefore, Samantha downloads from the company net the videos belonging to previous campaigns and analyses their associated semiotic annotations in order to understand how meanings have been articulated and distributed across the various semantic layers constituting the artifacts. In particular, she wants to identify which design variables have been consistently used to communicate brand personality and values in the various products under analysis. Therefore, she compares the annotations searching for similarities and differences. This comparison is inspirational. Samantha discovers that brand values have been mainly communicated by the audio tracks, e.g., by a leitmotif that recurs in all the videos with different orchestrations and sound design [13]. So she decides to design a new video where the same values are communicated by images (story) instead of by the music.

In this scenario, semiotic annotation has been exploited to generate insights particularly useful for addressing a design problem.

Semiotic annotation can be useful also for generic users in order to make more informed choices, i.e., to better understand if a product is adequate with respect to their values, needs, desires, preferences. Moreover, the annotation can be an auxiliary to educate to critical analysis and evaluation, contributing to cultivate/enhance users' perceptual sensitivity (making people better at learning to see and hear) and interpretative skills. Consider the following use scenario

Scenario-2. George teaches a course of Multimedia Design at his University. During his lectures, he exemplifies theoretical claims using existing videos. The search and selection of appropriate videos is a difficult and demanding task since they must be carefully analyzed before the lectures in order to understand if they are (or not) suitable to the intended ends. Again design knowledge could be very useful to understand how they function, and why they function in the way they do. The next lecture will be devoted to introduce and discuss various types of narrative structures. So George exploits semiotic annotation to search the web for commercial videos that represent an instance of the Hero's Journey or Greimas' canonical model. The annotation is then used to select the segments of the video that represent specific phases of each considered model to be shown to the students. A critical discussion is then started to assess the degree of fit among the visual and auditory modalities and their coherence with respect to the representational, interpersonal and compositional meanings expressed by each segment.

In this scenario, semiotic annotation has been exploited to search for appropriate videos with respect to their discursive structure and to support discussion and critical judgments. Students can, therefore, improve their understanding and interpretative skills. At the end, they can be helped to better master their craft in designing mediated experiences.

B. *Semiotic annotation and technological mediation*

An important concept arising from the field of Philosophy of Technology is *technological mediation*. As claimed by Verbeek in [86] the use of a particular technology or artifact affects the relation between the user and the world in two ways: by a process of transformation of perception of the world (*mediation of perception*) and by transforming the user's praxis or action in the world (*mediation of action*). The effect of mediation of perception is realized by an amplification or reduction of the experienced aspects of reality while the effect of mediation of action is realized towards an invitation or inhibition to perform certain actions instead of others.

Although all artifacts involved in the semiotic annotation (i.e., the meta-model/ontology, the video and the annotation itself) exert some kind of technological mediation, we are interested, here, in the role played by the ontology.

The ontology realizes a mediation of perception process toward its conceptualization and axioms. The conceptualization brings some aspects of the world into sharp focus at the expense of blurring other aspects. It invites the user to look at the reality through a specific type of glasses that amplify or reduce some experienced aspects of the domain of application. The mediation of action is strictly linked to the ontology's competence questions since they specify the functional aspects of the ontology: its scope, and possible uses. In other words, the ontology invites the user to enquire reality by making certain queries instead of others. As an instance, viewing (and conceptualizing) a video at the computer level as a technological artifact (e.g., a set of digital resources and execution programs; a functional tool) is different from viewing it (also) at the cultural level as a semiotic text (e.g., a cultural interface, a work of rhetoric or a mediator of experience). In the second case, a set of complex aspects related to meaning, ethics, etc. emerge that are usually ignored at the computer level. As an instance, if the artifact is a tool, ethics is irrelevant since the ethical agency is situated in the user. If ontologies can affect people's behavior and relationship with the outside world, the design or adoption of an existing ontology is an ethic activity and ontology itself is a materialization of values and ethical choices [87].

When ontologies are pushed into artifacts or are embedded in working environments/applications as meta-models they shape them and guide, in this way, the user's experience and expectations. Their mediation effect is thus indirect; it occurs through the artifact in which the ontology is embedded and merges with the mediation effect of the artifact itself. The mediation effect is usually made transparent (i.e., not visible) during use. Transparency of the meta-model during video use is important since it enhances the possibility of uncritical and intense processing that is at the base of transportation effect and narrative persuasion. However, recent studies in the field of Philosophy of Technology and Persuasive Design claim that mediation effects should be made opaque and comprehensible to users [88][89]. A semiotic annotation may support this claim by unfolding contextual information that is information *around* the video (e.g., purpose, assumptions, articulation of meanings, and intended effects). By separating the narrative (video) from the information about how the narrative has been constructed (the annotation) we are able to guarantee both ease of use (transparency of use) and control of mediation effects (opacity of context) that is a kind of semi-opacity of the video artifact. This is useful for the user in order to better understand how the video has been designed to satisfy the author's intended goals, why it functions as it does, what rhetorical mechanisms are at the base of its persuasive and informative functioning, what sort of culture it will encourage or resist. In this way, semiotic annotation may contribute to the diffusion of a critical attitude toward video commercials (and audio-visual products in general) and a greater awareness of the social effects this kind of products may produce. This opens to the last issue we wish to address.

C. *Semiotic annotation and criticism*

Criticism refers to "an expert of a given domain's informed exercise of judgment" [82]. Semiotic annotation has much to offer to the discipline of interface and interaction criticism [80][81]. Quoting Bardzell [81]: "[by Interaction Criticism] we mean rigorous interpretive analysis that explicates how elements of the interface, through their relationships to each other, produce certain meanings, affects, moods, and intuitions in people that interact with them". Then Bardzell moves into the nature of the concept "rigorous": "...we say rigorous to stress that interaction criticism, like the best film and literary criticism transcends anything-goes subjectivism and offers instead systematic, evidence-based analyses of subjective phenomena ..."

It should be evident from the above citation that semiotic analysis and annotation converges and largely overlaps with the notion of criticism [83].

Another issue that is strictly correlated with criticism, concerns the "value" of an artifact intended, here, not in economic terms (e.g., exchange value, use value) but more specifically, as a quality of the artifact that concerns its "inner logic" or the "human good" as discussed by recent theories about aesthetics [90] or cultural quality of new media [91]. We suggest that the annotation can change the value of an artifact. To support this claim we will draw on Danto's concept of *transfiguration* in his Aesthetic Theory [92]. As it is known, the issue Danto wants to address is the relationships between art and reality. In particular, the problem can be stated as follows: how can it happen that two objects that are phenomenologically indistinguishable - e.g., the Brillo Box artwork by Andy Warhol at MoMA and a similar object, the Brillo box containing soap pads at the supermarket - have so different values. The answer provided by Danto is that an object can change its value by means of a transfiguration process that is a particular kind of interpretation - called artistic interpretation - made in a context or atmosphere of art theory (the Art World). The interpretation does not change the physical appearance of the object but its ontological status: it changes the object into a work of art.

We can try to apply these concepts to annotated videos. Here the video is the object and the annotation is a semiotic interpretation playing the role of transfiguration. The interpretation is based on a theoretical background, the ontology that can be mapped to Danto's atmosphere of theory (the context). In our case, the informal ontology illustrated in Section IV takes inspiration from several semiotic theories (e.g., visual semiotics, enunciation theory, narrative semiotics, and social semiotics) as discussed beforehand. These theories provide a theoretical scaffolding for the ontology and the annotation as well. The video *with* the annotation has a value greater than the video alone because the annotation provides a surplus of information that can be used to interpret and understand the video, that is, to attribute some meanings that are not empirically available from the video alone. The value of the video is thus embodied in the product but it is external to it (i.e., it is in the interpretation materialized by the annotation) and cannot be captured by only looking at the tangible object. As a consequence, the semiotic annotation should be considered as a constitutive part of the video. They are strictly correlated and mutually informing: the annotation "illuminates" the artifact giving it value; the artifact provides the ground for and exemplifies the annotation [93].

What is interesting in Danto's theory is that the value is linked to interpretation: not a generic interpretation, however, but a theoretically grounded one. Moreover, Danto, stresses the fact that the interpretation must be *appropriate* to the formal and material characteristics of the objects. In other words, the meanings must be embodied in the form and materiality of the object. The modality of this embodiment affects the quality of the artifact. So, for example, the internal coherence is a kind of inner logic and a dimension of quality because it refers to how meanings are distributed among semiotic materials and how they fit together. This discussion opens up interesting research perspectives and poses critical problems to automatic annotation. If the value rests in an appropriate interpretation then it cannot be captured by automatic procedures that refer only to existence, i.e., to tangible and empirical features. It must be provided by some human. It is not strictly necessary that the interpretation is the designer's one; obviously, the designer is in a privileged position to provide this kind of knowledge since she is the main source of design choices. However, we can envisage other possibilities - and associated annotations - such as the exploitation of multimedia critics, semioticians, exhibition curators, and commentators. If the interpretation is not the designer's one, it should be, at least, an interpretation that the designers would consider as a possible one. Other important sources of information are represented by the script and the storyboard of the narrative.

VII. CONCLUSIONS

In this paper, we have presented an annotation method for narrative videos, along with a worked-out case study in the field of advertising and brand communication.

The standpoint is that of video production. We are interested in how purpose and meanings are intentionally constructed and articulated during the premeditate and message construction phases; how they are inscribed within the artifact and materialized through semiotic resources; how these meanings can be used to annotate the video for content retrieval, filtering, and content reuse.

The annotation method exploits a semiotic meta-model (an informal ontology) of the video genre. The meta-model articulates the semantic content of the video according to a set of interrelated layers each addressing a specific kind of meaning: structural decomposition, visual and auditory expression, narrative content (i.e., discourse and story), values and interpersonal relationships. A core conceptualization has been provided to represent each layer as well as the relationships existing among layers in a domain-independent way. These relationships are responsible for the global unity and consistency of the artifact. They form a semiotic ladder covering the conceptual gap existing between the shallow and concrete audio-visual qualities and the deep and abstract constructs related to discourse, story, and axiological values.

We highlight some features of the meta-model that on the base of our actual knowledge seem novel. First, the meta-model exhibits a strong separation of concerns that results in a modular conceptual architecture. However, what is important are the links existing between the various conceptualizations since these links are at the base of the articulation of meaning inside the product and of its internal coherence. They reflect design knowledge. Second, the introduction of a discourse model allows the annotator to explicitly aggregate basic story elements in a meaningful way in order to reflect important aspects of narrative products such as their rhetorical and dramaturgical structures that are ignored by traditional metadata standards. Moreover, the use of the concept of narrative program as the building block of discourse forces the annotator to focus simultaneously on several interrelated concepts - such as agent, action, state transition (event), object of value - that are strictly related to narrativity. Third, the introduction of a rich classification of agents inspired by Enunciation Theory provides the vocabulary for describing various roles involved in the development, communication, and use of an audio-visual product as well as their interrelationships.

The role of the meta-model is to guide the annotator during semiotic analysis by focusing her attention on specific features and relationships. Furthermore, it provides the vocabulary and concepts used as descriptors during the annotation process. Semiotic annotation is different from pure keyword or concept annotation. The task is not simply to attach subjective comments, notes, pre-existing opinions or remarks to audio-visual segments but to unfold the generative process of sense-making inscribed within the product.

We have briefly discussed the potential contribution of this kind of annotation for research in the fields of Research Through Design and Technology Mediation. The annotation, by unfolding the design knowledge inscribed within the product, is proposed as a viable means for communicating design thinking in a descriptive yet generative and inspirational fashion. It supports moving from theory/ideal (the meta-model) and practice/concrete (the artifact) and vice versa. Moreover, it makes visible the design decisions that were taken during the construction of the message opening the door to the assessment of technological mediation. This prompts designers and users to put particular attention to this issue.

Much of the job of semiotic annotation resonates with criticism. At the heart of criticism is the attempt to explain abstract meanings and impressions by referring to the properties and forms of the artifact or the way the artifact has been produced. This is the case, for example, of past research in computational media aesthetics [94] where film grammar (i.e., cinematic techniques used during production) is used to explain high order qualities of video resources such as, for example, rhythm and pace or tempo. Our approach is different in two main aspects. First, we use a semiotic model of the video genre to guide analysis and annotation. Second, while in computational media aesthetics design and production knowledge remains hidden in the algorithm for the analysis and annotation, in our proposal design knowledge is explicated in the annotation itself with the benefits we have already explained.

Semiotic annotation is inevitably complex if we try to capture the whole articulation and richness of intended meanings inscribed within a communicative artifact. Doing it well requires expertise. Automatic tools can be used to support low-level analysis of expressive qualities such as shot detection, dominant color identification, spectro-morphological analysis of sound objects, basic video statistics, etc. However, for the more abstract levels, the human intervention is still needed. We do not claim or expect that the average video producer will be able to follow the procedure without prior training. To what extent semiotic annotations can be replicated? If two or more analysts use the meta-model described in Section IV to annotate the same product are their results consistent? This is an important issue that requires further research.

Manual annotation is time-consuming but the case study we have worked out and our past experience with students showed that, for video commercials, it is a feasible approach due to the limited time extension of these kinds of products. The effort, in this case, is largely rewarded by the benefits connected with the unfolding of new design knowledge as discussed beforehand. Moreover, it should be noted that completeness of analysis is not always necessary. In many cases, only those segments of a video artifact that are deemed interesting and relevant for the purpose of the analysis are annotated. For longer texts such as films and documentaries, the manual approach is surely unfeasible without appropriate supporting tools. This is a direction of possible future research work, together with the construction of a formal ontology based on the proposed meta-model and its integration with existing top-level ontologies such as the OIO design pattern and DOLCE.

Semiotic annotation can be very useful during product use in order to compare actual interpretations with the intended interpretation embodied in the artifact. Intended meanings (or experience) is the golden standard in order to evaluate the effectiveness of communication. Moreover, the means/ends structure of the annotation can be exploited to make a kind of "communication diagnosis", i.e., to link symptoms (e.g., discrepancies between a user's interpretation and the author's intended meaning) with possible causes (e.g., the structural segments of the video that could be responsible for the observed symptoms). This is another future direction of research.

A final remark regards the scope of applicability of semiotic annotation. Although semiotic theories can be fruitfully applied for the analysis of a wide range of genres of texts (and recently to physical artifacts as well) we consider persuasive discourses (such as video commercials, advertising images, learning objects and advergames) the most interesting fields of application. Quoting De Sousa: " ... semiotic methods are often looked upon with skepticism and rarely taken into consideration regardless their usefulness to address interpretative analysis in a rigorous and systematic way..." [95]. We hope that this situation could change in the future and more semiotic aware models and tools could be proposed for a more effective content analysis and annotation. This research aims at being a step toward this end.

ACKNOWLEDGMENT

The authors thanks the reviewers for their constructive and thoughtful critiques.

REFERENCES

[1] E. Toppano, "Semiotic annotation of video commercials: why the artifact is the way it is?," Proc. WEB 2017: The Fifth International Conference on Building and Exploring Web Based Environments, IARIA, Barcelona, Spain, pp. 45-51, 2017.

[2] J. L. Aaker, "Dimensions of brand personality," Journal of Marketing Research, Vol. 34, No. 3, pp.347-356, 1997.

[3] F. R. Esch, "Brand identity: the guiding star for successful brands," in Schmitt, B.H., Rogers, D.L. (Editors). Handbook on Brand and Experience Management. Edward Elgar Publishing Limited, UK, Cheltenham, Chapter 4, pp. 58-76, 2008.

[4] B. H. Schmitt and D. L. Rogers, Handbook on Brand and Experience Mangement, Edward E. Northampton, MA, USA, 2008.

[5] IAB, "A digital video advertising overview," Interactive Advertising Bureau, 2008.

[6] IAB, "Digital video in-stream ad format guidelines," Interactive Advertising Bureau, 2016.

[7] J. Bruner, "Life as narrative," Social Research, Vol.71, No. 3, pp. 691-710, 2004.

[8] M. C. Green and T. C. Brock, "The role of transportation in the persuasiveness of public narratives," Journal of Personality and Social Psychology, Vol. 79, No. 5, pp. 701-721, 2000.

[9] H. Bilandzic and R. Busselle, "Narrative persuasion," in The SAGE Handbook of Persuasion, J. P. Dillard and L. Shen (Eds.), Sage Publications, Chapter 13, pp. 200-219, 2013.

[10] R. Busselle and H. Bilandzic, "Measuring narrative engagement," Media Psychology, 12, pp. 321-347, 2009.

[11] T. M. Karjalainen, "It looks like a Toyota: Educational approaches to designing for visual brand recognition," International Journal of Design, Vol.1, No.1, pp. 67-81. 2007.

[12] E. Toppano and A. Toppano, "Ethos, in sound design for brand advertisement," in Proc. ICMC|SMC, Athens, Greece, pp. 1685-1692, 2014.

[13] K. Krippendorff, "On the essential contexts of artifacts or on the proposition that design is making sense (of things)," in The Idea of Design, V. Margolin and R. Buchanan (Eds.), The MIT Press, pp. 156-184, 1995.

[14] E. T. Kazmierczak, "Design as meaning making: from making things to the design of thinking," Design Issues, Vol. 19, No. 2, pp. 45-59, 2003.

[15] R. Buchanan, "Declaration by design: rhetoric, argument, and demostration," Design Issues, Vol. 2, No. 1, pp. 4-22, 1985.

[16] P. Desmet and P. Hekkert, "Framework of product experience," International Journal of Design, Vol.1, No. 1, pp. 57-66, 2007.

[17] N. Crilly, A. Maier, and P.J. Clarkson, "Representing artifacts as media: modelling the relationship between designer intent and consumer experience," Journal of Design, Vol. 2, No.3, pp.15–27, 2008.

[18] R. Troncy, B. Huet, and S. Schenk, Multimedia Semantics, Metadata, Analysis and Interaction, Wiley, 2011.

[19] F. M. Nack, "Capture and transfer of metadata during video production," CWI Report INS-E0513, 2005.

[20] E. Toppano and V. Roberto, "Semiotic design and analysis of hypermedia," in Proc. 20th ACM Conference on Hypertext and Hypermedia, HT2009, Turin, Italy, 367-368, 2009.

[21] E. Toppano and V. Roberto, "Semiotic-based conceptual modelling of hypermedia," Proc. Image Analysis and Processing, ICIAP2013, Napoli, Italy, Lecture Notes in Computer Science, Vol. 8157, pp. 663-672, 2013.

[22] M. Agosti and N. Ferro, "A formal model of annotations of digital content," ACM Trans. on Information Systems, Vol. 26, No. 1, Article 3, 2007.

[23] A. Hanbury, "A survey of methods for image annotation," Journal of Visual Languages and Computing, Vol. 19, Issue 5, pp. 617-627, 2008.

[24] P. Andrews, I. Zaihrayeu, and J. Pane, "A Classification of semantic annotation systems," Journal of Semantic Web, Vol.3, Issue 3, IOS Press, pp. 223-248, 2012.

[25] E. Oren, K. H. Moller, S. Scerri, S. Handschuh, and M. Sintek, "What are semantic annotations," Technical Report, DERI, Galway, 2006.

[26] W3C, "Open annotation data model," Open Annotation Comunity Group, 2013.

[27] W3C, "Semantic Web," https://www.w3.org/standards/semanticweb/ Accessed: 11 Dec. 2017.

[28] J. M. Martinez, "MPEG-7 Overview," ISO/IEC JTC1/SC29/WG11 N6828, Palma de Mallorca, Spain, 2004.

[29] A. B. Benitez, J. M. Martinez, H. Rising, and P. Salembier, "Description of a single multimedia document," in Introduction to MPEG 7: Multimedia Content Description Language," B.S.Manjunath, P.Salembier, T.Sikora (Eds.), Wiley, pp.111-138, 2002.

[30] S. Dasiopoulou, V. Tzouvaras, I. Kompatsiaris, and M.G. Strintzis, "Enquiring MPEG-7 based multimedia ontologies," Journal of Multimedia Tools and Applications, Vol. 46, Issue 2-3, pp.331-370, 2010.

[31] R. Arnd, R. Troncy, S. Staab, and L. Hardman, "COMM: a core ontology for multimedia annotation," Handbook on Ontologies, Springer, Berlin, Heidelberg, pp. 403-421, 2009.

[32] M. Hausenblas, "Multimedia vocabularies on the Semantic Web," W3C Incubator Group Report, 2007.

[33] P. Schallauer, W. Bailer, R. Troncy, and F. Kaiser, "Multimedia Metadata Standards," in R. Troncy, B. Huet, and S. Schenk (Eds.), Multimedia Semantics, Metadata, Analysis and Interaction, Wiley, pp.129-144, 2011.

[34] L. Hardman, Z. Obrenovic, F. Nack., B. Kerherve B., and K. Piersol, "Canonical Processes of semantically annotated media production," Multimedia Systems, 14(6), 327-340, 2008.

[35] M.L. Ryan, "Narrativity and its modes as culture-transcending analytical categories", Japan Forum, 21(3), BAJS, pp. 307–323, 2009.

[36] S. Kinnebrock and H. Bilandzic, "How to make a story work: introducing the concept of narrativity into narrative persuasion," International Communication Association Conference, ICA-2006, Dresden, 2006. Retrieved from: http://publications.rwth-aachen.de/record/50885/files/3638.pdf Accessed: 11 Dec. 2017.

[37] F. de Saussure, Cours de linguistique generale, Payot, Paris, 1922.

[38] C. S. Peirce, Collected Writings, C. Hartshorne, P. Weiss, and A. W. Burks (Eds.), Harvard University Press, Cambridge, MA, 1931.

[39] T. van Leeuwen, Introducing Social Semiotics, London: Routledge, 2005.

[40] R. Eugeni, "Media experiences and practices of analysis. For a critical pragmatics of media," International Workshop "Practicing Theory", University of Amsterdam, March 2-4, 2011.

[41] C. S. de Souza, The Semiotic Engineering of Human-Computer Interaction, the MIT Press, Cambridge, MA, USA, 2004.

[42] S. Vihma, "Design semiotics- Institutional experiences and an initiative for a semiotic theory of form," in Design Research Now: Essays and Selected Projects, R. Michel (Ed.), pp. 219-232, 2007.

[43] C. Scolari, "Transmedia storytelling: implicit consumers, narrative worlds, and branding in contemporary media production", International Journal of Communication, Vol.3. pp. 586–606, 2009.

[44] T. Gruber, "A translation approach to portable ontology specification," Knowledge Acquisition, Vol. 5, No. 2, pp. 199-220, 1993.

[45] L. Manovich, The language of new media, Cambridge, MA: the MIT Press, 2001.

[46] S. Grimaldi, S. Fokkinga, and I. Ocnarescu, "Narratives in design: a study of the types, applications, and functions of narratives in design practice," in Proc. DPPI 2013, ACM NY, USA, pp. 201-210, 2013.

[47] M. Davis, " Knowledge representation for video," in, Proc. of Twelfth National Conference on Artificial Intelligence (AAAI-94), Seattle, Washington, AAAI Press, pp. 120-127, 1994.

[48] C. G. M. Snoek and M. Worring, "Multimodal video indexing: a review of the state-of-the-art," Multimedia Tools and Applications, Vol. 25, pp. 5-35, 2005.

[49] S. Pfeiffer, R. Lienhart, and W. Effelsberg, "Scene Determination based on video and audio features," Multimedia Tools and Applications, 15, pp.59-81, 2001.

[50] P. von Stackelberg, "Creating transmedia narratives: the structure and design of stories told across multiple media," Master's Thesis, State University of New York, 2011.

[51] V. Lombardo and R. Damiano, "Narrative annotation and editing of video," in Proc. ICIDS'10, Third Joint Conference on Interactive Digital Storytelling, pp.62-73, 2010.

[52] A.J. Greimas and P. Courtès, Semiotics and language. An analytical dictionary. Indiana University Press, Bloomington, IN, 1982.

[53] C. Bianchi, "Semiotic approaches to advertising texts and strategies: narrative, passion, marketing", Semiotica 183, 1/4, pp. 243-271, 2011.

[54] C. Colombo, A. Del Bimbo, and P. Pala, "Retrieval of commercials by semantic content: the semiotic perspective," Multimedia Tools and Applications13, pp. 93-118, 2001.

[55] J. M. Floch, Semiotics, Marketing, and Communication: Beneath the Signs, the Strategies, Palgrave, Hampshire, 2001.

[56] J. A. Bateman, "Towards a grande paradigmatique of film: Christian Metz reloaded," Semiotica, 167-1/4, pp. 13-64, 2007.

[57] C. Tseng, "Analysing characters' interactions in filmic texts: a functional semiotic approach," Social Semiotics, 23:5, pp. 587-605, 2013.

[58] A. J. Greimas, F. Collins, and P. Perron, "Figurative Semiotics and the Semiotics of the Plastic Arts," New Literary History, Vol.20, No. 3, pp. 627-649, 1989.

[59] D. Smalley, "Spectromorphology: explaining sound-shapes", Organized Sound, Vol.2, No.2, Cambridge University Press, pp.107-126, 1997.

[60] G. Kress and T. van Leeuwen, Reading images. The grammar of visual design. Routledge, New York, 2003.

[61] L. Hébert, Tools for text and Image analysis: An introduction to applied semiotics, Département de lettres Université du Québec à Rimouski, Version 3, 2011.

[62] J. Campbell, The hero with a thousand faces, New World Library, 2008.

[63] B. Rolfe, C. M. Jones, and H. Wallace, "Designing dramatic play: story and game structure," Proc. HCI2010, Int. Conf. on Human-Computer Interaction, Dundee: British Computer Society, pp. 448-452, 2010.

[64] E. Benveniste, Problemes de linguistique generale, Gallimard, Paris, 1966.

[65] C. Harrison, "Visual social semiotics: understanding how still images make meaning," Technical Communication, Vol. 50, no. 1, pp. 46-60, 2003.

[66] J. L. Lemke, "Travels in hypermodality," Visual Communication, Vol. 3 (1), pp. 299-325, 2002.

[67] J. F. Allen, "Towards a general theory of action and time," Artificial Intelligence, 23, pp. 123-154, 1984.

[68] A. Galton, "Towards an integrated logic of space, time and motion," in Proc. 13th Int. Joint Conf. on Artificial Intelligence (IJCAI-93), Chambery, France, pp. 1550-1555, 1993.

[69] W. C. Mann and S. A. Thompson, "Rhetorical Structure Theory: toward a functional theory of text organization," *Text*, Vol. 8, No. 3, pp. 243-281,1988.

[70] A. Gaeta, M. Gaeta, G. Guarino, and S. Miranda, "A smart methodology to improve the story building process," Journal of e-learning and knowledge society," Vol. 11, No. 1, pp. 97-124, 2015.

[71] N.J. Lowe, "A cognitive model," in Bernstein, M., and Gerco D. (Eds.) Reading Hypertext, Eastgate Systems, pp. 35-57, 2009.

[72] K. Rohlfing, D. Loehr, S. Duncan, A. Brown, A. Franklin, I. Kimbara, J. T. Milde, F. Parrill, T. Rose, T. Schmidt, H. Sloetjes, A. Thies, and S. Wellinghoff, "Comparison of multimodal annotation tools," Workshop report, Gesprächforschung - Online-Zeitschrift zur Verbalen Interaktion, 7, pp. 99-123, 2006.

[73] B. Hellwing and D. Uytvanck, "EUDICO linguistic annotator (ELAN)," Version 2.0.2, software manual, 2004.

[74] P. Boersmimedia and D. Weenink, "Praat: doing phonetics by computer," available from: http://www.fon.hum.uva.nl/praat/ Accessed: 11 Dec. 2017.

[75] A. Chebotko, Y. Deng, S. Lu, F. Fotouhi, and A. Aristar, "An Ontology-Based Multimedia Annotator for the Semantic Web of Language Engineering," in A. Sheth, M. Lytras (Eds.) Semantic Web-Based Information Systems. State-of-the-Art Applications, Cybertech Publishing, pp. 140-160, 2007.

[76] Pepsi Cola clip [online]. Available from: http://www.youtube.com/watch?v=edfRG9IREHc Accessed: 11 Dec. 2017.

[77] W. Gaver, "What should we expect from research through design?," Proc. CHI'12, ACM Press, pp. 937-946, 2012.

[78] J. Bardzell, S. Bardzell, and L. K. Hansen, "Immodest Proposals: research through design and knowledge," Proc. CHI'15, ACM Press, pp. 2093-2102, 2015.

[79] P. Brey, "Philosophy of Technology after the empirical turn," Techné: Research in Philosophy and Technology, 14(1), pp. 36-48, 2010.

[80] O. W. Bertelsen and S. Pold, "Criticism as an approach to interface aesthetics," in Proc. NordiCHI'04, ACM Press, New York, pp. 23-32, 2004.

[81] J. Bardzell and S. Bardzell, "Interaction criticism: a proposal and framework for a new discipline of HCI," Proc. CHI-08, ACM Press, pp. 2463-2472, 2008.

[82] J. Bardzell, "Interaction criticism: an introduction to the practice," Interacting with Computers, 23, pp. 604-621, 2011.

[83] J. Bardzell, "Interaction criticism and aesthetics," Proc. CHI'09, ACM Press, pp. 2357-2366, 2009.

[84] J. Lowgren, "Annotated portfolios and other forms of intermediate-level knowledge," Interactions, pp. 30-34, 2013.

[85] B. Gaver and J. Bower, "Annotated portfolios," Interactions, pp. 40-49, 2012.

[86] P. P. Verbeek, "Materializing morality: design ethics and technological mediation," Science, Technology & Human Values, Vol. 31, No. 3, pp. 361- 380, 2006.

[87] L. Anticoli and E. Toppano, "Technological mediation of ontologies: the need for tools to help designers in materializing ethics," International Journal of Philosophy Study, Vol.1, Issue 3, pp. 23-31, 2013.

[88] Y. Van Den Eede, "In between us: on the transparency and opacity of technological mediation," Found. Sci. 16, pp.139-159, 2011.

[89] D. Berdichevski and E. Neuenschwander, "Toward an ethics of persuasive technology," Communication of the ACM, Vol. 45, No. 5, pp. 51-58, 1999.

[90] L. Hallnas and J. Redstrom, "From use to presence: on the expressions and aesthetic of everyday computational things," ACM Trans. on Human-Computer Interaction, Vol.9, No 2, pp. 106-124, 2002.

[91] P. Brey, "Theorizing the cultural quality of new media," Techné: Research in Philosophy and Technology, 11(1), pp. 2-18, 2007.

[92] A. C. Danto, The transfiguration of the commonplace. A philosophy of art. Harvard University Press, CA: Massachusetts, 1990.

[93] J. Bowers, "The logic of annotated portfolios: communicating the value of Research Through Design," Proc. DIS 2012, ACM Press, pp. 68-77, 2012.

[94] C. Dorai and S. Venkatesh, "Bridging the semantic gap with computational media aesthetics," IEEE MultiMedia, Vol. 10, Issue 2, pp. 15-17, 2003.

[95] C. S. de Souza, "Viewpoint: semiotic perspectives on interactive languages for life on the screen," Journal of Visual Languages & Computing, Vol. 24, Issue 3, pp. 218-221, 2013.

ModRef Project: Data Migration into CIDOC-CRM Triplestores and Factorisation

Pascaline Laure Tchienehom

Université de Paris 10 - Labex "Les passés dans le présent"
Nanterre, France
Email: pkenfack@u-paris10.fr

***Abstract*—ModRef is a project from the laboratory Labex "Les passés dans le présent", which coordinates various projects on digital humanities. ModRef focuses more precisely on the semantic web and linked open data. The goal is to move heterogeneous data into triplestores also called data warehouses or collections of RDF files in order to improve the sharing, exchange and discovery of new knowledge. For this purpose, the CIDOC-CRM norm has been chosen since it is, at present, the reference for the semantic description of museographic data or cultural heritage data. In order to realise the proof of concept of ModRef, a general architecture has been defined, a semantic modelling and data mapping of selected sub-projects of ModRef have been proposed, triplestores have also been created. A web application has been implemented and deployed. This web application describes the ModRef project, as well as it enables visualising, querying and exploring created triplestores. We also present and discuss the simplification or factorisation of the migration of data into CIDOC-CRM triplestores.**

Keywords–Digital Humanities; Semantic Web; Linked Open Data; Triplestores; CIDOC-CRM.

I. Introduction

The laboratory Labex "Les passés dans le présent" accompanies several projects in Social and Human Sciences (SHS) on issues related to digital humanities [1][2]: from dematerialisation of data to their structural description and even to their semantic description as well. ModRef (Modelling, References and Digital Culture) is a project from Labex that gather together a set of sub-projects with the goal of migrating their data into triplestores or data warehouses or collections of RDF (Resource Description Framework) files in order to improve the sharing, exchange and discovery of new knowledge. For this purpose, the CIDOC-CRM (International Committee for DOCumentation-Conceptual Reference Model) norm [3] has been chosen because it is currently the reference for the semantic description of museographic data or cultural heritage data [4]. The aim is globally to move from non-structured or semi-structured data to structured data and afterwards from structured data to semantic data. The semantic web then provides a solution to perform these data migrations.

The semantic web [5][6] is not only a concept but also an architecture [7], which is increasingly used in several applications. The semantic web architecture is a set of independant layers that collaborate to perform various tasks. This architecture describes data from their representation to their exploitation by applications or semantic web agents. Hence, various norms of data representation exist. The CIDOC-CRM is an example of semantic norm and more precisely a conceptual reference model or ontology. The aim of semantics and also the aim of the various metadata languages or semantic norms that define semantics is to provide an homogenous framework for representing and querying heterogenous data in order to reduce information silence and therefore improve the discovery of knowledge. Hence, ModRef project aims at realising a migration of data towards CIDOC-CRM triplestores using core data originally from heterogenous data sources where heterogeneity is based on contents and initial logical structure (spreadsheets, relational databases, XML files) as well.

In this paper, we present the ModRef project through: a general description of the semantic web, the linked open data and the CIDOC-CRM norm, in Section II; the general architecture of the ModRef project, in Section III; a CIDOC-CRM semantic modelling and data mapping of the three pilot sub-projects of ModRef with the CIDOC-CRM graph, in Section IV; a migration of data into CIDOC-CRM triplestores with and without factorisation, in Section V; a visualisation and exploitation of triplestores through the web application [8] that has been developped and deployed, in Section VI; the evaluation procedure and results, in Section VII.

II. Semantic Web, Linked Open Data and CIDOC-CRM General Presentation

The semantic web architecture is made of different layers [7] (see Figure 1). Those layers can be grouped in several categories: representation, reasonning, querying, trust and interaction (of web applications). This architecture describes a set of norms that any semantic web application should meet.

Representation layers define a common socle for all other layers of the semantic web architecture. These layers describe the representation of addresses (URI, Unicode), logical structures (XML) and semantics of data (RDF).

Addressing guaranties a unique reference to every resource by using namespaces that define prefixes of URIs (generic types of URLs) for a set of data.

Structuring data allows to describe the organisation of descriptive elements of a given data. It then defines the logical structure of the data. There are different types of generic model [9] describing logical structures (description of data that shows its components):

1) *attribute-value or key-value or flat structure model.* Resources are described by a list of attribute-value pairs. This model is easy to manage though it has a drawback pertaining to the lack of structure for the representation of complex information such as hierarchies for instance and hence prevent from making complex analysis related to structure. In this

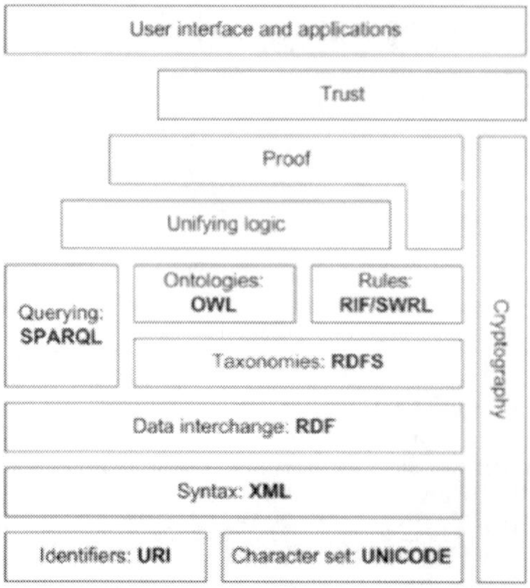

Figure 1. Semantic Web Architecture.

model, attributes are independant to each other for the attribute is considered as key. Consequently, it is forbidden to have two attributes with the same name since the name is the key of the descriptive element;

2) *hierarchical model* allows the structuration of logical structure, generally in the form of a tree like XML. This model allows a more precise description and analysis of data structure by creating composition links between nodes or attributes. Several nodes can then have the same name but different paths in the tree. XML is a standard for information exchange on internet. An XML document can describe databases or complex spreadsheets. There are also many XML norms such as: XML-EAD (Encoded Archival Description) for archives description, XML-TEI (Text Encoding Initiative) for text documents.

On the other hand, models based on logical structure are generally bound to the context or applications for which they have been defined and then are less re-usable. So, from one application to another, identical characteristics can be described by different logical structures. It will then be very difficult without a consensual semantics (metadata languages norms or standards) to query heterogenous data models.

Semantics of data is an answer to homogenise heterogeneous data sources. There are various data representation models based on semantics [10] [11] by using metadata languages that describe concepts and/or links between concepts (Dublin Core, RDF/RDFS/OWL, FOAF, Wordnet, CIDOC-CRM). These languages will enable more interoperability given the fact that their semantics is public and published through namespaces. Most of those metadata languages rely on RDF representation formalism which is an oriented graph with graph's paths define by a sequence of triples generally describe as follows: *[subject, predicate, object]* or *[domain, property, range]*. Note that various metadata languages can be used within the same semantic model and some of those metadata languages already define a conceptual model or ontology.

There are many standards for metadata languages. *RDFS and OWL* extend the *RDF* language and are more reasonning languages (use of properties such as: specialisation, generalisation -rdfs:subClassOf-, inverse -owl:inverseFunctionalProperty-, equivalence -owl:equivalentClass, owl:equivalentProperty-, identity -owl:sameAs-, symmetry, transitivity) of the semantic web whereas RDF is more of a representation language. In the same way, *FOAF* (Friend Of A Friend) describes people and organizations, what people do, links between people and is mainly used in social networks.

Wordnet is an ontology (formal descriptive model of the common vocabulary within a community in order to share information in a given domain), a lexical database developped by linguists of the laboratory of cognitive sciences of Princeton University (cf. http://wordnet.princeton.edu/wn20/). It aims at listing, classifying and linking in various ways the semantics and lexical contents of languages. There are different versions of Wordnet for different languages: english, french. Wordnet has been converted in RDF format. Note that lexiques, dictionnaries and thesaurus are used to construct ontologies and by that means contribute to the semantic description of data.

There are various data representation models based on semantics [10][11] that use metadata languages to describe concepts and/or links (properties or predicates) between concepts or instances of concepts. Those metadata languages are: Dublin Core, RDF, RDFS, OWL, FOAF, SKOS, Wordnet, CIDOC-CRM and so on.

The *CIDOC-CRM* [3] is a conceptual reference model for describing museographic data or cultural heritage data. The version of the CIDOC-CRM norm that we have worked with is the version 6.2 of may 2015. It describes 94 classes and 168 properties. In 2006, the CIDOC-CRM has become a norm ISO 21127:2006 but work on that norm has started since 1996. This norm describes general characteristics of objects (identifier, type, title, material, dimension, note) but also history of objects through events or activities (transfer of custody -former localisations, current localisation-, origin, discovery, curation, attribute assignement, measurement), as well as relations between objects or parts of objects (bibliography, composition, similarity, other representation -photo, drawing, painting-, inscription). An OWL implementation of the CIDOC-CRM by the University of Erlangen-Nuremberg is available [12] and the namespace of that implementation of CIDOC-CRM is usually prefixed by "*ecrm*".

The general structure of the CIDOC-CRM is described in Figure 2. The root class of all CIDOC-CRM entities is the class *E1 CRM Entity* and it is subdivided in direct sub-classes, among which the two main classes are:

1) *E77 Persistent Item*, which is the generic class of persistent entities. A persistent entity is an entity that can survive over an indeterminate time, such as: persons, objects, ideas, concepts. Those entities can have a beginning or an end of existence;
2) *E2 Temporal Entity*, which is the generic class of temporal entities. A temporal entity is an entity bounded by time (with a beginning and an end time), such as: event, beginning of existence, end of

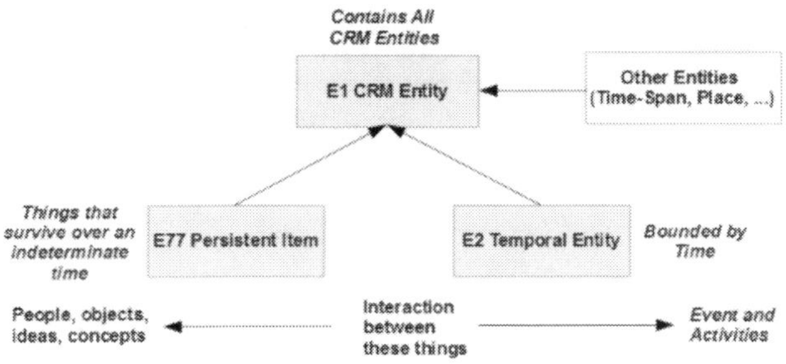

Figure 2. General Structure of CIDOC-CRM Entities.

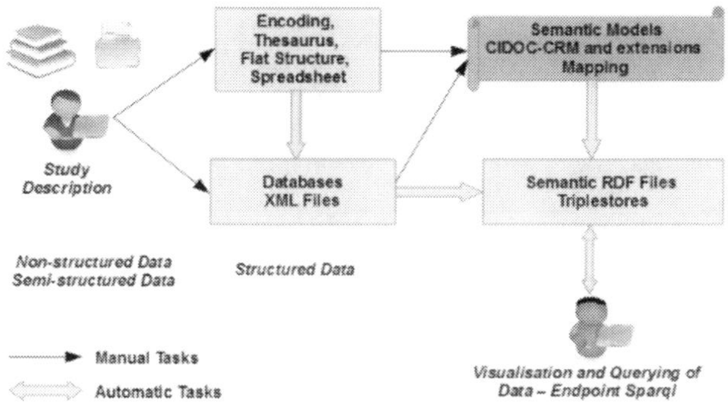

Figure 3. Architecture of ModRef project.

existence, activity, creation, production, modification, transfer of custody, curation, attribute assignement, measurement.

The other direct sub-classes of the root class *E1 CRM Entity* are the classes *E52 Time-Span, E53 Place, E54 Dimension, E92 Spacetime Volume*. In general, the CIDOC-CRM describes entities but also interactions that can exist between entities: interactions between persistent entities; interactions between temporal entities; interactions between persistent and temporal entities; general interactions between entities (for instance, interactions that exist between persistent or temporal entities and other general entities describing time-span, place, dimension). There also exists interactions between entities and primitive values (string, number, date time).

Besides, various projects around the world work on the migration of data into triplestores (CIDOC-CRM or not):

1) The *British Museum* [13], which is a museum on history and culture and that uses the CIDOC-CRM;
2) *Arches* [14], which is a collaboration between the Getty Conservation Institute (GCI) and the World Monuments Fund (WMF) on immovable cultural heritage (monuments, bridges) and that uses the CIDOC-CRM;
3) *DBPedia* [15], which is an online encyclopedia widely used [16] and that does not use the CIDOC-CRM norm but various metadata languages, such as: *dbpedia, foaf, umbel, schema.org, dublin core, geo*;
4) *Nakala* [17], which is an online service to upload, document and exhibit (museographic) data and that does not use the CIDOC-CRM norm but various metadata languages, such as: *foaf, skos, dublin core, vcard*.

The specificity of our web application is that it deals with heterogeneous data sources according to the contents and the logical structures (spreadsheets, relational databases, XML files) of data. Data migrated into triplestores are opened through our web application. This application provides a visualisation service of triplestores under three differents formats: *rdf, triples, attribute-value summary*. The web application also allows querying triplestores separately or together by using *"Endpoint Sparql"* (interface for typing and executing Sparql query, where Sparql is a querying language for RDF files) and *general query forms* that are useful for those who do not know the Sparql query language [18] and the CIDOC-CRM language.

III. Architecture of the ModRef project

The architecture of the ModRef project, illustrated in Figure 3, describes the various processes of data digitisation from the creation of digital data based on an expert knowledge for instance to the visualisation and querying of data by a user. Data can go through several transformations before being available in triplestores. Hence, we can move from non-structured or semi-structured data (notes, reports, books, web sites) to structured data described by logical structure. This logical structure can be a flat structure of the form *attribute-value* or *spreadsheet*, but it can also be more structured using *relational databases* or *XML files* that are, in our context, XML-EAD (Encoded Archival Description) files [19]. These various descriptions usually make use of thesaurus (controlled vocabulary of descriptive terms or not). From those structural descriptions, we can build a semantic description of data with a semantic RDF graph which relies on standards or norms. In our context, we have used the CIDOC-CRM norm to generate triplestores through a mapping between data and the CIDOC-CRM graph. These triplestores can then be used by semantic web applications or "Endpoint Sparql". The first stage of data transformation (from non-structured or semi-structured data towards structured data) is performed within each sub-project of ModRef whereas ModRef project itself focuses more on the second stage of data transformation (from structured data to semantic data).

Therefore, to realise the proof of concept (POC) of ModRef, three pilot projects have been selected:

1) *CDLI (Cuneiform Digital Library Initiative)*: Digital museum on antique documents in cuneiform writing [20];
2) *ObjMythArcheo*: corpus of antique archaeological objects with mythological iconography [21];
3) *BiblioNum*: Digital library on history of France during the 20th century [22].

Table I compares data of the three pilot projects of ModRef based on 5 criteria: descriptive texts size, number of objects, logical structure type, number of elements of the logical structure and data description language.

IV. ModRef CIDOC-CRM Modelling and Data Mapping

We have identified the useful CIDOC-CRM classes, for which at least one path leads to a non-null value, for the data

TABLE I. DATA COMPARISON.

	CDLI	ObjMythArcheo	BiblioNum
Texts size	300 Mo	100 Mo	100 Mo
Number of objects	313 332 objects	17 424 objects	77 collections - 62 392 files
Logical Structure	Database of type Spreadsheet	Relational Database	XML-EAD
Number of elements of the structure	1 table with 61 attributes	59 tables	146 XML-EAD elements
Language	English	French-English	French

modelling of our three pilot projects. This modelling represents extracts related to the four following themes or subjects:

1) general characteristics of objects (identifier, type, title, material, dimension, note or description), bibliography, composition and similarity of objects;
2) events of beginning of existence (origin) and end of existence;
3) miscellaneous activities (transfer of custody, attribute assignement, measurement);
4) inscriptions and other representations (photo, drawing, painting).

In general, those extracts are constant because with the CIDOC-CRM, it is possible to identify all potential paths that lead to a given information. A semantic graph is thus a set of nodes and oriented arrows that fulfill some constraints and rules (shortcut, entailment, inverse). These constraints and rules define the consistency and validity of the model.

In the following sections, we will describe the four different themes (graph's extracts) for the CIDOC-CRM modelling of our pilot projects and also an instance of data mapping with the corresponding CIDOC-CRM semantic graph snippet. Note that the mapping or alignment principle is globally the same for all themes and for all pilot projects.

A. Modelling of general characteristics

General characteristics of an object is defined more often by interactions through short graph's paths. Those characteristics describe for an object various information, such as: identifier, type (categorisation), title, material, dimension, note or general description.

The modelling of the general characteristics of objects of the ModRef project is illustrated in Figure 4. In this figure, there are two different graph's paths for defining the dimension of an object:

1) a *short path* or *shortcut path* that links class *E70 Thing* to class *E54 Dimension* with the property *P43 has dimension* by the triple *[E70 Thing, P43 has dimension, E54 Dimension]*;
2) a *long path* with more nodes to fill. This path is described by the following triples: *[E1 CRM Entity, P39i was measured by, E16 Measurement]*, *[E16 Measurement, P40 observed dimension, E54 Dimension]*. With this path, we can fill more information related to the activity of measurement *E16 Measurement*. Actually, the class *E16 Measurement* is a type of activity because classes *E13 Attribute Assignment*, *E7 Activity* and *E5 Event* belong to its hierarchy (see Figure 5).

Besides, it is authorised to fill various paths leading to the same information in a CIDOC-CRM graph. Therefore, we sometimes have to choose between the different possibilities when we do not have the necessary information to describe a given path. This is the case mostly when a temporal entity is used in the path.

On the other hand, Figure 4 also illustrates other interactions between persistent entities, such as: *P70i is documented in* for bibliographic references, *P46 is composed of* for objects composition, *P130 shows features of* for objects similarity, *P128 carries* for relation between an object and an entity carried by or engraved on the described object, such as an inscription for example.

B. Modelling of events of beginning and end of existence

An important activity on museographic data is the description of their origin (beginning of existence) in order to define their date of origin, their place of origin and eventually the participants to their origin or creation. The modelling of beginning and end of existence events of objects in the ModRef project is illustrated in Figure 5. The CIDOC-CRM allows to define for each event three main information: date or period, place and participants.

For the beginning of existence (origin), we use the event *E63 Beginning of Existence* and the following patterns of triples: *[E77 Persistent Item, P92i was brought into existence by, E63 Beginning of Existence]*, *[E2 Temporal Entity, P4 has time-span, E52 Time-Span]*, *[E52 Time-Span, P78 is identified by, E49 Time Appellation]*, *[E4 Period, P7 took place at, E53 Place]*, *[E53 Place, P87 is identified by, E44 Place Appellation]*, *[E5 Event, P11 had participant, E39 Actor]*, *[E63 Beginning of Existence, rdfs : subClassOf, E5 Event]*, *[E5 Event, rdfs : subClassOf, E4 Period]*, *[E4 Period, rdfs : subClassOf, E2 Temporal Entity]*. Besides, for the beginning of existence (origin) we may also start from activities *E65 Creation* or *E12 Production*, which have as super-classes the classes *E63 Beginning of Existence* and *E7 Activity* (see Figure 5).

For the end of existence, we use the class *E64 End of Existence* or any of its sub-classes and we will then be able to define the date, the place and the participants to the end of existence of an object.

C. Modelling of miscellaneous activities

Figure 6 illustrates an extract of our model for the description of activities in general, and for the description of the activity *transfer of custody* in particular. Hence, to link an object to an activity of transfer of custody, we use the property *P30 transferred custody of* (or its inverse *P30i custody transferred through*) between the target activity (*E10 Transfer of Custody*) and the physical object (*E18 Physical Thing*). Moreover, for a transfer of custody, we can describe the various protagonists of the transfer (*P29 custody received by, P28 custody surrendered by*) and also describe eventually a history of the different transfers of custody related to a specific object or document. Note that there also exists a shortcut path that does not use the transfer of custody activity but that allows to define the current or former keepers or owners of an object (*P49 has former or current keeper, P50 has current keeper, P51 has former or current owner, P52 has current owner*).

Generally, for an event or an activity, we can describe the date (or period), the place and the participants (or actors)

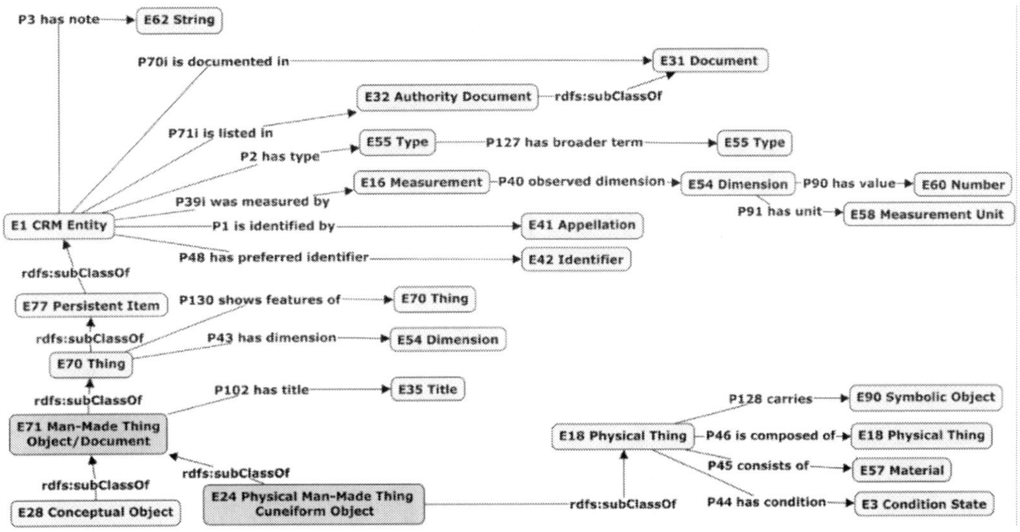

Figure 4. Modelling of general characteristics.

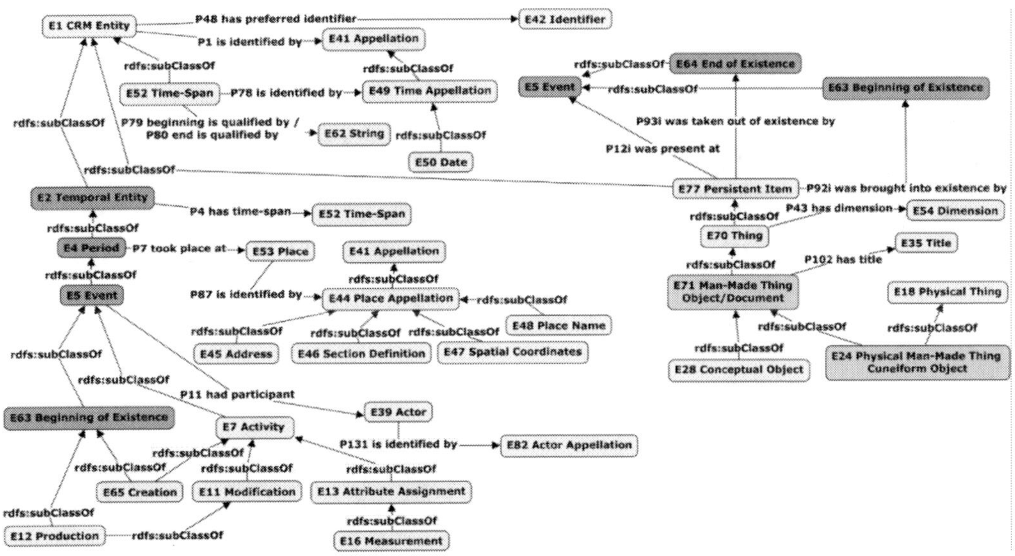

Figure 5. Modelling of events of beginning and end of existence.

of the event or activity. Specifically, for an activity (transfer of custody, attribute assignement, measurement, curation), we will be able to define more information, such as: the procedure or technique used (*P33 used specific technique, P32 used general technique*), the various objects used (*P16 used specific object, P125 used object of type*), the purpose of the activity (*P20 had specific purpose, P21 had general purpose*).

D. Modelling of inscriptions and other representations

Figure 7 illustrates a snippet of the model for the description of inscriptions engraved on objects or the description of other representations (photo, drawing, painting) of these objects (physical or conceptual). Hence, to link an object to its inscription, we use the property *P128 carries* between a physical object (*E18 Physical Thing*) and a symbolic objet (*E90 Symbolic Object*) that is inscribed on the target described object. This will then help to find, for instance, all objects engraved with a given inscription (seal, signature).

Besides, to link a photo or drawing or painting to an object (physical or conceptual), we can use a set of properties:

1) *P62 depicts* for describing the link between the photo or drawing or painting (here, *E24 Physical Man-Made Thing*) and the target entity *E1 CRM Entity* (physical or conceptual object) represented by the photo, drawing or painting. This property does not

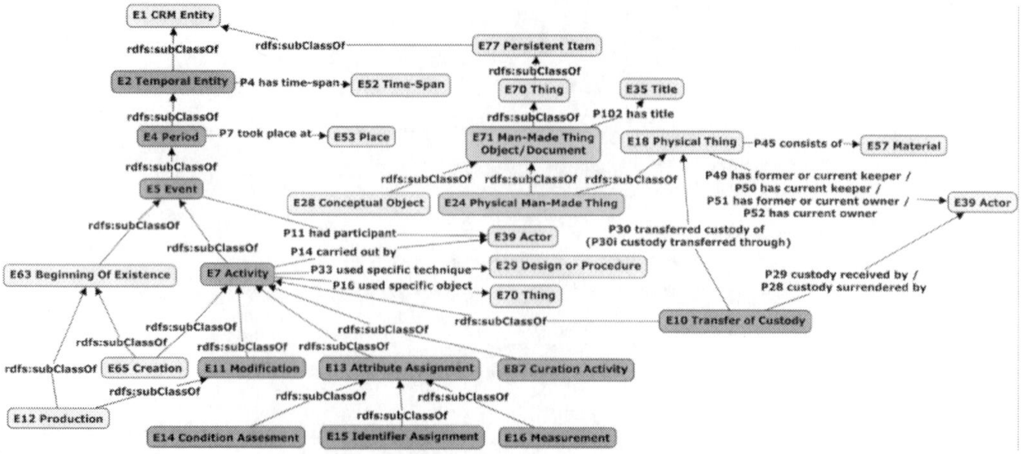

Figure 6. Modelling of miscellaneous activities.

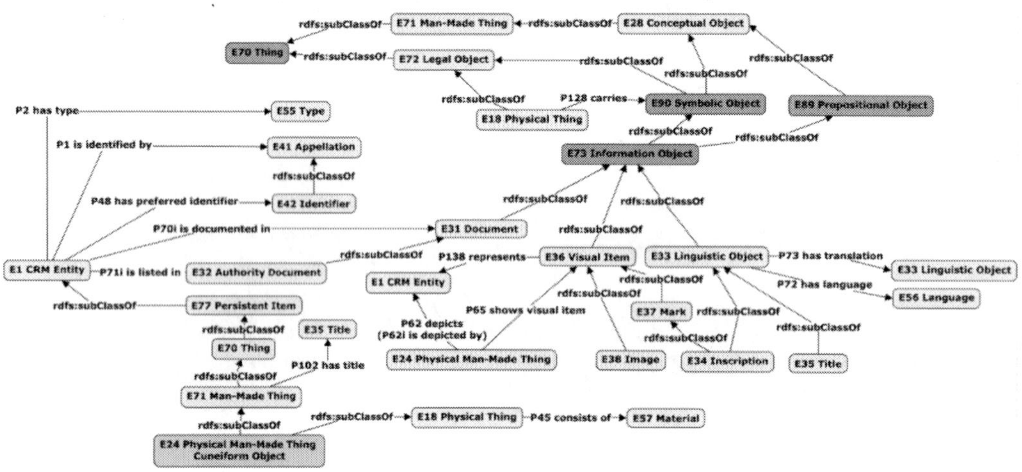

Figure 7. Modelling of inscriptions and other representations of an object.

describe inscriptions or other information engraved directly on objects;

2) *P65 shows visual item* that links the photo or drawing or painting to a visual representation (*E36 Visual item*) of the described object represented by the photo or drawing or painting;
3) *P138 represents* that links a visual representation (*E36 Visual item*) of an object to the target described object (*E1 CRM Entity*).

Note that the property *P62 depicts* is a shortcut of properties *P65 shows visual item* and *P138 represents*. The photo or drawing or painting is usually described with the class *E24 Physical Man-Made Thing*.

E. Data Mapping or Alignment

Data migration into triplestores requires an alignment stage of data with extracts of the CIDOC-CRM graph proposed. This mapping is essential due to the heterogeneity of initial data structured description and also due to the diversity of pilot projects. This matching is not properly a programmatic task but relies on logical structure details specific to the structural descriptive model chosen by each sub-project. It is a task halfway between modelling and programming that it enables to oversee more clearly. Note that this task should not be confused with the alignment between ontologies or owl/rdf files [23][24] since here it is rather an alignment between the CIDOC-CRM ontology and raw data from databases or XML files (in our context, XML-EAD files).

Primarily, the mapping consists in filling a semantic graph's nodes. Terminal nodes will be filled with values extracted from data logical structures of the corresponding sub-projects whereas non-terminal or intermediary nodes will be filled with URIs and will then define by that means paths to terminal nodes. Note that a particular attention must be drawn to the construction of URIs for their readability, as well as for the consistency of graph's paths in order to avoid paths' conflicts and warrant the uniqueness of a given path compared to another.

Figure 8 illustrates an extract of data mapping, initially in XML-EAD [19] and that corresponds to the first theme of our semantic modelling (see Figure 4). In XML-EAD, for instance, dimensions of an object is obtained with xpath */ead/archdesc/did/physdesc/dimensions* or */ead/archdesc/dsc/c/did/physdesc/dimensions*, according to the target information level that can be either the collection level or the document level.

Hence, to describe the dimensions of an object, we use a sequence of triples of the form:

[http://www.modref.org/biblionum/document_id/e70_thing, rdf : type, ecrm : E70_Thing],

[http://www.modref.org/biblionum/document_id/e70_thing, ecrm : P43_has_dimension, http://www.modref.org/biblionum/document_id/e54_dimension],

[http://www.modref.org/biblionum/document_id/-e54_dimension, rdf : type, ecrm : E54_Dimension],

[http://www.modref.org/biblionum/document_id/-e54_dimension, rdfs : label, "/ead/archdesc/dsc/c/did/physdesc/dimensions"],

[http://www.modref.org/biblionum/document_id/e71_man-made_thing, owl : sameAs, http://www.modref.org/biblionum/document_id/e70_thing].

Finally, the mapping realised will be translated into a programmatic data structure that will be then used to automatically generate files that follow RDF and CIDOC-CRM syntax: it is the data migration into triplestores or the creation of triplestores.

V. Data Migration into Triplestores and Factorisation

Efficiently migrating data into triplestores involves various skills. The sustainability of the whole procedure implies to define a general and rigorous architecture for the workflow of the different types of data handled. This architecture explicits the global method applied to all projects that wish to move their data into triplestores. This method is subdivided in different well-identified steps: data preparating (study and structural description), semantic modelling and data mapping from structural to semantic description and at last creating and exhibiting triplestores that can then be visualised and queried by users or semantic web applications. Initially, data are often non-structured or semi-structured (notes, reports, books, html) and first need to be converted into a structured representation (spreadsheets, databases, XML files) in order to easily construct their semantic representation thereafter. This continuum of steps requires several skills and needs some of in-between profiles skills to enable moving data from one format to another: (1) non-structured data or semi-structured data to structured data; (2) structured data to semantic data.

Besides, the key element of the architecture for migrating data into triplestores is the modelling and mapping of data with the semantic graph model chosen. In order to achieve data migration of ModRef project, we have performed an alignment between their data structural description and their semantic description by filling some nodes of the semantic graph with data retrieved from databases or collections of XML-EAD files. This migration into triplestores implies at the same time the reading of databases and the parsing of XML-EAD files (see Table I). Nodes filled with values are terminal nodes and non-terminal nodes are filled with URIs.

On the other hand, on instances, when we are mapping data with the CIDOC-CRM model, we do not need to explicit all the hierarchy of the classes used since we already have an implementation of the whole model of the CIDOC-CRM ontology. Subclasses inherit properties from all their superclasses. Hence, we can perform what we call here a *factorisation* and then reduce de number of use of the identity property *owl:sameAS* between the hierarchy of classes.

A. Factorisation

For the first modelling theme *"General characteristics of objects"*, the simplification is straightforward. *E24 Physical Man-Made Thing* is the most specialized reference class. Then all its super-properties are inherited and we finally get Figure 9. The other main simplification is that we no longer need to keep track of the hierarchy from *E24 Physical Man-Made Thing* to *E1 CRM Entity*. Hence, this is going to reduce the number of non terminal nodes in our triplestores and we can guess easily that the number of terminal nodes will remain the same.

For the second theme *"Events of beginning of existence (origin) and end of existence"*, the simplification is two-fold because we have a persistent part (*E24 Physical Man-Made Thing*) and a temporal part (*E63 Beginning of Existence* or *E64 End of Existence*) to deal with at the same time. Then all super-properties of classes *E24 Physical Man-Made Thing*, *E63 Beginning of Existence* or *E64 End of Existence* are inherited and in the end we obtain Figure 10. The other main simplification is that we no longer need to keep track of the hierarchy of our three main classes *E24 Physical Man-Made Thing*, *E63 Beginning of Existence* or *E64 End of Existence*. Hence, as for the first modelling theme, this is going to reduce the number of non terminal nodes in our triplestores and we can also guess easily that the number of terminal nodes will remain the same.

For the third theme *"Modelling of miscellaneous activities"*, the simplification is the same as for the second theme because we have also a persistent part (*E24 Physical Man-Made Thing*) and a temporal part (miscellaneous activities with classes such as: *E10 Transfer of Custody, E13 Attribute Assignement, E16 Measurement, E87 Curation Activity*). Once again, the consequences are the same, all super-properties of target classes *E24 Physical Man-Made Thing* or *E10 Transfer of Custody* for instance are inherited and finally we obtain Figure 11, which illustrates only the persistent item *E24 Physical Man-Made Thing* and the activity *E10 Transfer of Custody* though we can easily guess that the model remain the same for others activities (*E13 Attribute Assignement, E16 Measurement, E87 Curation Activity*). Of course, the other main simplification is that we no longer need to keep track of the hierarchy of our target main classes *E24 Physical Man-Made Thing, E10 Transfer of Custody, E13 Attribute Assignement, E16 Measurement, E87 Curation Activity*. Hence, this is going to reduce the number of non terminal nodes in our triplestores and we can also guess easily that the number of terminal nodes will remain the same.

For the fourth theme *"Modelling of inscriptions and other representations"*, the simplification is two-fold between a persistent part (*E24 Physical Man-Made Thing*) and another persistent part (inscriptions and other representations represented

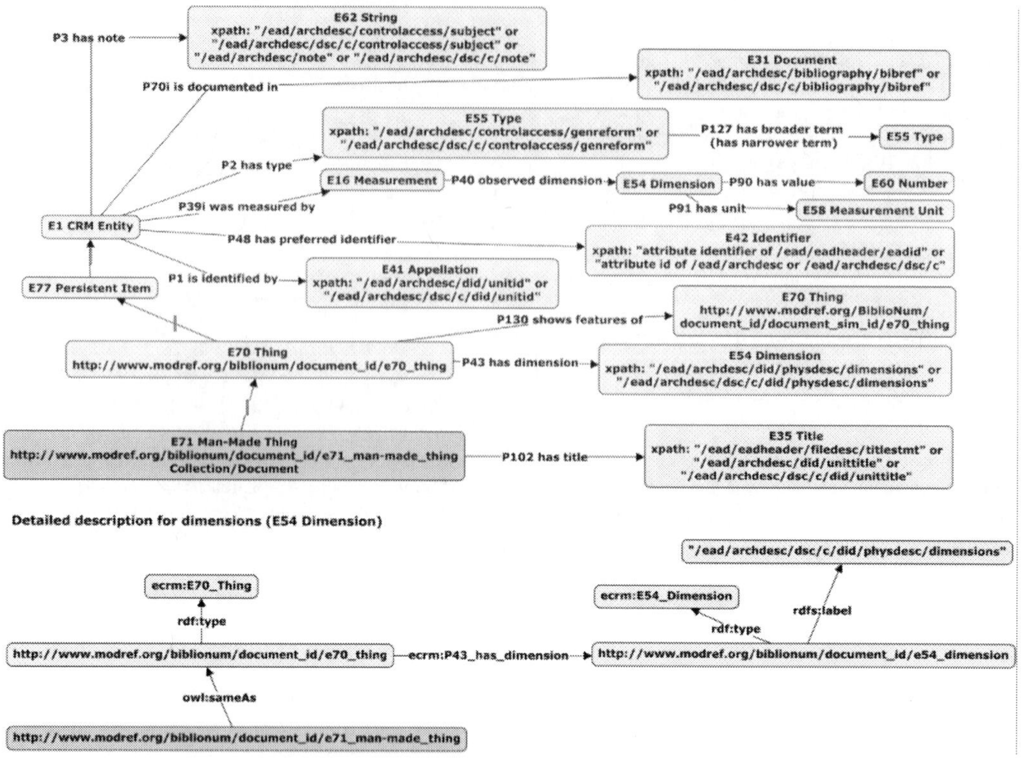

Figure 8. Data mapping snippet between XML-EAD and CIDOC-CRM.

by the super-class *E90 Symbolic Object*). Indeed, there is an interaction between the two persistent classes *E24 Physical Man-Made Thing* and *E90 Symbolic Object* thanks to the property *P128 carries*. In this specific case of modelling inscriptions and other representations of a given object, *inscriptions (E36 Visual Item or E33 Linguistic Object, E34 Inscription)* are sub-classes of class *E90 Symbolic Object* (see Figure 12). If we are interested in any of *E90 Symbolic Object* sub-classes then we can move the property *P128 carries* form class *E24 Physical Man-Made Thing* to our target specific class (rule of inheritance). Hence, this will reduce that specific part of the hierarchy and also the number of non terminal nodes in this specific part. On the other hand, *other representations* of a given object is considered and described the same way as the original or target object using interactions through properties such as: *P62 depicts, P65 shows visual item, P138 represents* (see Figure 12).

The proof of concept of ModRef or the validation of data migration into triplestores is a set of tasks uphill (preparating and structuring of data, semantic modelling, alignment of data) and downhill (publishing, visualising, querying and exploring triplestores) the migration process. Hence, exploiting triplestores by querying and exploring them and the avantages that can be then got through triplestores is the other major aspect around those new data warehouses of RDF documents.

VI. Visualisation and Exploitation of Triplestores

Created triplestores are available for visualising (under three different ways: rdf, triples and attribute-value summary) and querying through our web application. The interest of triplestores is that we have a public and published model of information representation that enables querying triplestores indifferently with the same procedures. We have defined two procedures for exploiting triplestores: interfaces similar to "general query forms" and "Endpoint Sparql" (see Figure 13).

As they are really close to natural language, "general query forms" are simple and intuitive means for querying triplestores. Special knowledge is not necessary, all that is needed is to fill target fields on a given form and launch the query execution. A Sparql query is automatically constructed using values of filled fields and the query obtained is then used to retrieve information from triplestores. At the end of query execution, a list of objects is selected and returned as results to the user who can then visualise them in three ways: *rdf, triples and attribute-value summary*.

Besides, we can also query triplestores by using "Endpoint Sparql". This second query mode requires Sparql query language knowledge that is, at present, the reference language for querying RDF documents. Sparql is a simple language but not always at everyone's comprehension level. Hence, "general query forms" can be seen as a first query step for triplestores whereas "Endpoint Sparql" guarantee a more complete exploitation of triplestores by a free formulation of

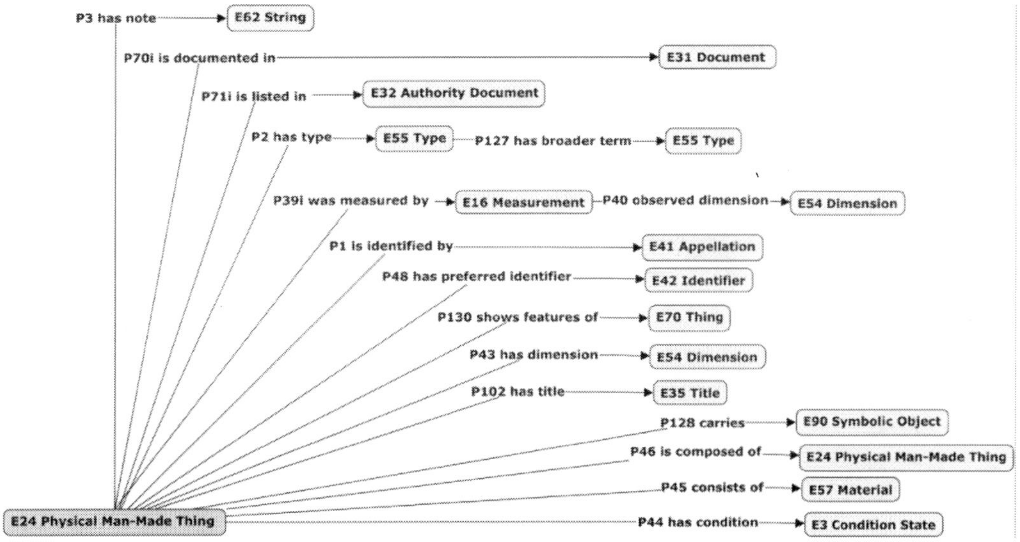

Figure 9. Factorisation of the modelling of general characteristics.

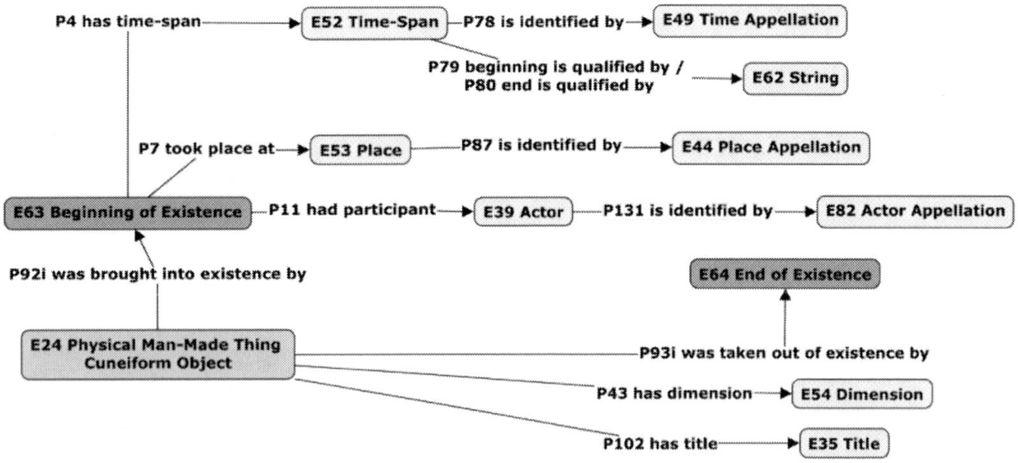

Figure 10. Factorisation of modelling of events of beginning and end of existence.

Sparql "Select" query type.

Our web application allows to visualise, query and explore triplestores separately for each pilot project of ModRef but also together by using the LOD (Linked Open Data) of ModRef. The web application provides, for each project and for the LOD of ModRef, a service to visualise triplestores data under three forms but also provides a service to query triplestores by using either "general query forms" or "Endpoint Sparql". Hence, as results to a query, the LOD allows to retrieve various information (statue, tablet) coming from different triplestores (see Figure 13). Several Sparql queries have been executed to validate data migration and a list of queries samples is provided with the web application. We have developped our own web application "Endpoint Sparql" and we also provide a Virtuoso "Endpoint Sparql" (Virtuoso is a software that allows to create an instance of "Endpoint Sparql") [25].

Note that the notion of exploiting triplestores refers to notions of querying and exploring semantic graphs. Hence, querying triplestores is executing Sparql queries that are pre-defined (general query forms) or free (Endpoint Sparql) whereas exploring triplestores is a kind of querying only performed through "Endpoint Sparql" for it allows to discover various paths in a semantic graph towards a given data. Actually, different paths can lead to the same information inside a graph (by the use of various notions: shortcut, refinement, inheritance/entailment, inverse) even if those paths are not always all filled. We can then write Sparql queries to discover if different paths that lead to a given data exist or write queries to know paths that lead to terminal nodes associated to values. Exploring is then very important to master a specific

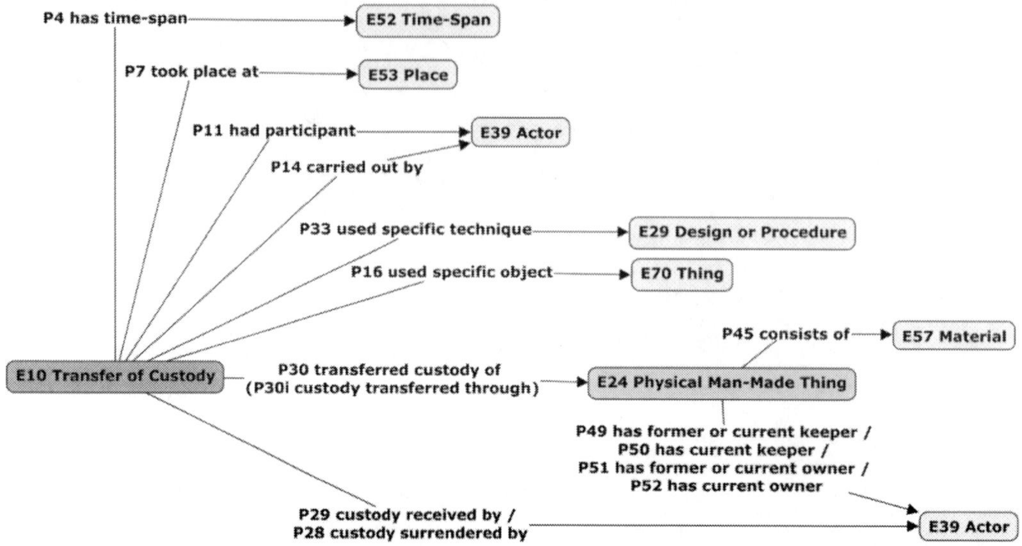

Figure 11. Factorisation of modelling of miscellaneous activities (eg. Transfer of Custody).

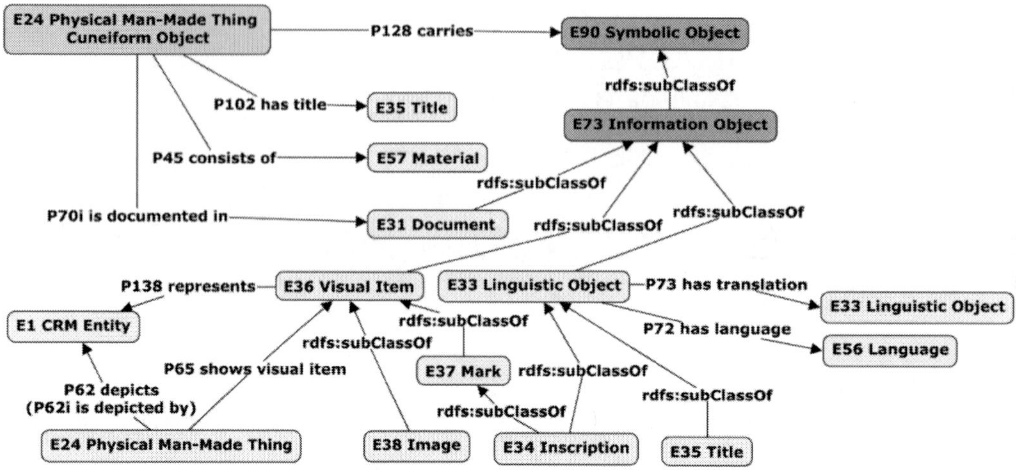

Figure 12. Factorisation of modelling of inscriptions and other representations of an object.

triplestore.

VII. Evaluation Procedure and Results

We have perform several Sparql queries types to validate the various datasets of our triplestores. The queries can be divided into two groups, one group related to the general RDF syntax schema (*list of concepts or predicates used, list of terminal triples (see Table II), list of triples of a given resource, extracts of paths leading to non-empty terminal nodes*) and another group related to the CIDOC-CRM schema (*checking instanciation of a given class, checking labels of given entity or resource (see Table III), characteristics of a given object (see Table IV), information on origin or custody of a given object*).

Moreover, triplestores are subdivided into constant parts (number of objects or triples) and queries are executed each time on one part and gradually on the other parts if the user asks so. The results are then progressively merge. The user chooses to execute its queries bit by bit and can stop the execution on any part of the triplestore. The current part

TABLE II. LIST OF TERMINAL TRIPLES WHERE THE TERMINAL NODE IS NON-EMPTY.

```
SELECT Distinct ?subject ?predicate ?object
WHERE
{
?subject ?predicate ?object .
Filter ( isLiteral(?object) && ?object != "" )
}
```

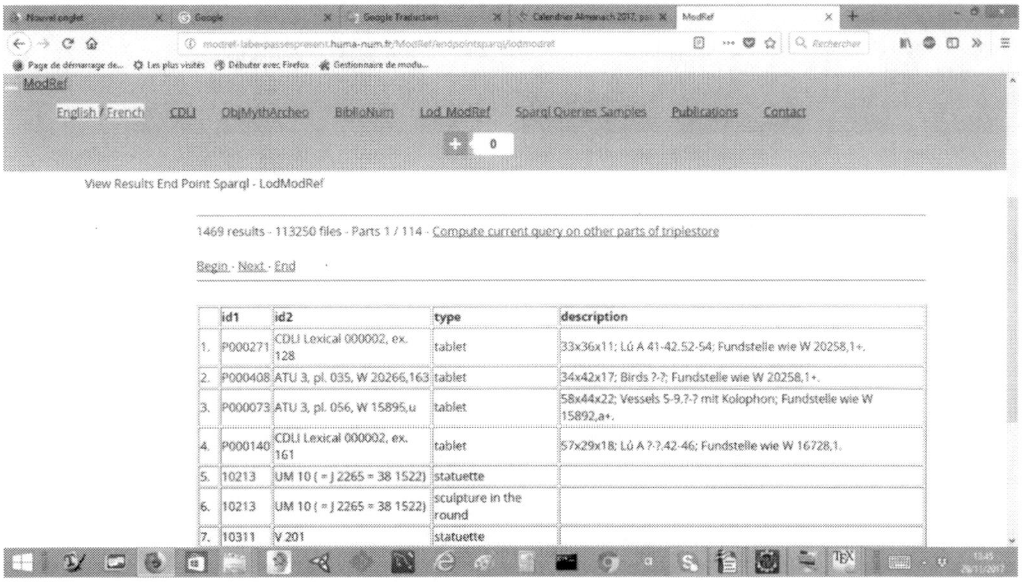

Figure 13. ModRef Project Web Application: Endpoint Sparql.

TABLE III. LIST OF TYPES OR CATEGORIES OF OBJECTS.

```
PREFIX ecrm: <http://erlangen-crm.org/150929/>
PREFIX rdf: <http://www.w3.org/1999/02/22-rdf-syntax-ns#>
PREFIX rdfs: <http://www.w3.org/2000/01/rdf-schema#>

SELECT Distinct ?type
WHERE
{
?type_uri rdf:type ecrm:E55_Type .
?type_uri rdfs:label ?type .
Filter ( ?type != "" )
}
```

TABLE IV. LIST OF CHARACTERISTICS THAT COME FROM ROOT ENTITY "E1 CRM Entity".

```
PREFIX ecrm: <http://erlangen-crm.org/150929/>
PREFIX rdf: <http://www.w3.org/1999/02/22-rdf-syntax-ns#>
PREFIX rdfs: <http://www.w3.org/2000/01/rdf-schema#>

SELECT Distinct ?id1 ?id2 ?type ?description
WHERE
{
?e1_obj ecrm:P48_has_preferred_identifier ?id1_uri .
?id1_uri rdfs:label ?id1 .
?e1_obj ecrm:P1_is_identified_by ?id2_uri .
?id2_uri rdfs:label ?id2 .
?e1_obj ecrm:P2_has_type ?type_uri .
?type_uri rdfs:label ?type .
?e1_obj ecrm:P3_has_note ?description .
}
```

number (on which the current query has been executed) and the total number of parts are always shown. Figure 14 shows that queries average time execution (in seconds) is rather constant on a given triplestore's part (*1000 objects*) and the execution speed of these queries is quite good for the users. Therefore, the cumulative time execution increases as triplestore's parts

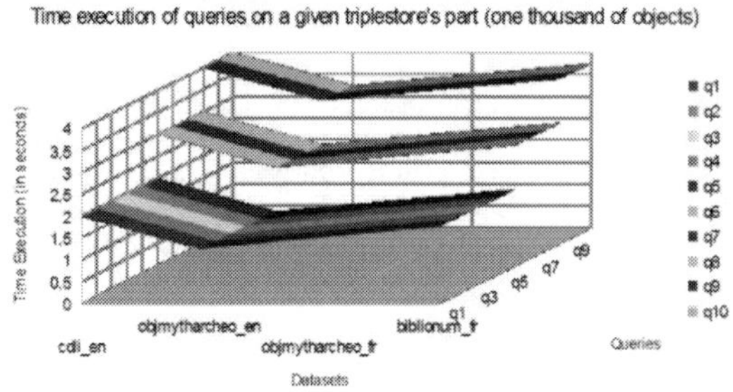

Figure 14. Queries Execution for ModRef Project.

are combined.

TABLE V. MIGRATION PROCEDURE GENERAL STATISTICS.

	CDLI	ObjMythArcheo	BiblioNum
Number of Logical Structure Queries	1 SQL query	32 SQL queries	36 XML-EAD paths
Number of Literal Values	5 300 000	280 000	930 000
Number of Concepts	36	36	36
Number of Predicates	39	39	39

Once the modelling and alignment tasks were done, we proceeded to the implementation of the architecture of the migration process and thereafter we implemented the modules for visualising and querying (General Query Form, Endpoint Sparql) triplestores. All these implementations took about one year. The time execution of the migration process itself, on a 2.13 GHz processor with 4 GB RAM, takes: 6 hours for the project *CDLI* involving one long SQL query; 30 minutes for the project *ObjMythArcheo* involving 32 SQL queries; 2 hours for the project *BiblioNum* involving 36 XML-EAD paths.

Table V describes general statistics of the migration results for the three pilot projects of ModRef based on the following criteria: number of logical structure queries, number of literal values, number of concepts and predicates. Finally, the factorisation procedure has reduced the number of non-terminal nodes by around 30 percent.

VIII. Conclusion

The ModRef project allows to realise the proof of concept (POC) of data migration into CIDOC-CRM triplestores through: a general architecture that identifies the various steps; modelling and data mapping with the CIDOC-CRM semantic graph; data migration into triplestores; publishing of triplestores through a bilingual "*English-French*" web application [8] that provides services for visualising, querying and exploring triplestores.

Further work is directed towards:

1) *integration to others existing internet LOD (Linked Open data)* [26][27] in order to improve the sharing, exchange and discovery of knowledge at a greater scale. LOD should increase the discovery of new knowledge, because of the amount and diversity of linked data but mainly due to the use of semantic web formalisms, metadata languages, thesaurus published, standardised and even normalised;
2) *comparison of various triplestores (DBPedia, Nakala, British Museum, ModRef)* that describe similar data [28] (similar objects, objects of same historical period, objects of same type, identical objects) in a LOD context. This will lead to mutual enrichment of the various actors of the LOD;
3) *inference implications or issues or consequences* on CIDOC-CRM triplestores as well as on integration with others triplestores using factorised or non-factorised CIDOC-CRM triplestores.

Acknowledgment

The author would like to thank the laboratory Labex "Les passés dans le présent" of the University of Paris 10 Nanterre and the ANR project ModRef referenced by ANR-11-LABX-0026-01.

References

[1] P. L. Tchienehom, "Modref project: from creation to exploitation of cidoc-crm triplestores," The Fifth International Conference on Building and Exploring Web Based Environments (WEB 2017), 2017, pp. 52–60.

[2] D. Oldman, M. Doerr, G. de Jong, B. Norton, and T. Wikman, "Realizing lessons of the last 20 years : A manifesto for data provisioning and aggregation services for the digital humanities. http://www.dlib.org/dlib/july14/oldman/07oldman.html [retrieved: November, 2017]," D-Lib Magazine, vol. 20, no. 7/8, 2014.

[3] P. L. Boeuf, M. Doerr, C. E. Ore, and S. Stead, "Definition of the cidoc conceptual reference model, version 6.2," Produced by the ICOM/CIDOC Documentation Standards Group, Continued by the CIDOC CRM Special Interest Group. http://www.cidoc-crm.org/ [retrieved: November, 2017], May 2015.

[4] S. V. Hooland and R. Verborgh, Linked Data for Libraries, Archives and Museums. How to Clean, Link and Publish Your Metadata, A. L. Association, Ed., 2014.

[5] N. Shadbolt, T. Berners-Lee, and W. Hall, "The semantic web revisited," IEEE Intelligent Systems, vol. 21, no. 3, 2006, pp. 96–101.

[6] T. Berners-Lee, J. Hendler, and O. Lassila, "The semantic web," Scientific American, 2001, pp. 34–43.

[7] T. Berners-Lee, "Axioms, architecture and aspirations," W3C all-working group plenary Meeting. https://www.w3.org/2001/Talks/0228-tbl/slide1-0.html [retrieved: November, 2017], 2001.

[8] "Modref cidoc-crm project," http://modref-labexpassespresent.huma-num.fr [retrieved: November, 2017] or http://triplestore.modyco.fr [retrieved: November, 2017].

[9] P. L. Tchienehom, Modélisation et Exploitation de Profils : Accès sémantique à des Ressources, E. U. Europennes, Ed., 2015, iSBN 978-3-8416-7617-7.

[10] R. Heartfield and G. Loukas, "A taxonomy of attacks and a survey of defence mechanisms for semantic social engineering attacks," ACM Computing Surveys (CSUR) - DL (Digital Library), vol. 48, no. 3, 2016.

[11] J. Scarinci and T. Myers, "A semantic web framework to enable sustainable lodging best management practices in the usa," Information Technology and Tourism, vol. 14, no. 4, 2014, pp. 291–315.

[12] "Cidoc-crm implementation," http://www.erlangen-crm.org/ [retrieved: November, 2017], 2015.

[13] "British museum cidoc-crm project," http://collection.britishmuseum.org/ [retrieved: November, 2017].

[14] "Arches cidoc-crm project," http://www.getty.edu/conservation/our_projects/field_projects/arches/ [retrieved: November, 2017].

[15] "Dbpedia project," http://www.dbpedia.org/sparql [retrieved: November, 2017].

[16] T. Ruan, Y. Li, H. Wang, and L. Zhao, "From queriability to informativity, assessing "quality in use" of dbpedia and yago," In proceedings of the 13th Extended Semantic Web Conference ESWC'16, 2016, pp. 52–68.

[17] "Nakala project," http://www.nakala.fr/sparql [retrieved: November, 2017].

[18] P. Haase, J. Broekstra, A. Eberhart, and R. Volz, "Comparison of rdf query languages," In proceedings of the third International Semantic Web Conference ISWC'04, 2004, pp. 502–517.

[19] "Xml-ead elements," https://www.loc.gov/ead/tglib/element_index.html [retrieved: November, 2017].

[20] "Cdli cidoc-crm project," http://www.cdli.ucla.edu [retrieved: November, 2017].

[21] "Objmytharcheo cidoc-crm project," http://www.limc-france.fr and http://medaillesetantiques.bnf.fr [retrieved: November, 2017].

[22] "Biblionum cidoc-crm project," http://www.argonnaute-u.paris10.fr [retrieved: November, 2017].

[23] D. Faria, C. Martins, and A. Nanavaty, "Agreementmakerlight results for oaei 2014," ISWC Workshop on Ontology Matching - Proceedings of the 9th International Conference on Ontology Matching (OM'14), vol. 1317, 2014, pp. 105–112.

[24] D. Faria, C. Pesquita, E. Santos, M. Palmonari, I. Cruz, and F. Couto, "The agreementmakerlight ontology matching system," The 12th International Conference on Ontologies, DataBases, and Applications of Semantics (ODBASE), 2013, pp. 527–541.

[25] "Modref virtuoso endpoint sparql," http://3s-passespresent.huma-num.fr/sparql [retrieved: November, 2017].

[26] W. Beek, L. Rietveld, S. Schlobach, and F. van Harmelen, "Lod laundromat: Why the semantic web needs centralization (even if we don't like it)," IEEE Internet Computing, vol. 20, no. 2, 2016, pp. 78–81.

[27] E. Daga, M. d'Aquin, A. Adamou, and S. Brown, "The open university linked data - data.open.ac.uk. semantic web," Semantic Web, vol. 7, no. 2, 2016, pp. 183–191.

[28] W. Beek, S. Schlobach, and F. van Harmelen, "A contextualised semantics of owl:sameas," In proceedings of the 13th Extended Semantic Web Conference ESWC'16, 2016, pp. 405–419.